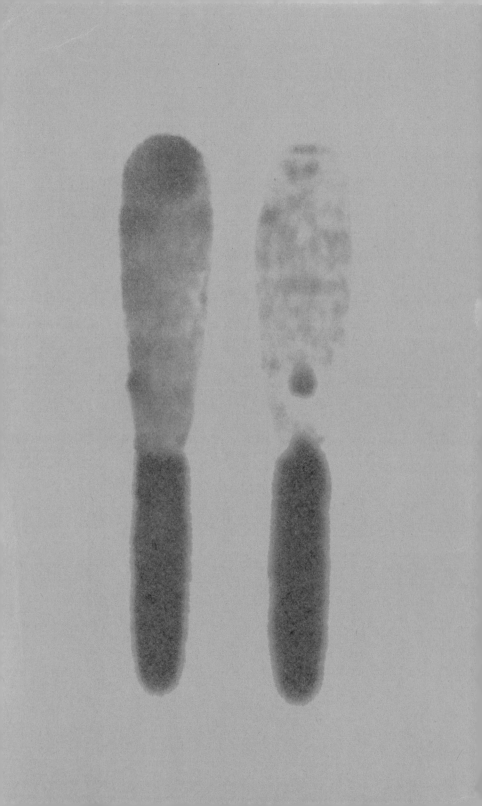

The
Tycoons
Arthur M. Louis

Simon and Schuster
NEW YORK

Copyright © 1981 by Arthur M. Louis
All rights reserved
including the right of reproduction
in whole or in part in any form
Published by Simon and Schuster
A Division of Gulf & Western Corporation
Simon & Schuster Building
Rockefeller Center
1230 Avenue of the Americas
New York, New York 10020
SIMON AND SCHUSTER and colophon are trademarks of Simon & Schuster.
Designed by Irving Perkins
Printed and Bound by Fairfield Graphics
Manufactured in the United States of America
1   2   3   4   5   6   7   8   9   10

Library of Congress Cataloging in Publication Data

Louis, Arthur M
The tycoons.

Bibliography: p.
Includes index.
1.   Executives—United States—Biography.   I.   Title.
HF5500.3.U54L68   658.4′00973   80-25817
ISBN 0-671-24974-6

To Matt and Rich,
and in memory of Ida Sylvia Louis

Contents

"*There are geniuses in trade, as well as in war, or the State, or letters; and the reason why this or that man is fortunate is not to be told. It lies in the man; that is all anybody can tell you about it.*"

—RALPH WALDO EMERSON, "*Character*"

The
Tycoons

Chapter One

Born to Succeed

BEFORE THE turn of the century, the leaders of American business ranked among the great celebrities of their day. Communications weren't nearly as swift or as overpowering as they are now; yet almost everyone was familiar with the names and exploits of the mighty empire builders—men like Andrew Carnegie, E. H. Harriman, James J. Hill, Collis P. Huntington and John D. Rockefeller. They had their detractors, of course. The term "robber barons" was first applied to them by contemporaries—not, as commonly supposed, by a later generation in jaded retrospect. Although the robber barons were essentially selfish and entirely ruthless, they were grudgingly admired by common, workaday people. To the public they were the princes of an industrial renaissance, and in their way a force for good. Not only did they provide employment for the masses, but they also stirred hopes and ambitions among the lowly, while kindling a sense of national purpose in the wake of the Civil War. Their achievements were regarded with the kind of awe, envy and excitement that we now lavish on sports stars, entertainers and the gaudier politicians.

As the century turned, the face of American business changed dramatically. The robber barons were dying, or slipping into retirement, and their fiefdoms were consolidated into what came to be known as "modern" corporations, with newly issued stock scattered among thousands of absentee owners. The watershed, historians suggest, was the formation in 1901 of the United States Steel Corporation, which brought together many large producers, the most notable being the fiercely independent Carnegie Steel Company. Andrew Carnegie, by then in his mid-sixties, succumbed to the blandishments of the financier J. P. Morgan—the impresario of this and many other combinations—after exacting from him the fabulous sum of $492 million in bonds and stock. Carnegie was so devoutly entrepreneurial that he refused to consider salaried administrators as businessmen. "Strictly speaking," he wrote, "a man, to be in business, must be at least part owner of the enterprise which he manages and to which he gives his attention, and chiefly dependent for his revenues not upon salary but upon its profits."

How strange those words were to seem just a few decades later, when salaried administrators occupied the very top positions in practically all of America's leading companies. The large entrepreneurial organization never disappeared entirely, of course. Empire builders stubbornly continued to rise, bulling their way to the forefront of American business, and into the consciousness of the American public. Men like Henry Ford and H. L. Hunt, though in spirit they belonged to the nineteenth century, built their companies and their gigantic fortunes during the twentieth, and they managed to get by without sharing the ownership with outsiders. But despite such glaring exceptions, by 1950 only 5 percent of the top executives of the nation's largest railroads, utilities and industrial companies could be classed as entrepreneurs.

Today it is almost impossible for an individual to build a giant company and still retain a major portion of the stock. "Giant" now means revenues of several billion dollars, and companies normally attain that size only by issuing new stock to finance their expansion, or by acquiring or merging with other companies. Either way, the original proprietor's holdings will be diluted. Some of the more aggressive acquisitors of the modern era, the men who built the great conglomerates, can technically be described as entrepreneurs and proprietors. But it is the rare conglomerator who continues to hold even 5 percent of the stock in his company, let alone 50 percent. The merger movement, which reached the proportions of a mania during the sixties, has ebbed and flowed in recent years, but the general direction is clear. More and more economic power is becoming concentrated in fewer and fewer companies, which in turn are headed by men with less and less of an ownership stake.

These men exert tremendous leverage. Today's chief executive, even if he rose through the ranks and holds only a token amount of stock, has effective control of the entire company, with all its assets and all its power to do good or ill. There is no practical way for the shareholders, dispersed as they are, to interfere with his day-to-day operation of the business, and the board of directors is unlikely to intervene either, unless the chief executive is guilty of flagrant misconduct—or still worse, of extreme ineptitude. The chief executive has all the powers and prerogatives of a demigod, and in some companies "demi" merely describes the half of it.

The leaders of Big Business today are only dimly perceived—when they are perceived at all—by the general public. Their names are a matter of public record, of course, as are the financial statements of their companies. And if one happens to be an attentive reader of the business journals, it is possible to learn something about the personalities and backgrounds of at least some of the more prominent businessmen. But by and large, modern businessmen are highly trained professionals, with little of the flamboyance or the taste for glory that animated the robber barons, and they shy away from publicity. As a former chairman of one of the very largest companies has declared: "The more able the man, the less he stands out, the greater his relative anonymity outside his own immediate circle." In an era when business is subject to increasingly hostile scrutiny from regulatory agencies, the consumer movement and the press, a desire for anonymity is easy to understand.

But today's tycoons are too powerful and too important to remain hidden behind a veil. They control the destinies of tens of millions of employees, and can make or break tens of millions of shareholders as well. Their decisions and actions have a direct impact on customers, suppliers, consumers—in short, everyone. And their words carry considerable weight in the highest councils of government, both at home and abroad.

The purpose of this book is to pull aside the veil, to explain who the tycoons* are, what drives them, and why and how they reach the top. What is it that gives the tycoons their special edge? How do they differ from the unsuccessful American, and in particular from the unsuccessful businessman? Why do they succeed where others fail?

The answers are as fascinating as they are complex.

It was a pleasant Friday afternoon in the summer of 1973, and Irving Saul Shapiro, a senior vice president of the giant E. I. du Pont chemical company, was playing golf with his wife. Like most businessmen, Shapiro loves golf, and takes it very seriously, but there is scarcely an athletic fiber in his body, and he plays the game poorly. The spectacle of Shapiro hacking a path along a neatly tailored fairway in the lush Delaware countryside is enough to make a grounds keeper weep, or a pursuing foursome wriggle in frustration. After years of dedication he rarely breaks a hundred. Shapiro's sporting talents come to the fore only in sedentary, cerebral pursuits. By all accounts, he plays an exceptionally crafty hand of poker or gin rummy.

While Shapiro golfed, his boss, back at the Du Pont headquarters in Wilmington, was trying to reach him. Charles Brelsford McCoy, the chairman and chief executive officer of Du Pont, hadn't realized that Shapiro was taking a holiday. When Shapiro's secretary offered to track him down at the country club, McCoy told her not to bother. "It's not important," he said. "I'll try him on Monday." Brel McCoy is a reserved man, with a considerable gift for understatement, but that time he outdid himself. The news that he chose to save for next week was of the greatest importance to both Du Pont and Shapiro, and it was to cause quite a public stir as well.

* The word "tycoon" is derived from the Japanese, and its literal meaning is "great lord." The late tycoon Henry R. Luce, through the publications of Time Inc., made the word popular in this country. Many people think it applies only to businessmen who founded their own companies. But Luce, who was himself a founder, endorsed the use of "tycoon" to describe any highly successful businessman.

Shapiro strolled over to McCoy's cozy walnut-paneled office on Monday morning. He figured that McCoy wanted him to present a routine progress report, and after sitting down he seized the initiative, dilating on the various projects he had been handling. Shapiro was a member of Du Pont's top managerial body, the Executive Committee. A lawyer by training, he was in charge of matters relating not only to law, but also to public policy and finance. After Shapiro finished his presentation, McCoy started talking—at first about inconsequential matters. But then the conversation took an unexpected turn, and Shapiro, dumbfounded, asked for a piece of paper so he could take notes.

"He was laying out a course of action," Shapiro recalls, "in which I would be named vice chairman of the corporation. If all went well, by the end of the year I would be chairman and chief executive officer. I was in a state of surprise. I was hearing him, but he sometimes speaks in an elliptical manner. I wanted to make damn sure I understood. I wrote it down, and I read it back to him. He said, 'That's right.' " Shapiro preserved his notes for a while, initially to convince himself that he hadn't been dreaming, later as a souvenir of his climactic moment in business. Alas, the document eventually was lost, swept away in the continual flow of papers that pass through an executive's hands.

It was no surprise that McCoy, approaching the mandatory retirement age of sixty-five, was about to choose a successor. But nobody thought it would be Shapiro—least of all Shapiro himself. What made the appointment remarkable, and gave it historical significance as well, was the fact that Shapiro was a Jew, the son of humble immigrants from Lithuania. No one with a background even remotely similar had ever reached the top at Du Pont. Most of the chief executives of the company—which was founded in 1802—had belonged to the Du Pont family either by blood or marriage. Brel McCoy, the twelfth man to head the company, wasn't a Du Pont himself, nor had he married one. But two of his children did marry into the family, and his own father had served as a high-ranking officer of the company. McCoy was a secure and valued member of the Wilmington establishment. Of Scotch-Irish descent, and a Protestant like each of the chief executives before him, McCoy, a patrician in his own right, could trace his American roots back to pre-Revolutionary days—further back than the Du Ponts themselves. In choosing Shapiro to succeed him, he was bucking centuries of tradition.

As Shapiro himself gratefully observes, McCoy's action was exceptional not only for Du Pont, but for Big Business in general. Today, in what we like to consider an enlightened age, it still is rare for *any* major company to select a chief executive who is not white, male and Christian. Thanks to various new laws and regulations, women and minorities are currently getting more of a boost in business, and they may one day become commonplace among the tycoons—the chief executives of our largest companies. But the great majority of the present tycoons were helped to the top by prejudice, their success facilitated by an accident of birth. Many of them might justly wonder where they would be today if they had been forced to compete on fairer terms. Their situation calls to mind the old-time major-league baseball stars who would play exhibition games against the Negro teams and come away thankful that they didn't have to bat regularly against Satchel Paige or pitch to Josh Gibson.

Big Business still is awaiting its Jackie Robinson. There is not a single black at the head of any of the major American companies, if we define "major companies" as those listed in the annual *Fortune* directory. The directory includes 1,300 companies in all. First and foremost are the celebrated *Fortune* 500, the largest industrial companies ranked by revenues. There also is a Second 500, which includes the next-largest industrials, and there are fifty each of the largest commercial-banking companies, life insurance firms, diversified financial enterprises, retailers, transportation companies and utilities. Taken all together, they constitute the cream of American business—unsullied by black leadership.

It is only fair to point out that there is *some* trace of racial integration among the Big Business tycoons. William S. Anderson, the chief executive of the NCR Corporation, a *Fortune* 500 company that makes business machines, was born in Hankow, the son of British citizens, and is one-quarter Chinese. And one of the Second 500 companies, Wang Laboratories, a manufacturer of small computers, is headed by a full-blooded Chinese. But Dr. An Wang, who is a native of Shanghai, did not have to worry about bigoted personnel policies on his way to the top, since he founded the company himself.

Only one female heads a company listed in the *Fortune* directory. She is Katharine Graham, of the Washington Post Company, who became nationally renowned as the guardian angel of the Watergate journalists Woodward and Bernstein. Mrs. Graham did not have to work her way to the top. She inherited the job, which had been held by her father, Eugene Meyer, and later by her husband, Philip Graham, who committed suicide in 1963.

It is unlikely that significant numbers of women will join the ranks of the tycoons anytime soon. A recent study of the companies in the *Fortune* directory indicates that very few women are even within striking distance of the top. The author of the study, Wyndham Robertson, inspected all the proxy statements issued in 1978 by the companies in the directory. The companies were required to disclose the names of their three highest-paid officers and to indicate which directors earned more than $40,000 a year. In all, there were 6,400 executives and directors who fitted those categories, and ten of them—one-sixth of one percent—were women. Miss Robertson had made a similar survey of proxy statements issued six years earlier, and at that time there were eleven women in a universe of 6,500 executives and directors. It is difficult to discern any progress.

Women have found it nearly impossible to rise through the ranks of major companies. To get even *near* the top, they have been forced to take shortcuts. Of the ten high-ranking women executives in the 1978 study, five got there as entrepreneurs in partnership with their husbands, while two others (one of them Kay Graham) served in companies that were controlled by their families. Only three of the ten succeeded strictly as professionals, even though this is manifestly the era of professional management in Big Business. Two of the three women professionals actually began as secretaries—the stereotyped role for women in business. Joan Manley, a group vice president of Time Inc., had spent six years as a secretary for another publishing firm, and Dorothy Moore, corporate secretary of Michigan General, a financial holding company, had previously been personal secretary to the man who founded the firm. The third, Juliette Moran, an executive vice president of the GAF Corporation, the chemical manufacturer, started as a chemist during World War II. "I would never have been hired as a chemist if there had been a man in sight," she remarked.

For the greater part of this century, the Roman Catholics were among the principal victims of discrimination in Big Business. Social historians have suggested that Catholics were excluded from the upper reaches of business in retaliation for bumping the Protestants out of big-city politics. But whatever the reason, Catholics found it extremely difficult to reach the top in the nation's major companies. A survey made as recently as 1970 found that only 9 percent of the companies in the *Fortune* directory were headed by Catholics, a meager showing considering that Catholics accounted for 23 percent of the general population.

Lately, the Catholics have made an impressive surge. A survey of essentially the same companies, taken six years later, disclosed that the Catholics had increased their share to 14 percent of the chief executives. More-recent figures are not available, but it seems clear that the Catholics are continuing to gain ground and may soon achieve parity. They have been rising to the top in some of the very largest, most prestigious companies. In one notable demonstration of the new tolerance, the nation's largest insurance company, Prudential, appointed its first Catholic chief executive, Robert Arthur Beck, in 1978. Beck was born in 1925—in the Bronx, no less—and came of age during the postwar economic boom, a period when Big Business, desperate for talented young people, was forced to become less snooty. A fair share of Catholics got onto the managerial "fast track," and in the past decade or so the most talented of all have emerged as the top men in their companies.

When Thomas Aquinas Murphy joined General Motors four decades ago, he assumed that he would never be the top boss. As he recalls it, "If anybody had said, well, sometime in the future, there will be an Irish Catholic who would head not just General Motors, but probably any of the leading companies of the time, I would probably have said, 'You are out of your mind. The Irish are not going to get there, nor the Catholics.'" But as things turned out, the Catholics developed something of a dynasty at GM. In 1967, while Murphy was serving as comptroller, the company selected its first Catholic chief executive, James M. Roche, and Roche was followed by another Catholic, Richard C. Gerstenberg. Murphy succeeded Gerstenberg in 1974.

The Jews have few such happy stories to relate, although superficially they seem to be well represented among the tycoons. In one recent survey, Jews were shown to occupy 6 percent of the top jobs in companies listed in the *Fortune* directory, while their share of the general population was only 3 percent. The author of the study went so far as to assert that "Jews are now overrepresented." But the statistics in themselves are deceptive. The great majority of the Jewish chief executives either organized their own companies or are descended from men who did. Among the one hundred largest industrial companies, for example, there are four chief executives readily identifiable as Jewish, and three of them are entrepreneurs—Armand Hammer, of Occidental Petroleum; Leon Hess, of Amerada Hess; and Charles G. Bluhdorn, of Gulf and Western Industries. The only professional manager is the anomalous Irving Shapiro, of Du Pont. Unlike the Catholics, the Jews have enjoyed little success rising through the ranks as professional managers. When they do climb to the top, it is usually in companies with a history of Jewish leadership. In short, the Jewish tycoons are confined almost exclusively to "Jewish" companies.

Against this background, Shapiro's achievement at Du Pont seems absolutely astounding. In the heady aftermath of his rise to the top, he declared, "It's the American system that has paid off"—meaning, no doubt, the idealized American system, where the opportunities are the same for all and the most diligent and talented people inevitably succeed. But it would be more accurate to say that Shapiro succeeded in spite of the real American system, where people who happened to be of the right race, sex and religion were deemed more equal than others.

Shapiro's religion originally prevented him from even getting a job at Du Pont. An early job offer from the company had to be hastily and apologetically withdrawn after it was vetoed by an executive who didn't like Jews. That executive eventually moved elsewhere in the company, and the future chief executive of E. I. du Pont de Nemours and Company was finally permitted to join the legal staff in 1951. When Shapiro and his wife went house hunting in the Wilmington area, they found that many of the more desirable residential communities were restricted. They bought a house in Westwood Manor, and later they bought a tract of land in the suburb of Greenville, where they built their own house. Even in the early seventies, on the eve of his appointment as chief executive, Shapiro still had not been invited to join some of the fashionable clubs that had long since embraced his colleagues in top management. The Brandywine Country Club, where he persisted in his version of golf, had been organized by Jews who couldn't get into the other clubs in the area.

All sorts of clubs opened their doors to Shapiro after it was learned that he would be the chairman of Du Pont. He had the satisfaction of rejecting an invitation from an ultra-exclusive country club, where he could have become the first Jewish member ever. But he did join a dining club whose few Jewish members had been limited to the local judiciary. He explains that the contacts he makes there are helpful to his company.

On first inspection Irving Shapiro does not seem cast in the heroic mold. He is only five feet nine, and his 170 pounds, though about normal for his height, are poorly distributed, making him look plump. He has a large head and thick jowls, and his eyes peer out from heavily wrinkled pouches, set beneath dark, arched eyebrows. His black hair, tinged with gray, has receded slightly along his broad forehead. He looks very much like a gnome, or as some have suggested, "a wise old owl."

In conversation one begins to appreciate the true dimensions of the man. He speaks in a pleasant baritone, precisely and with great self-assurance. He is cool, but not cold, and has a quiet, sardonic sense of humor. He knows how to put people at their ease, and he tries to maintain friendly contact with the lowlier Du Pont employees. He used to stand in line and hobnob with the troops in the company cafeteria, but he had to give that up after he became chairman. "It doesn't work," he explained. "The whole place comes to a stop." He likes to visit the Du Pont plants and chat with the workers, asking them to explain their work and to offer opinions about the way things are run. "The employees are thrilled that you'll come and see them in their workplace and treat them as equals," he told one interviewer. "Well, they are equals, so it's no big deal, but from their perception the fact that the c.e.o. will come to the plant and try to get acquainted with them is very flattering." He believes strongly in the importance of *listening.* "People who accomplish things do more listening than talking," he has said. "It is deeds, not words, that count."

Shapiro is alert, quick and obviously intelligent. "No one else in Du Pont's top management," *Fortune* declared, "has his ability to analyze risks, to comprehend complex issues of law and politics, to negotiate, and to devise solutions that the company—and those watching it—can accept." He traveled far on intelligence, but he was helped as much by an extraordinary determination. The climb to the top was never easy, and he sometimes had to swallow his pride. There is a very tough and durable man beneath the cordial veneer.

Shapiro's parents came to the United States in the great wave of immigration around the turn of the century. His father, Samuel, had left Lithuania after a miserable interlude as a draftee in the Tsar's army. Sam Shapiro knocked around Europe for a few years, picking up seven different languages, before sailing to the U.S. in 1912 and settling in Minnesota, to which some friends had preceded him. He was a scholarly man whose greatest ambition was to practice law, but he couldn't afford the education, so he went to work instead as a pants presser in a dry-cleaning plant. A decade later, he started his own dry-cleaning business. Irving's mother, the former Freda Lane, had come over much earlier. Orphaned as a child, she traveled alone to New York City during the 1890s and got a job working twelve hours a day in a garment factory. She was to spend the next twenty years in the sweatshops, and on at least one occasion she was jailed overnight as a striker. While visiting a brother in Minneapolis, she met Sam Shapiro, and they were married after a brief courtship. Irving, the first of three sons, was born in July 1916.

Physically, young Irving was virtually a basket case. His manual dexterity was so poor that he actually flunked kindergarten. And he suffered throughout his childhood from asthma and eczema. But once he got past kindergarten, he proved to be an excellent student, with a special talent for mathematics, and even as a youngster he was poised and articulate.

The family dry-cleaning plant wasn't very profitable, and Irving and his brothers, Leonard and Jonas, were expected to work there in the evenings and on weekends. Irving didn't have enough mechanical ability to be trusted with the cleaning equipment, but he was allowed to drive a delivery truck, and he also would sort the dirty clothing. He came to loathe the work and would cast about for any excuse to avoid his chores. In later years a doctor told him that the lint-laden atmosphere probably had aggravated his asthma.

Shapiro was in his teens when the Great Depression struck. He recalls that there was rarely enough food around the house, nor could his family afford enough coal to heat their home adequately during the bitter Minnesota winters. He and his brothers would insert strips of cardboard in their shoes to replace worn-out soles. His childhood sweetheart, Charlotte Farsht, whom he later married, recalled that their dates were "something less than glamorous." They would walk his dog around a lake, and the only refreshments he could afford were two ice cream cones—one for Charlotte and one for the dog. Today, despite a salary of several hundred thousands per year, Shapiro retains his frugal habits. During a convention weekend at The Homestead, in Virginia, he was heard exhorting his wife to buy at Sears rather than at a high-priced boutique nearby.

Because of the economic pinch, Shapiro's father could afford to send only one son to college, and as the eldest, Irving was selected. He attended the University of Minnesota, where he received a bachelor's degree in 1939 and a law degree in 1941. He was an honor student, and never finished lower than tenth in a law-school class of 133. His father was able to give him $5 a week for expenses, and he earned a few dollars more at odd jobs. He also borrowed $200 a year, interest-free, from a special law-school fund. His skill at poker proved particularly helpful. He and a half-dozen other law students would get together for a game every Saturday afternoon, and by happy chance the group included an inept player with a wealthy father.

Left to his own devices, Shapiro might not have chosen law. His mathematical skill prompted him to consider a career in accounting. But his father, the frustrated lawyer, applied heavy pressure. Long after it was clear that he would never practice, Sam Shapiro would buy law books—and read them for pleasure! If he couldn't be a lawyer, at least his son could. Irving was doubtful even as he entered law school. It was only after his first exam that he thought things might work out all right. "I did rather well, which convinced me that I could be a successful lawyer. I had led a sheltered existence and had no decent measure of my own abilities. I had to demonstrate them to myself."

As one of the top students, Shapiro assumed that he wouldn't have much trouble landing a job. But the fact that he was Jewish proved a formidable barrier. Thurman W. Arnold, the assistant U.S. attorney general in charge of antitrust, was recruiting from the law schools, and Shapiro was one of four graduates from the University of Minnesota who applied. "Three of us were Jews," he recalls. "Only the one who wasn't Jewish made it. That was the New Deal, and the great liberal Thurman Arnold." He tried for another government job, with the Tennessee Valley Authority, which was known to have openings for lawyers. "We exchanged a series of letters, but nothing came of it. I don't know what happened." He made the rounds of the Minneapolis law firms—"a less than exhilarating experience. Anyone named Shapiro just didn't crash through in most of the law firms." Some of the younger lawyers, taking pity on him, sat him down and explained, "You're not going to make it unless you change your name." "The hell with that!" Shapiro retorted. "My parents labored to bring me up—I'm not going to give up their name." He finally found a local lawyer who provided him with office space in return for occasional services. He spent much of his time searching titles for prospective home buyers.

Shapiro had been carrying on this mundane practice for only a few months when the Japanese bombed Pearl Harbor. The government hastily organized the Office of Price Administration, and the call went out for lawyers to help draw up the regulations. An OPA recruiter visited the University of Minnesota, and a professor recommended Shapiro. Shapiro agreed to serve and hopped a train to Washington in January 1942. On arriving at Union Station, he caught sight of the Capitol dome. "I walked over there and walked around. I was absolutely out of my skin. I reported late to work." Today's young people, he contends, are too blasé to be deeply affected by such an experience. Not long after he started with the OPA, Shapiro was called for his draft examination, but he was declared ineligible because of his history of asthma.

He remained for more than a year in the OPA's rationing division. "We spent half our time responding to mail," he recalls. "I found I could write better than *some* people who were lawyers. It gave me a clue for the future." The lawyer at the next desk, a young man from California named Richard M. Nixon, left after a few months to join the Navy. Shapiro got to know Nixon pretty well during their brief time as colleagues. "He was different then —one of the boys—and he got along very well with people." They met to compare notes several years later, when Nixon was a Communist-hunting congressman, and Shapiro, by then with the Justice Department, was serving as an assistant prosecutor in the famous Communist Eleven trial. They didn't meet again until two decades later, in a receiving line, while Nixon was President. "He didn't know who I was," Shapiro says, "or at least he played it that way."

Having decided that the OPA was "no place for a lawyer," Shapiro went to the Justice Department, hoping for something better. He couldn't get a job with the civil division, but the criminal division hired him. Still in his twenties, he proved to be something of a boy wonder. By one account, he "quickly earned a reputation at Justice as a superb writer of briefs, with an ability to grasp the critical issue in a case, clarify it, and argue convincingly in support of the government's position." Early in his career he was assigned to argue a case concerning the draft before the Supreme Court. He had never before argued in any court, let alone the highest in the land. What was more, the case was considered a sure loser—which is why it was handed to a novice. But Shapiro sensed an opportunity and spent countless hours preparing for his courtroom debut. He lost, as expected, but he managed to make it close, with three of the eight participating justices favoring his case. Shapiro's appearance before the Court was witnessed by a battalion of high-powered lawyers, who were waiting to argue a major antitrust case, and his reputation at Justice was greatly enhanced.

His assignment to the Communist Eleven trial was a token of esteem from his superiors. It was one of the most important and difficult trials of the century, and also among the longest. The trial was controversial at the time, and in retrospect it seems to have been one of the more dubious extravaganzas of the Cold War. Eleven leaders of the American Communist party were indicted in 1948 by a federal grand jury on charges of conspiracy to advocate the overthrow of the government by force and violence—a crime under the Smith Act. The trial began in January 1949 at the Federal Courthouse on Foley Square in Manhattan, and continued for nine stormy months. All eleven defendants were found guilty by a jury and were fined and imprisoned. Ten of them received prison terms of five years each, while the other got three years after Judge Harold R. Medina took note of his outstanding war record. Six defense lawyers also were sentenced to prison, for contempt of court.

There was strong feeling among civil libertarians that the Smith Act was unconstitutional. No actual attempt at violent overthrow was charged. The act permitted the government to prosecute the Communists for their words alone—an apparent abridgement of their freedom of speech. But an appeal of the verdict was rejected by the Circuit Court in 1950, and the Supreme Court declined to reverse the judgment.

Shapiro concedes that he felt uneasy about the law he was enforcing. "If I had been a legislator, I would not have voted for the Smith Act," he remarks. But he never considered turning down the assignment, nor did he go about it halfheartedly. "It wasn't up to me to decide which laws I liked and which I didn't." He now says he doesn't think it was necessary to send the Communists to jail—which may or may not be a consolation to the surviving defendants. But he believes he still can offer a rationale for the trial. "The case was useful for ventilating the facts about the Communist party," he explains. "It exposed the internal operations, the underground, the aliases, all the conspiratorial aspects. It was a revelation. The behavior of the defense lawyers, trying to take over the courtroom, opened the eyes of the country. The resident intellectuals in this country thought the Communist party was a strong force that couldn't be contended with. Things ring in my memory—like the confidential informants who refused to go on the witness stand, on the grounds that 'you guys aren't good enough to take on the Party.' The U.S. Attorney in New York wouldn't use his own staff. He said, 'If Washington

wants to prosecute, they're gonna have to send me a staff.' It was
totally different than in today's world."

Shapiro lived in New York hotels throughout the trial while his
wife and children remained behind in Washington. He was able
to visit them only on alternate weekends. He rarely spoke up
during the trial proceedings, spending most of his time on backup
work for U.S. Attorney John F. X. McGohey, who handled the
bulk of the prosecution. When the case was appealed, however,
Shapiro not only prepared the government briefs, but also argued at length in court.

His prominent participation in the appeal led to a job offer
from Du Pont. His former boss at Justice, Oscar A. Provost, had
joined Du Pont's legal department. Provost happened to be in
New York while the case was being argued before the Circuit
Court, and he noticed Shapiro's name in the New York *Times*. He
reached Shapiro at the courthouse, and they got together for
lunch. Provost offered Shapiro $12,000 a year to join the legal
staff—$2,000 more than he was making at Justice. Provost had
made a similar overture a couple of years earlier, but Shapiro had
been blackballed because he was Jewish.

Despite the earlier snub, Shapiro eagerly accepted. He was
lured by the $2,000 raise, which was big money in those days.
Moreover, his prospects at Justice seemed murky. He had risen
to assistant chief of the criminal division's appellate section, which
placed him outside the protection of Civil Service. He was a Democrat, and if a Republican administration was to take over, he
probably would be dismissed. He pondered whether to join a law
firm or a company and decided that a company would be more
suitable. "I felt I could be more effectively employed in a legal
department with clients whom I knew, and who knew me, and
with whom I had a continuing relationship. It was a bit of intro-
spection. I tried to figure where my talents were, and where my
shortcomings. I figured I would not be a scintillating personality
in dealing with clients. I was a quiet young man, not very distinguishable from a lot of other young men, and I felt I played
better in this setting. In a sense, it was a matter of security. I felt
more comfortable in a familiar setting rather than working with
strangers."

A friend from the Anti-Defamation League of B'nai B'rith tried to talk Shapiro out of going to Du Pont. "He said, 'You're out of your mind,' " Shapiro recalls. But Du Pont had "persisted in coming after me"—so it must really have wanted him. Besides, he might have had to face bigotry almost anywhere he worked. In the Justice Department itself his attempt to join Thurman Arnold's trustbusters had been foiled for what seemed to be reasons of religion. And he remembered another unpleasant occasion, while he was working at Justice, when Attorney General Tom C. Clark had complained that there were too many Jewish names on government briefs.

Shapiro had no experience with the problems that concerned a Du Pont lawyer most—trade regulation and antitrust. He bought a lot of books and spent his first few weeks getting educated. He was placed in the antitrust section of the legal department, where he advised sales managers how to avoid government lawsuits. Later he was promoted to senior lawyer, serving in effect as general counsel for several industrial departments. The industrial managers were accustomed to lawyers who seemed almost eager to squelch their bright ideas. But in Shapiro they found a lawyer with a positive attitude, one who would not simply tell them "no," but would suggest an alternative. Shapiro, it seemed, was more than just a lawyer—he had a talent for business. The word spread, and executives from all over the company started flocking to his office. "People started coming around saying that they had a legal problem," he remarks, "but what they really had was a business problem. There is nothing more important to a businessman than to have someone who will solve a problem, particularly someone who will shed some tears with him when he's feeling pain." He made valuable alliances with many of Du Pont's rising young managers. "I built my own clientele, and it was natural for me to move along as they moved along."

His progress was not entirely smooth, however. Once he nearly quit the company, after failing to receive a promotion he felt he had earned. "The most traumatic experience I had at Du Pont," he says, "was being passed over for a division manager's job in the legal department in fifty-three or fifty-four. The job went to someone else whom I didn't consider as qualified. The choice was made by the general counsel. I think it was a personal choice, related to intramural considerations, with nothing to do with merits." Shapiro vowed that he would leave Du Pont in a year if his prospects didn't improve. But he kept the vow to himself. "Anyone who advertises for a promotion is slitting his throat," he observes, "though I don't think there was any question about my views. The job has to seek the man. If the merit is there, it's gonna be obvious to people who make the appropriate decisions. I think people are able to communicate messages about their ambitions, but not by unsheathing a weapon. In our culture, it's the wrong tactic. An organization looks for talent, and seeks to promote it. You don't get ahead by confrontation, but by demonstrating that someone misjudged you."

Before the one-year deadline was reached, Shapiro received his first big bonus—$17,000. "It looked like an absolute fortune to me," he says. "It was a lot of money, and took care of a lot of pain. Don't ever discount money as a palliative for this kind of pain." He was persuaded to linger awhile, and later, under a new general counsel, he became assistant general counsel, leapfrogging the man who had beaten him out for the division manager's job.

A couple of years before Shapiro joined Du Pont, the company had been hit with a monumental antitrust suit. The Justice Department demanded that Du Pont get rid of its immense holdings in General Motors—63 million shares, or nearly one-quarter of the total outstanding. The stock was a throwback to the second decade of the century, when Du Pont's management had helped reorganize the auto company. The Justice Department charged Du Pont's latter-day managers with using the holdings to control GM's purchasing policies.

It was four years before all the documents were examined, all the depositions were taken, and the case was ready for trial. By that time, Shapiro had begun to make his mark at Du Pont. Although he was not assigned directly to the trial, he did play a crucial role. He provided a link between the trial lawyers—marooned in Chicago, where the government chose to wage the battle—and top management in Wilmington. He served as an interpreter to management, explaining the proceedings in laymen's terms, and offering advice when asked. The more they saw of Shapiro, the more the top bosses were impressed, and the assignment gave his career a substantial boost. Shapiro recalls one memorable meeting in the office of Walter S. Carpenter, Du

Pont's chairman at the time. Carpenter was obviously pleased with Shapiro's presentation. As Shapiro was leaving, Carpenter warmly remarked, "Mr. Shapiro, my name is Walter." Very few people at Du Pont were on a first-name basis with the chairman, and Shapiro was startled. He did have enough wits about him to make the obvious reply: "My name is Irving."

The General Motors case ground through the courts for over a decade, and at the end Shapiro was Du Pont's lawyer in charge. Although Du Pont's executives were cleared of personal wrong-doing, the company was forced to get rid of the stock, as the Justice Department had demanded. The company had a choice of selling its huge block on the market—which would have griev-ously depressed the price of all GM shares—or distributing the stock to its own shareholders, in proportion to their holdings in Du Pont. It preferred to distribute the shares, but under the law the Du Pont shareholders would have to pay tax on the full share value. Shapiro then launched a successful lobbying effort in Washington to ease the shareholders' tax burden. Congress passed a law that permitted the recipients to treat the GM shares as a return of capital, cutting the tax liability in half. In 1965, around the time the distribution of shares was completed, Sha-piro was promoted to the Number Two position in the legal de-partment.

In 1970, Ralph Nader sent a team of his "raiders" to study Du Pont's role in the state of Delaware. Shapiro acted as liaison man for the company, and he kept the raiders on a short leash. "When they came in," he declared, "they thought they had the right to wander through the halls, walk into any man's office, and talk about anything they wanted. We said no dice." Shapiro attended the interviews within the company and recorded them all on tape. The Naderites eventually published a highly unfavorable book-length report, entitled *The Corporate State*, which contended that Du Pont dominated the social and political affairs of Delaware and abused its power with a heavy hand.

The report sorely disappointed Brel McCoy, by then the chief executive of Du Pont, but he was pleased with Shapiro's handling of the matter. Not long after the raiders cleared out, he promoted Shapiro over the heads of the general counsel and several other high-ranking managers, onto the powerful Executive Committee and the board of directors. Shapiro was given the title of vice president, and he became a senior vice president less than two years later. McCoy put Shapiro on the Executive Committee against the strenuous advice of other Du Pont officers, who protested that it was too big a jump. Shapiro thought it was "gutsy" of McCoy to take a gamble on him, and wondered whether he would have had the courage to make such a move himself.

After joining the Executive Committee, Shapiro played an important role in merging Du Pont with the Christiana Securities Company. Christiana was a holding company whose principal asset was a 28 percent stake in Du Pont itself. It was controlled by the Du Pont family, and was the vehicle through which the family had, in turn, controlled the chemical company. By the 1970s, however, there were hundreds of family members scattered across the landscape, and they no longer functioned as a unit. The Du Pont management feared that Christiana might be taken over by some other company and that control of Du Pont would pass to outsiders. Under the terms of the proposed merger, the shareholders of Christiana would receive a nice premium over the market value of their shares. It was up to Shapiro to convince the Securities and Exchange Commission, which oversees such matters, that the merger also would benefit the Du Pont stockholders. He did convince the SEC, but some Du Pont stockholders objected anyway, and the matter went to court. The merger finally took effect in 1977.

Despite Shapiro's string of triumphs, the odds against his reaching the top seemed much too strong. It wasn't only that he was Jewish, though that was certainly handicap enough. Du Pont ordinarily got its top men from operations, not staff, and no lawyer had ever been chosen chief executive. A Du Pont chief executive was supposed to be a chemist or engineer, who thoroughly understood the arcane details of the multi-billion-dollar production process. Moreover, Shapiro was a latecomer to Du Pont, having arrived in his mid-thirties. The company's top managers typically came to Du Pont straight out of school and spent their entire adult lives learning the business.

McCoy had led everyone to assume that his successor would be Edward R. Kane, who fitted the mold perfectly. A handsome, hard-driving man, two years younger than Shapiro, Kane had joined the company in 1943, after earning a doctorate in chemistry at the Massachusetts Institute of Technology. He started out doing experimental research with nylon, then moved through a succession of supervisory positions in both research and manufacturing. He was appointed to the Executive Committee in 1969, a year ahead of Shapiro, and was promoted to vice chairman of the committee—second only to McCoy in the managerial hierarchy —in 1971. At the time, the promotion was meant to herald the succession.

Then McCoy changed his mind. He perceived that Du Pont— to say nothing of American industry in general—had entered a period when public-policy problems overshadowed routine business matters. In the years ahead Du Pont would need, above all, a leader who could deal effectively with the growing challenges from government and consumers. Shapiro had a genuine zeal for public affairs, taking an active role in charities and other community projects around Wilmington. And he served as chairman of Du Pont's Public Affairs Committee, which advised and guided the company on social and governmental issues. Ed Kane, by contrast, took only a passing interest in such matters. In earlier, less-troubled times, Kane, a first-rate operating man, might have become chairman. Instead he was appointed president and chief operating officer, taking charge of Du Pont's inside activities, while Shapiro, as chairman and chief executive, roamed the world outside.

Today Shapiro estimates that he devotes between 30 and 40 percent of his time to external affairs. That estimate seems borne out by his schedule during one typical week in the spring of 1980. On the first day, Monday, he confined himself to intramural matters. There were meetings with the Finance Committee and the board of directors, then luncheon with the board, then a series of management meetings. That evening he played host at a formal dinner for 200 members of management. On Tuesday the outside activities predominated. Shapiro went to New York to attend the board meetings of Citibank and its parent, Citicorp, both of which he serves as a director. He returned to Wilmington by helicopter, eating lunch aboard. At his office he was visited by Dean Graham Allison, of the John F. Kennedy School of Govern-

ment at Harvard, and Elliot L. Richardson—*the* Elliot Richardson
—who like Shapiro is a member of the school's Visiting Committee. Shapiro had been too busy to attend the previous committee
meeting, and the pair brought him up to date. In the evening
Shapiro attended a dinner for some Mexican dignitaries, sponsored by Du Pont's International Department. On Wednesday he
flew to Atlanta, where he gave a speech entitled "Managing
Safety" to the Institute of Nuclear Power Operations. He flew
back to Wilmington to take care of his mail and telephone calls
and to hold a few quick meetings. Then it was dinner out again,
this time with some local civic leaders. On Thursday he held an
early meeting with the managers of Du Pont's Finance Department. Then he flew to Washington to talk with two assistant attor-
neys general about criminal-code legislation. He was acting on
behalf of the Business Roundtable, a powerful national lobby.
Back in Wilmington he met with the Delaware Roundtable, a
group of businessmen concerned with the state economy and
other matters of public policy. Then he was off and flying again
—to upstate New York, where he had dinner with a major customer. Friday was almost entirely taken up with a meeting of the
Du Pont Executive Committee. And Shapiro spent Saturday and
Sunday reviewing staff reports that would require decisions the
following week.

He *does* manage to keep occupied.

Shapiro says some of his colleagues were concerned that Jewish
organizations might make heavy demands on him and that this
would divert him from the business of running Du Pont. He
acknowledges that the organizations have indeed made their demands, but says he doesn't let this conflict with his job. "Most of
the demands have been involved with fund raising," he remarks.
"The president of a Jewish university called on me the other day,
to put pressure on an investment banker. I felt it was ethically
improper since the investment banker earns money from Du
Pont." He is also frequently asked to speak at banquets and other
gatherings sponsored by Jewish groups, but he generally refuses.
"I feel that most of my speaking engagements should be for the
benefit of Du Pont."

Shapiro's performance in the public arena has earned him the
deep respect of his fellow tycoons. He now ranks as one of the

most influential men in American business—a leader among leaders. He served for a time as chairman of the Business Roundtable and remains an extremely active member. The Roundtable is limited to the upper crust of business management, its membership consisting of 190 chief executives of major companies. (Precisely *which* companies is a closely kept secret.) The organization's chief goal is to combat what Shapiro calls "an unprecedented government regulation of business."

As one of the few Democrats at the head of a blue-chip company, Shapiro was helped by an unusually good relationship with President Carter. In fact, the President tried in vain to recruit Shapiro as secretary of the treasury at the start of his Administration. Carter and his aides frequently called Shapiro to the White House for consultation, and Shapiro influenced many important decisions.

In one highly publicized episode, he helped frame the legislation—signed by Carter in June 1977—that restrains American business from cooperating with the Arab boycott of Israel. While serving as chairman of the Roundtable, he approached the leaders of the Anti-Defamation League, which was urging Congress to pass such a law. He suggested that instead of fighting each other the two organizations should work out a compromise. They did, and Congress passed their draft of the bill essentially unchanged. Although he has been a supporter of Jewish causes, Shapiro did not forget which hat he was wearing on this occasion. Congress already opposed the boycott, and some political observers say the Anti-Defamation League might have obtained stronger legislation on its own.

Shapiro has often expressed misgivings about letting private citizens make public policy, and he concedes that his activities in the boycott matter "came close." "In a democratic society it's necessary and appropriate that people make their views on policy known," he says, "but there has to be a sharp line between people who are in public office and those who aren't. The boycott case is as close as you can come without overstepping the boundaries. The intensity of the problem justified it."

Having had the benefit of Shapiro's leadership and counsel, some of his fellow tycoons appear to have modified their attitudes toward Jews within their own companies. It has occurred to them that it might actually be a good idea to let Jews have a shot at the top jobs. For the first time in memory, the American Telephone and Telegraph Company has a Jewish executive within reach of the pinnacle. Morris Tanenbaum, a chemist by training, was recently promoted to executive vice president, and he is considered a dark-horse candidate to succeed the present AT&T chief executive, Charles Lee Brown, Jr., who is scheduled to retire in 1986. If a seemingly impregnable WASP fortress like AT&T were to fall, and if some women and blacks were to join the ranks of the tycoons as well, then it really would be time to acclaim the "American system."

Chapter Two

The Crucible

PRACTICALLY ALL of today's tycoons were raised during the Great Depression. It was not a time when Big Business enjoyed the highest esteem. Millions of Americans looked upon the prominent businessmen of the day as greedy, grasping villains who had helped drag the nation to disaster. Franklin D. Roosevelt himself, in his first inaugural address, lashed out at the "unscrupulous money changers"—as he called the leaders of the financial community—and demanded "an end to a conduct in banking and in business which too often has given to a sacred trust the likeness of callous and selfish wrongdoing." Many of the New Deal reforms were designed to bring business firmly to heel.

Even in this hostile atmosphere the future tycoons learned to revere the free-enterprise system. They were, by and large, a privileged breed—members of relatively affluent families who were intimately bound up with the system. A recent survey of the heads of several hundred major companies indicates that nearly half of them were themselves the children of business proprietors or managers. Most of the others had fathers in the professions, or in white-collar jobs just below the managerial level. Only one tycoon in six grew up in a blue-collar family. And only one in eleven claims to have been poor. Scarcely a household in the nation was not squeezed to some degree by the Depression, but the tycoons were generally more comfortable than most. They were well housed, well clothed and well fed, and they were able to go to college—which was quite a distinction in their day. Not only did seven out of every eight chief executives graduate from college, but nearly half of them earned advanced degrees as well.

Many of the older tycoons attended college during the early and middle thirties, when radical organizations were flourishing on campuses throughout the country. Irving Shapiro, of E. I. du Pont, recalls that there were groups at the University of Minnesota, his alma mater, agitating for free love and against the military, as well as those seeking the downfall of capitalism. He spurned them all. While his bank account might have been proletarian, his background and temperament were emphatically bourgeois. His father's dry-cleaning plant was, after all, a business —if not a large or prosperous one. "I grew up identifying with that, never knowing just how small it was," he remarks.

Nor did the radical causes hold any appeal for John Thomas Connor, a future head of both Merck and Company and Allied Chemical. Born in 1914, Connor was the oldest of five children of an oil distributor in Syracuse, New York. The business did well enough during the Depression, and all the children went to college. But their father had suffered heavy losses in the stock-market crash, so a certain amount of frugality was required. John wanted to go to Dartmouth but had to attend college locally instead. He graduated from Syracuse University in 1936. There were several radical groups singing their siren songs on the Syracuse campus. One group that Connor remembers in particular was called Veterans of Future Wars—"arising from disillusionment with U.S. participation in World War I, and fueled by the Depression." But Connor remained, as he puts it, "a straight arrow," who confined himself to his studies and to the more conventional extracurricular activities. "I was in the top 5 percent scholastically," he recalls. "I was captain of the golf team; for three years I was manager of the football team; I was president of the senior class, president of the fraternity, and so forth. I got a taste of managing things in those days, and discovered I enjoyed it. I think I played a constructive role and did some good work for the class and the school. I generally supported institutions, including the university. I thought the U.S. was a great place in which to live, full of opportunities for ambitious and energetic young people. I heard all the antibusiness arguments and understood the need to control excesses, but I felt that the private sector had a function to fulfill."

Of all the present-day tycoons, perhaps the closest to a radical hell-raiser was Charles Franklin Luce, today the chief executive of the Consolidated Edison Company. To meet him now, one would never suspect that Luce had nearly been kicked out of college for challenging faculty censorship of a student newspaper, or that he had helped organize a boycott against restaurants that underpaid their workers. Slender and over six feet tall, with carefully groomed gray hair, he speaks softly and precisely, and his bearing is prim and proper. He seldom smiles, as befits the head of New York City's star-crossed utility. He could easily pass for a British aristocrat, an Episcopalian divine or the stereotype of a successful businessman.

Luce had a rockier childhood than most tycoons. He was born in the little town of Platteville, Wisconsin, in 1917, the older of two sons of James Oliver Luce, a farm boy who had married a girl from a prosperous family. James Luce took charge of the furniture store and mortuary that were left by his father-in-law. Under his care the businesses went broke well before the Depression. He also lost a bundle of money by investing heavily in farm real estate during 1919 and 1920, just before the bottom fell out of the market. He was forced to take a job as a manual laborer in a plant that produced sulfuric acid, and he rose to the rank of foreman before the plant shut down during the early thirties. Over the next few years he worked sporadically for the federal and state governments. Finally, in 1936, he was appointed postmaster, and the family's financial problems ended.

Charles Luce recalls that his father was "a very intelligent man, very bright—he had almost total recall." But he is clearly disappointed that his father failed to use that intelligence effectively. The elder Luce had dropped out of college in his sophomore year, upon getting married, and although he was a top student, he never went back. "He was quite impulsive, kind of a dreamer," says Charles. "There's a theory of negative learning. You either emulate the faults or virtues of parents, or you turn them around —reverse them." Charles vowed that he would become a success.

His determination was spurred by a physical handicap. He had contracted polio before he was old enough to walk, and was forced to wear a brace until he was eight years old, when an operation relieved his condition somewhat. (He still wears corrective shoes and walks with a pronounced limp.) Luce felt acutely aware that he was different, particularly when other children taunted him about his limp. On one occasion he got a job as a caddie at the local golf course, but the other caddies laughed at him and called him "Stepin Fetchit," and one of them beat him up. His mother went to the club the next day and got the bully fired. To prove that he was just one of the gang, Luce would join in even the roughest sports, such as football, or the most implausible, such as hiking. But his stamina was limited, a fact that others couldn't always appreciate. "We had a gym teacher who was a nut on running," he recalls. "He was ahead of his time, it would seem. I couldn't run for a long stretch—only in sprints. I got sick and threw up. I talked to my mother about it. My father went and got that gym teacher, and beat the pants off him. He didn't tell me about it—I just found out. He was very supportive." Nowadays, Luce rides a bicycle for exercise, pedaling a few miles each weekend near his home in Westchester County.

While still a fifth-grader, Luce decided that he wanted to be a lawyer. His interest in the law had been stimulated by an uncle who was a county judge. Judge Roscoe Luce would regale the family with colorful accounts of his court cases. Young Charles was fascinated, and he also couldn't help noticing that his uncle was financially well heeled. One evening at dinner, Uncle Roscoe told him, "Charles, you study hard and go to law school. By then I'll be ready to retire as a judge, and we'll go into the practice of law together." Charles took him seriously, and he was nearly finished with law school before he realized that the judge had forgotten. He did clerk for his uncle a couple of summers, but the old man didn't step down from the bench until Charles was in his mid-forties. "I never reminded him of his promise," Charles remarks. "I wouldn't have wanted to make him feel bad." Luce spent fifteen years practicing law, and the next six as an administrator with the federal government, before finally going into business. Con Edison was his first corporate employer, and he started there as chief executive.

After having attended Platteville State Teachers College for two years, Luce had switched to the University of Wisconsin, where he received both his undergraduate and law degrees. He was a fanatically dedicated student, and he graduated with high honors. He worked so hard that his parents, always protective where he was concerned, would urge him to take it easy. "The Depression was a strong motivator to study hard," he recalls. "I saw what unemployment meant. I knew by the time I entered law school that not many graduates got jobs, and the top students were more likely to get jobs." Perhaps as a legacy of the Depression, Luce today lives unpretentiously. He prefers hamburgers and hot dogs from a lunch cart to more lavish fare, and he wears his drab, conservatively tailored suits until they start to disintegrate.

Luce's education nearly came to an abrupt halt while he was at Platteville State. He wasn't on the staff of the school paper, the *Exponent,* but he had sent the paper a letter attacking faculty censorship. Not surprisingly, the faculty publications committee wouldn't let it be printed. When Luce protested this decision, a faculty member suggested that he publish the broadside himself. Luce took the advice, and carried it a step further. He published a newspaper of his own, containing not only the attack on censorship but articles on other subjects as well. For six dollars he was able to use the printing press at the Grant County *News,* where he had been working part-time, and he got the money back in fees from his readers. But Luce's little exercise in free speech and free enterprise angered Asa Royce, the president of the college. "He was getting ready to bust me," Luce recalls. Luce went to see a member of the state board of regents—"he was a liberal"—and the man interceded for him. A year or so later, after Luce had moved along to the University of Wisconsin, Platteville State abandoned censorship.

At Wisconsin, Luce joined a group called the United League for Liberal Action, whose chief aim was to reform the economic system. He says it was a natural step, since he was descended from a long line of liberals. "Father was a Democrat and a political liberal to his dying day," Luce remarks. "FDR was a hero in our family. I can remember the family sitting around the radio. When he said, 'The only thing we have to fear . . . ,' the whole family just cried. We would have died for that man." The United League waged a campaign to ensure that restaurant workers around the campus were adequately paid. The members checked the restaurants to see whether they were honoring the legal minimum wage, which at the time was 23 cents an hour. Then they staged a boycott—with picket lines and blacklists—against those that didn't comply with the law.

Some tycoons seem embarrassed at having gotten through the Depression without suffering. They know that a rise from rags to riches makes more exciting copy, and they become a trifle inventive in recounting their early days. Thomas Murphy, for example, in his official General Motors biography, is quoted as stating flatly, "I didn't have enough money to go to college." He graduated from high school in 1932, but couldn't afford to resume his education until the fall of 1934—so the story goes. The official account seems a mite puzzling, however, when one considers that Murphy's father held a good job throughout the Depression as manager of a City Products Company icehouse. Many youngsters of that era were less fortunate in their choice of parents, but still managed to make it through college without a two-year delay.

In person, Murphy tells a somewhat different story. A tall, genial man, with wavy gray hair and dark horn-rimmed glasses, he recalls that he was an able but unenthusiastic scholar at St. Leo High School in Chicago. By the time he graduated, he felt that college would be a waste of money and time. Employment seemed much more precious than education in those days, and he knew a lot of young people who had skipped college or even dropped out of high school when they found a job. There was no telling when they might find another. "I would say that our horizons were shortened, because we couldn't see beyond," Murphy remarks. "You know—things are down, and they had been down, and it didn't look like there was any ready way that they were going to come up."

Despite his earnest efforts, Murphy couldn't find steady employment. He performed heavy labor at the City Products icehouse during the summers, when business was at its peak; but he would be out of work the rest of the year, and after spending his meager earnings, he would have to live off his parents. "I don't think I would have settled for the icehouse," he says, "but if I could have gotten a job someplace else that would have given me year-round employment, I certainly would have been willing to take it, and forget the education." That's how close General Motors came to missing Tom Murphy.

Murphy says he never felt seriously deprived by the Depression —although he did have a $100 savings account in a bank that suddenly closed. "But I think that atmosphere kind of left a mark on anybody who was, let's say, conscious at the time," he remarks. "The very fact that you had that experience of living through an era like that—it left you with some mental scars." Most significantly, he says, it made him conservative in business, quick to pull the reins when his young subordinates got carried away with their bright ideas. One of Murphy's colleagues at GM joked that the boss suffered from "depression-induced brain damage."

It took considerable prodding to get Murphy into a college classroom. He had become friendly with a coworker at the icehouse named Al Adams, who was an upperclassman at the University of Illinois. "Why don't you go back to school?" Adams demanded. "You're going to be around here breaking your back the rest of your life if you don't get more of an education." Adams said the money he earned during the summers covered most of his college expenses and that he was able to make up the rest by taking odd jobs. "You could do it," Adams remarked, "if you really wanted to." Their supervisor overheard the conversation and suggested that they all ride over to the university campus and have a look. They visited the dormitory where Adams stayed— "not the most palatial in the world," Murphy thought. And they picked up some literature describing the undergraduate program. "And then my mother kind of got on my back," Murphy recalls. "At any rate, I finally decided to give it a shot. All it took to get into the University of Illinois at that time was a transcript of your credits from high school and the matriculation fee. And I truthfully don't remember whether that was five dollars or ten dollars. I have a feeling it was ten." Not taking any chances, Alma Murphy accompanied her son to the registrar's office and stood in line with him.

As they neared the registration window, she asked him what he was planning to study. He hadn't given it much thought. His friend Adams was majoring in physical education, and Murphy himself—strong and lanky—was a good baseball player. "But then I thought, well, I'm interested in athletics, but not to the extent where I'd want to think about it as being my livelihood. I guess at one time I would have given my right arm to be a professional baseball player, but I didn't have quite the ability." He had taken some postgraduate courses in bookkeeping, typing and shorthand at a public high school. "So I thought, well, maybe business wouldn't be a bad idea." He certainly didn't harbor any antibusiness sentiment. In fact, he claims that he never even encountered any during his youth—"perhaps because of the background of my parents. They were good, solid, hardworking Christian people. And I'd say that most of the people that we came in contact with, and the education that I got, certainly was not in any way prejudicial to business."

Murphy did well at Illinois, although he was rusty at first, after his long absence from study. In retrospect he is glad he waited to go to college, because the delay gave him time to mature. He had skipped a grade in grammar school, so he was only sixteen years old when he got out of high school. "I think probably that academically it would have been a lot easier for me if I'd gone straight from high school into the university," he says. "But I don't think it would have been as beneficial for me. I think those two years that I was out made me appreciate probably more fully the importance of education, and made the education, let's say, a broader experience." He graduated in 1938 with a degree in accounting and went directly to work for GM.

The head of the American Telephone and Telegraph Company is one tycoon who will freely concede that the Depression had no harsh or enduring impact on his life. Charles L. Brown, Jr., the first of two children, was born in 1921, so the Depression coincided with his youth. His father himself worked for AT&T, having joined the company after a brief fling as a college mathematics teacher. He was to stay with the company for thirty-seven years, serving as a traffic manager in the Long Lines Department.

While the elder Brown never lost his job, he did work only part-time for a while. Even the telephone company was forced to retrench during the Depression, since many customers couldn't pay their bills and their phones had to be removed. But the period of retrenchment didn't impress Charles, Jr., as hard times. "We were always a reasonably frugal family," he relates. "I didn't feel as though I was badly restricted, or that we were suffering deeply, though I certainly realized we couldn't have all the things we wanted. We were on a fairly low budget in the twenties, and this was more a continuation of the same thing. I had a home life that was satisfactory, not lavish or, on the other hand, in any way poverty-stricken. I was able to attend school, to work in the summers and have a fairly balanced view of what money meant." When it came time to choose his own career, he never hesitated to enter business. "I don't recall that I ever had anything else in mind."

There *are* some tycoons whose families were genuinely poor, even by Depression standards. They might conceivably have turned to crime, or even revolution, but they were kept in line by parents who had a strong respect for institutions. They acquired an appetite for money, not rebellion, and they vowed, like Scarlett O'Hara before the intermission, that they would break the bonds of poverty. A career in business struck them, not as something odious or shameful, but as their greatest opportunity for success.

By all odds Jean Paul Lyet, the chief executive of the Sperry Corporation, should have come to a bad end. Born in 1917, he was raised in a poor neighborhood of Philadelphia called Brewerytown. His parents, Louis and Elizabeth Lyet, were divorced when he was eight years old, and his father, who played the trumpet in a traveling dance band, stopped contributing to the family's upkeep. Mrs. Lyet, forced to support not only Paul but her widowed mother as well, went to work as a telephone operator. Delinquency was the rule among the children of Brewerytown, and many of them wound up in jail. Even the more law-abiding youngsters would steal coal to heat their homes. But Mrs. Lyet was a devout Episcopalian who demanded impeccable behavior from Paul. A friend from those days later remembered that the boy was "revoltingly honest."

Lyet toyed for a while with the idea of becoming a journalist, but by the time he got out of high school in 1935 he had resolved on a business career. "I wanted not to be poor," he recalled, "and I'm still very much interested in making certain that my family is not. To that extent I've been scarred—I'll never shake it." He attended evening classes at the University of Pennsylvania's Wharton School, while working days as a real estate agent, and after six years he finally graduated.

He became a certified public accountant, and by the age of twenty-six he was earning $35,000 a year as the chief financial officer of a company that made farm machinery. After the company was bought by Sperry, Lyet moved up through the ranks, becoming the chief executive in 1972. He is now a millionaire, and he also earns around a half-million dollars a year. That is pretty good even in these inflationary times, and it goes a long way toward allaying the fear of poverty. But probably no amount of money can ever be quite enough for someone who grew up poor.

David Joseph Mahoney, Jr., the head of Norton Simon, Inc., is another tycoon who rose from blighted beginnings. He was born in 1923, the son of a construction worker, and was brought up in a lower-class neighborhood of the Bronx. The construction industry collapsed early in the Depression, and Mahoney's father couldn't find steady work for six years. It was the kind of situation that could cause a young boy to stray, but Mahoney, like Lyet, had a strong mother who held him to a high standard of conduct and prodded him to get ahead in life. Mahoney was also strongly influenced by his *spiritual* mother, the Catholic Church. He received a strict Catholic upbringing and submitted to the rigorous discipline of the church schools. "A lot of us kids went to jail, a lot of kids became priests," he remarked, while reminiscing about the old neighborhood. He didn't become a priest, of course, but he did manage to stay out of trouble.

As a university trustee during the sixties, Mahoney found himself amazed by the student demonstrators who disrupted the campus routine. "I could in one way understand the injustices that were being done," he says, "whether it be the Vietnam war or whatever, but I could never shift gears to how the hell they could possibly go in and tell the head of the university how to run the school! I'm not making any judgments on them, but I used to think, from my point of vantage, that when I had the nuns and the brothers in grammar school, to think I'd go in and tell them how to run the school was just preposterous. If I was three minutes late for class, I would get hung up on the wall. But later, even when I got to college, I thought, 'Live and let live.' They had a job to do, I'm supposed to go to class and get some grades, and then I can do some other things. I didn't think they needed my advice."

Tall and handsome, sprightly and personable, with a celebrated penchant for gracious living, Mahoney today is the reigning glamor boy of American industry. But there is an old saying: You can take a boy out of the Bronx, but you can't take the Bronx out of the boy. Mahoney speaks loudly and rapidly, and the Bronx accent, together with what must have been the Bronx gestures and mannerisms, is still readily detectable. He recalls that after his father was thrown out of work, his mother, the former Laurette Cahill, became an operator with New York Telephone. The phone company, it appears, was a refuge for many a mother in distress. Mahoney himself is now a director of New York Telephone, and he regrets that his mother didn't live to see him join the board. "This, to her, would have been the more ultimate success of her son than chairman of Norton Simon or anything else," he remarks. He says he had been staunchly defending the telephone company's service for years, even before he became a director. "Me, who is the maverick, who is questioning everything, was accepting the phone company. It finally dawned on me that subconsciously I was defending my mother. My mother hadn't gone to high school or anything, so this was her real identity, the job with the telephone company."

In the depths of their financial crisis, the family, which included one other son, would gather for what Mahoney calls "kitchen talks." The principal items on the agenda were "whether you're going to eat or not, or you're going to be thrown out on the streets, or whether the furniture is going out." Although in later years he became a Republican, and now describes himself as a "fiscal conservative," Mahoney says he has "never felt very comfortable with some of the economists and politicians, or right-wing conservatives, constantly saying that what this country needs is unemployment to straighten out its budget."

The Depression all but destroyed his father's spirit, Mahoney says. "He was a very decent, hardworking man, who had been disillusioned by the whole process. My father and his friends

weren't an educated, intellectual group who could relate to a
Marx or Lenin or anything else like that theoretically. But prag-
matically, they joined the union."

Mahoney himself was a bit young to be affected by thirties
radicalism. What's more, as he points out, "In the world I grew
up in, kids were more interested in athletics and so forth." Still,
he might have been excused for sharing his father's disillusionment. But his mother was pushing him in a different direction.
"You can get out of this mess," she would tell him. She was
stronger than his father, he says, although that may simply have
been a quirk of circumstance. "My father was facing the unemployment line every day. Somebody that's hurt or bruised doesn't
share the optimism of someone else." Mahoney was convinced
that he could indeed pull himself out of the "mess," and it became
his overriding concern. "I just never wanted to be in that position
again, where money was going to be a problem."

He found salvation within easy reach—a few feet above his
head. He was an outstanding basketball player at high school, and
several colleges offered him athletic scholarships. "I used to kid
all the scholastic students," he recalls. "If you were in the top 2
percent you got a Regents scholarship, which gave you $100 a
year. If you're an athlete, you get $500. It makes you realize
where the game was. And there were more athletes than geniuses."

In 1949, after time out for service in the Army, he earned his
bachelor's degree at the Wharton School. He started his own advertising agency, then sold it to become a professional manager.
After skipping from one company to another for more than a
decade, he finally settled down at Norton Simon and became the
chief executive in 1969. The company, based in New York, owns
the Avis car-rental firm and also manufactures a large variety of
consumer products, among them Canada Dry Ginger Ale, Max
Factor cosmetics and Wesson Oil.

Mahoney's hunger for money is something of a legend in the
business world. He perennially ranks among the highest-paid
chief executives in the nation. During 1978, for example, he received a total of $916,667 in salary and bonus, placing him less
than $60,000 shy of GM's Tom Murphy, and well in front of

Clifton Canter Garvin, Jr., the chief executive of the Exxon Corporation, who had to settle for $767,500. GM and Exxon ranked first and second that year among the industrial companies, while Norton Simon ranked 120th. Its $2.4 billion in revenues represented only a fortnight's haul for either of the two giant companies.

Occasionally Mahoney is chided at the annual stockholder meetings for taking such a large bite of the proceeds. A few years ago two stockholders went so far as to sue Norton Simon, Inc., seeking to trim Mahoney's pay and fringe benefits. The company made some concessions and settled the case out of court, but Mahoney's contract remains extremely impressive. He regularly receives generous stock options, and in addition to his towering salary and bonus the company pays the bulk of the premiums on his $6,834,000 worth of life insurance. When Mahoney leaves Norton Simon he will receive $100,000 a year in consulting fees for five years, and if the directors decide to fire him they will have to give him two years' notice. If he becomes disabled or dies in office the company will pay out half the amount of his salary for the next five years. He also is entitled to pension and profit-sharing payments of well over $100,000 a year upon retirement.

Mahoney grows agitated when asked to defend his contract. Even his critics acknowledge that he has done a good job as the head of Norton Simon. The company has suffered some setbacks lately, but over the years its earnings per share have grown at an exceptional rate, and the stockholders are undoubtedly fortunate to have his services. Mahoney says he might have made more money if he had remained an entrepreneur rather than becoming a professional manager. "I have no regrets about what's happened to my career financially or anything like that," he remarks, "but it certainly has not had the rewards of others." He called attention to an article that appeared in *Fortune* during 1979, listing eighty-three entrepreneurs whose net worth ranged from $50 million to more than $500 million. It seems that Mahoney himself, after three arduous decades in business, is worth a mere $20 million, more or less. "There are always going to be people that have more," he says, "and there are going to be a hell of a lot more people that have less. So I'm content and satisfied."

As we have seen, the tycoons owe a lot to their parents, both directly and indirectly. The great majority, raised in relative comfort during the Depression, never lost sight of the potential rewards of the free-enterprise system, never wavered in their belief that skill and dedication would yield those rewards in the future. They embarked upon their business careers with just the right attitude for success. As children of the privileged, they also started out possessing those valuable credentials that privilege confers—solid educations, family connections, respectability. There can be no doubt that they enjoyed a head start over their contemporaries in the quest for success in business. But then, as more than one President of the United States has told us, life is unfair.

And yet it can be argued that the poor boys—those few who made it to the top—owe their parents even more. Their parents weren't able to offer them anything tangible, only moral support —but that made moral support all the more important. Often, as in the cases of Paul Lyet or David Mahoney, it spelled the difference between success and despair. Since the Lyets and Mahoneys are so rare, we must conclude that despair, the natural enemy of ambition, usually triumphed in those poor neighborhoods of long ago.

Whatever their upbringing, scarcely any of the future tycoons went overboard with compassion for their fellow men. While they might have sensed the suffering around them, they saw the Depression primarily as a personal, practical challenge. Changing the system, as the reformers so hotly urged, would have simply confused matters, making it more difficult for an ambitious young man to reach the top, and perhaps even doing away with the top entirely. The tycoons were imbued with the spirit of individualism—which boils down, during hard times, to *every man for himself*.

Chapter Three

The Fortunes of War

NOTHING IS more critical to a businessman than the ability to recognize and exploit opportunities. For many of today's tycoons, that ability received its first real test during World War II. The war may have inflicted misery upon much of mankind, but it also proved a bonanza for American business. Never before did so many businessmen find so much opportunity to exploit so fully.

This was especially true of the entrepreneurs, whose personal fortunes expanded in direct proportion to the fortunes of their companies. Many companies that hadn't gone anywhere during peacetime became robust and vigorous after converting to defense production. Thomas Mellon Evans, whose H. K. Porter Company was a small, sluggish producer of locomotive parts before the war, launched himself on a big-time industrial career by moving into the production of munitions. Jack Simplot, the Idaho potato processor, developed a profitable new sideline as a major supplier of dehydrated potatoes to the armed forces. Edwin Land's Polaroid Corporation, which grossed barely a million dollars during 1941 as a manufacturer of headlight filters and sunglasses, built its annual volume to more than $16 million in 1945, as a supplier of goggles for antiaircraft gunners. By 1947, Polaroid's revenues had dropped almost to the pre-war levels, and the company was losing money. But the profits earned during wartime helped finance Dr. Land's development of the sixty-second camera, which, after it was placed on the market in 1948, revolutionized the photographic industry.

Most of the modern-day tycoons were too young to spend the war years in the comfort of the countinghouse. They had to interrupt their careers—or even their educations—to enter the service. And most of those who were of draft age but exempt for one reason or another felt constrained to take government jobs in support of the war effort. Rather than write off the war as a loss of time, however, quite a few of the tycoons were actually able to use it to get ahead in business.

In many cases they acquired knowledge and developed skills that were to prove helpful after they returned to civilian life. Leon Hess, the proprietor of Amerada Hess, already an oilman when the war began, served as an Army officer in Europe, and after D Day he was assigned to procure and transport petroleum for General Patton's troops. "It taught him all about planning," a friend later recalled. "He became very orderly in his way of going about any problem." Charles Brown, the chief executive of AT&T, entered the Navy in 1943, after earning a degree in electrical engineering at the University of Virginia. He served aboard the U.S.S. *Mississippi* in the Pacific, maintaining the radar system that controlled the ship's guns. "It gave me a certain confidence that I could supervise successfully," he remarks, "as well as a feeling that I was able to master technical matters—both the theory and practice of apparatus and machinery." Fletcher Lauman Byrom, currently the head of the Koppers Company, a diversified industrial concern, became a project coordinator with the Naval Ordnance Laboratory in Washington. The Navy had rejected his request for a military commission because he was too short. Byrom imposed order and efficiency on a staff of several hundred highly individualistic research scientists—a task that might have stymied Hercules. After the war, at the invitation of Admiral Arleigh Burke, he led a study group that recommended development of the surface-to-air missile—now a staple in the Navy's arsenal. Byrom had been only a salesman before the war, but his stint in Washington brought forward and strengthened his administrative and analytical talents.

Some tycoons got a vital boost simply by meeting the right people during the war. The case of William Anderson, the head of the NCR Corporation, deserves mention if only because the circumstances were so bizarre: he made the crucial contact while serving as a prisoner of war. Anderson's father was a Scottish engineer who ran an ice plant in Hankow, China, and his mother, also a British citizen, was half Chinese. When the Japanese invaded China in 1937, William, still a teenager, fled to Hong Kong. That wasn't far enough. Four years later, after the Japanese captured Hong Kong, he was placed in a prison camp, where he nearly died from malnutrition. One of his fellow prisoners, George Haynes, had represented NCR—then the National Cash Register Company—in China. They became friends, and Haynes offered to get Anderson a job with the company if they both survived. After the war Anderson started out as a salesman in Hong Kong, and unlikely as it may seem, he later became the head of the company's Japanese subsidiary. There could be no plainer demonstration of that profound tautology "Business is business." Anderson was named chief executive of NCR in 1973, while Haynes did pretty well himself, rising to senior vice president for Europe.

Anderson's case was rather special, of course, but the truth is that very few men get to the top without being taken under the wing of an older man somewhere along the way. And for many of the tycoons, that *somewhere* had something to do with the war. John Connor, for example, who served with a government agency during wartime, profited mightily from his association with the agency's boss, Dr. Vannevar Bush, a man of considerable renown and many talents. It was through Bush that he met the head of Merck, the pharmaceutical company, and it was with Bush's hearty endorsement that he was eventually offered a job on Merck's legal staff. Bush himself later joined Merck as a director and was instrumental in getting Connor appointed chief executive.

Connor has often been described as brash, outspoken and free-spirited—far removed from the stereotype of the stuffed-shirted business bureaucrat. "I've always regarded myself as an independent thinker," he says. "It is a trait acquired from early childhood. Members of my family will affirm that I'm independent-minded.

I would explain this by my father's attitude. He always encouraged me to get the facts on both sides and come up with a view that reflected your own thinking. So in my studies, jobs and other activities, I followed almost instinctively that approach to problems."

Now in the twilight of his career, he seems to have mellowed somewhat. A six-footer of medium build, with gray hair and fuzzy sideburns, he speaks with a soft tenor, has a soft cherubic face, and in fact seems soft all over. During our interview his manner was mild and avuncular, and he remained unswervingly philosophical even when discussing some of the unhappier events in his past. Yet I could sense the fire still crackling behind the facade, ready to blaze forth if he thought himself ill used.

He graduated *magna cum laude* from Syracuse University, where he majored in political science, and he got his law degree from Harvard in 1939. From the start he intended to pursue a career in public administration. "I guess I was struck by the fact that the federal government would play a more important role in our activities," he remarks. "It sort of buttressed my feeling that law and public service would be an interesting career, with future growth possibilities. The New Deal epitomized what was happening, but it also was happening at the state and city level." He finished in the top 10 percent of his law-school class, but he narrowly missed getting an "A" in Felix Frankfurter's seminar on administrative law, so he was not included among the graduates that Frankfurter recommended for positions with the New Deal.

Instead, he went over to the enemy camp. "There was a smart-aleck saying that Harvard Law people were getting out of Cambridge and turning Left," he recalls. "I turned Right, to one of the most hidebound law firms in the country." The firm was Cravath, de Gersdorff, Swaine and Wood, of New York City—since renamed Cravath, Swaine and Moore. Connor had worked there one summer, and had concluded that it was "the best law firm in the country, if not the world. It was easy to see that they were perfectionists. They did an outstanding job for their clients." The firm specialized in corporation law and frequently challenged governmental regulation of business. One of the partners, Frederick H. Wood, squared off against New Deal agencies in a number of cases before the Supreme Court, including the landmark

Schechter Poultry case, in which the Court declared the National Industrial Recovery Act unconstitutional.

Connor occasionally worked with Wood—"trying to undo some of the things that the brighter students in my class were trying to do in Washington," as he later described it. Connor's father was a Democrat, friendly with the politicians in Syracuse, and Connor considered himself basically a New Dealer. "But some of these things I thought were too extreme," he says.

After Pearl Harbor, Connor wanted to get involved in the war. He already had a wife and child, so he decided that he wouldn't enlist in the armed services unless he was certain to be drafted. He got a job as general counsel of the Office of Scientific Research and Development, amid cries from his colleagues at Cravath that he was "deserting" them. The director of the OSRD, Dr. Bush, was twenty-four years older than Connor. He had served as dean of engineering at the Massachusetts Institute of Technology and president of the Carnegie Institution of Washington. "He was the reincarnation of the Renaissance man," Connor says. "He was absolutely brilliant, very versatile in his talents and his interests. He was an engineer, physicist, inventor, educator, writer, and just about everything else you'd want to think about." At their first meeting, Connor concluded that working for Bush would be a "delightful" way to spend the war, and he certainly wasn't disappointed. "Bush had a method of approaching and resolving problems that was sort of the same approach that Cravath had to legal problems," he recalls. "Something would come up, and I'd go into his office. He'd say, 'Where did we last leave this?' He'd summarize the background facts, then ask, 'What's new?' Then, 'What do we have to decide?' So we'd delineate the issues. Then he would say, 'What are the alternatives?' We'd think about them. Then, 'What seems to be the best alternative? What are the pros and cons?' Then, 'Is there any reason we shouldn't go ahead with that alternative?' If there was no reason, he'd say, 'Let's go ahead and do it.' He was sharp, factual, decisive—he was damn good! His judgment was unexcelled." Connor describes his decision to join Bush's agency as "the best I ever made in my life."

The OSRD supervised the great scientific projects of the war, and it was Connor's job to deal with any legal complications. The development of penicillin for practical use involved ten American companies and dozens of scientific laboratories throughout the U.S. and Great Britain. Connor arranged for the patents. He also was responsible for the legal work behind the development of the atomic bomb, drawing up contracts between the government and various companies and institutions. The atom-bomb project would often keep him late at the office, but of course he couldn't explain the details to his wife, Mary, and she sometimes got miffed. "I suppose you're working on the most important project in the world today," she chided. "That's right," Connor replied with an enigmatic smile. His wife might not have been impressed, but the government was, and his service with the OSRD earned him a Presidential certificate of merit.

While working for the agency he met George Wilhelm Merck, whose ancestors back in Germany had founded Merck and Company during the seventeenth century. Merck was a consultant to the Army's Chemical Warfare Service and a friend of Vannevar Bush. In 1944, Connor enlisted in the Marines. As he was saying his farewells at OSRD, Bush told him: "George Merck would like a chance to hire you. Why don't you go out and let the Japs shoot your big toe off, and he'll probably look you up."

Connor liked the idea of working for Merck and Company. "Merck was preeminent in medical research," he says, "and George Merck himself was farsighted, idealistic, and had a high sense of integrity." But Connor preferred to keep all his toes. He served as an intelligence officer with a dive-bombing unit in the Pacific and rose to the rank of captain. His unit was never in the thick of the fighting. "We happened to be in the Marshall Islands when the active front was in the Marianas, Iwo and Okinawa." After V-J Day he visited Japan as a member of a strategic-bombing survey group. Then he was ordered back to Washington, where he was made counsel of the Office of Naval Research, which was about to take jurisdiction over the contracts he had negotiated for the OSRD. One of his more excruciating chores was to dismantle the network of patents he had painstakingly assembled for the penicillin project.

His new job frequently brought him into contact with James V. Forrestal, who was then secretary of the Navy. Connor helped Forrestal a couple of times with some congressional testimony, and Forrestal hired him as a special assistant. Connor deeply admired Forrestal and watched in dismay as that tortured soul moved inexorably toward a nervous breakdown and suicide. In an unpublished memoir, Connor recalls being awakened early on Christmas morning in 1946 by a call from Forrestal, who wanted him to come out and play golf. "I felt sorry for anyone so lonely that he would leave home and hearth on Christmas for the golf course," Connor wrote. He took embarrassed leave of his own family and joined Forrestal for a quick round. He recalls that they both played quite well. The Secretary, after dropping Connor back at home, proceeded to his office.

George Merck caught up with Connor early in 1947, and offered him a job as a lawyer with Merck and Company. He promised that there would be "room at the executive level," and by the end of the year Connor had been promoted to chief counsel and secretary of the company. Connor attended meetings of the board of directors and eventually was elected a member of the board and chairman of its Management Committee. He also headed a task force that supervised the production, testing and marketing of cortisone, one of the company's more important discoveries. The promotions continued to come rapidly. Connor reached the rank of vice president in 1953 and became general manager of the international division in 1955.

He had been converted, rather abruptly, from a professional man to a generalist. He concluded that it was "more fun" to be a generalist, but also more of a challenge. It was more fun because he had a chance to make and implement decisions, not just recommend them. It was more of a challenge because he had to learn to work effectively with large numbers of subordinates. "You have to let other people make mistakes, if need be, to acquire the experience and judgment that goes with handling larger matters," he observes. "You have to learn to delegate authority— which is very hard to do for someone who is professionally trained. Professionals take pride in doing things for themselves —for example, writing briefs if you're a lawyer. If you're gonna be a generalist, you have to let others do things, and accept their conclusions. It requires a great self-discipline and self-restraint."

While Connor was doing just fine, the company was having problems. Merck had been good at developing new products but weak at marketing them. Its competitors did a better job of selling the very drugs that Merck introduced. In 1953, Merck merged with another pharmaceutical company, Sharp and Dohme, which was known for its strong marketing organization. On paper it seemed an ideal arrangement—but as so often happens, the executives of the two companies couldn't get along, and the merger wasn't working. The Merck people, oriented toward research, scorned the Sharp and Dohme people as "hucksters," while the Sharp and Dohme people thought the Merck people were ludicrously impractical. In 1954, the year after the merger, the revenues of the combined companies declined by 9 percent.

Chairman Merck decided that the company needed a tough new president to impose law and order. Early in 1955 a committee of five directors was appointed to choose a successor to the incumbent, James J. Kerrigan. The head of the committee was none other than Vannevar Bush, who had joined the Merck board in 1949, partly at Connor's urging. The committee interviewed thirty top executives of Merck, asking whom they would like to see appointed president. Connor received the most votes —among them his own. When the selection committee approached him, he declared, "I should be the new president." "I've always had the opinion," he says, "that personal advancement takes care of itself if you do the job and do it well. On the other hand, when there is a promotional possibility, I have never been too modest to prevent me from speaking out. It was easy to see who my competitors would be for the job of president. I began to compare their capabilities and experiences with mine as objectively as I could on a matter that's subjective." Although he tooted his own horn, he says he was careful to refrain from backbiting. "When it gets to a situation where there's internal politicking and gossiping, it can be counterproductive," he remarks. "If two executives are squabbling, the top man concludes that both have inherent deficiencies. I expressed it once in these terms: It's relatively easy to cooperate effectively with a broad-minded, fully competent, intelligent person. Since there are so few, the real test is to cooperate with another imperfect person like yourself. If one fellow isn't of that frame of mind, it certainly reflects credit on the cooperative one."

The committee agreed with Connor's assessment of the candidates, and he took office as president and chief executive officer in September 1955, while George Merck remained as chairman. When Merck died two years later, Vannevar Bush became chairman of the company. Cynics might conclude that the two old friends were playing favorites, but Connor points out that there were two other executives who stood a chance of beating him and that he had the broadest experience at handling important projects. Most significant, perhaps, he already had shown that he could bring the company's warring factions together. As head of the international division he had successfully merged the overseas operations of Merck with those of Sharp and Dohme.

Connor's expressions of self-esteem do appear to have been justified. Merck's revenues nearly doubled and its earnings nearly tripled during his nine years as president. When he left in 1965 to join the Johnson Administration as secretary of commerce, the company had been transformed from a bedraggled also-ran into a solid blue chip. His outstanding record at Merck made him a desirable catch later on, when Allied Chemical, another company in trouble, went looking for new leadership. Connor served as chief executive of Allied for eleven years, retiring in 1979 upon reaching his sixty-fifth birthday. He then became chairman of Schroders, Inc., the American holding company for an international banking organization based in London. Even as a senior citizen he continues to honor the men who nurtured and sustained him in his youth. Photographs of Bush and Forrestal were prominently displayed on the wall of his office, and there was also a striking life-size bronze head of Forrestal peering out from a shelf.

While Connor was helped immensely by his wartime experience, he was already well along the road to success before the war. The knowledge he gained, and of course the contacts he made, quickened the pace. But for other tycoons the war had an even more decisive impact, spelling the difference between success and mediocrity, and perhaps between success and failure.

A prominent case in point is Charles Bates Thornton, cofounder of Litton Industries. Known to friends, foes and strangers alike as "Tex," he was laboring in obscurity in the years before the war as a minor functionary in the Interior Department. It is intriguing to speculate where he would be today if there had been no war. He was certainly too restless to wait around for a Civil Service pension, and his natural ability might have yielded at least *some* measure of success. But it is entirely possible, if not probable, that he would never have scaled the heights he did if the war hadn't intervened.

When Thornton entered the war as an officer in the Air Force —or Army Air Corps, as it was called—he was given a chance to demonstrate his outstanding aptitude as a strategic and financial planner. He later drew on the friendships and associations he cultivated during the war to obtain executive positions first with the Ford Motor Company and later with Hughes Aircraft, the aerospace and electronics firm founded by Howard Hughes. By 1953, his reputation as a businessman firmly established, Thornton was able to raise $1.5 million to organize Litton Industries. The company went on to become a major conglomerate, and Thornton became a millionaire many times over. Today he is not only a leading industrialist but a prominent rancher as well, having acquired 330,000 acres of land in northern Nevada, where he raises 15,000 head of cattle.

A stocky man of average height, with a large, leonine head and heavy features, Thornton seemed cagey and uncomfortable when we discussed his career. With his feet propped on a chair, he doodled incessantly on a lined pad of paper. Constantly smoking cigarettes, and squinting suspiciously through the haze, he dodged many questions about himself, though he spoke in eloquent detail about other businessmen—usually off the record. Thornton is one of the more puzzling figures in American business. As *Time* pointed out in a cover story about him many years ago, he is a visionary with a strong practical streak, shy with strangers but outgoing and articulate with friends and associates, extremely rich, yet a penny pincher who haggles with shopkeepers and leaves miserly tips. "Everybody loves Tex," a good friend of his once said, "but nobody really knows him."

Litton Industries, which is based in a white colonial-style brick mansion in Beverly Hills, has been a troubled and controversial company over much of the past decade or so. Until 1968 it apparently could do no wrong, and both its earnings and its stock price seemed bound for infinity. But since then the company has had some serious financial setbacks, and it suffered substantial losses during the 1974 and 1978 fiscal years. Always heavily involved in defense work, Litton has been embroiled in some dramatic squabbles with the government over the cost and quality of its products. But despite the problems, there is no gainsaying Thornton's achievement in building one of the largest U.S. industrial companies virtually from scratch. Litton's revenues exceed $4 billion a year from the manufacture of ships, business machines, microwave ovens and many dozens of other goods.

As a major defense contractor, Litton has been a special target of the more radical critics of business. This was particularly true during the Vietnam war, when Litton and Thornton seemed the very embodiment of the dreaded "military-industrial complex." "Different people have called me different things," says Thornton. "I don't care what they call me. I sort of let it be." Frankly, I think he *does* care. He says he has had a bad press in the Soviet Union. "They called me the 'uncrowned king of the U.S.' They talked about 'starving people hanging from barbed wire around our palatial mansion.' " Nevertheless, he played host to visiting Soviet officials during the period of détente. A skilled pilot, he took one Russian on a morning flight over the California desert, then handed him the controls. The Russian, who didn't know how to fly, enjoyed himself at first, but when the plane went into a dive he howled for Thornton to take over again. The folks at Litton got a big laugh out of that, and at a party they introduced their guest as "the only Russian kamikaze pilot."

Thornton's business career actually began in his adolescence. He was born in 1913 in Knox County, Texas, and became the man of the family almost at once. His father, Word Augustus Thornton, was a swashbuckler who ran off not long after Tex was born. The elder Thornton made a pile of money fighting fires in the oil fields—he literally blew them out with nitroglycerin—but lost it in the 1929 stock-market debacle. Many years later he was murdered by hitchhikers. His wife, Alice Bates Thornton, worked hard to make a responsible citizen out of their son. When the boy was only twelve, she urged him to buy land with the money he earned from odd jobs, and he managed to accumulate nearly forty acres. At nineteen Tex invested his capital in a filling station, but he sold it soon afterward to open a Plymouth dealership with a partner, Buford Cox. Cars weren't selling well in those days—it was the trough of the Depression—but the partners made good money anyhow. In lieu of cash, they agreed to accept livestock and farm implements, which they sold to the better-heeled farmers in the area.

In 1934, at the age of twenty-one, Tex went off to seek his fortune in the burgeoning New Deal bureaucracy. His starting salary as a clerk in the Interior Department was $1,440 a year. He had studied engineering and business administration at Texas Technological University, before dropping out to run the filling station, and he resumed his education at George Washington University, receiving a bachelor's degree in 1937.

His big breakthrough came in the days just before Pearl Harbor, when he was discovered by Robert A. Lovett, the assistant secretary of war for air. Lovett had read a report by Thornton on the means of financing low-cost federal housing. He was impressed with Thornton's skill at sorting out and interpreting the great mass of statistics and other information. Lovett, who had been a partner in the investment-banking firm of Brown Brothers Harriman and Company, desperately wanted a planner who could organize the Air Force in a businesslike way. He had been studying the growth of Germany's air power since the mid-thirties, when he was still in private life, and he fully appreciated the coordination and discipline that were needed to build such a force. Upon entering the government in 1940, he had found to his astonishment that coordination and discipline were sorely lacking in the Air Force. He had asked to see the Air Force plans in the event the U.S. entered the war. The only plan anyone could find was a musty old document setting forth the procedure in case of an air raid on New York City. "Flying the ocean in those days," Thornton recalls, "you used a flying boat—a two-day affair. The oceans gave us time in America to convert our civilian industrial base to military. We had to train 95,000 pilots and 1,700 specialists. It had to be built almost from scratch. The next war is gonna be won with force in being. If that had been the case in forty-one, we wouldn't be a free nation today—it wouldn't be a free world."

At Lovett's urging, Thornton was already in uniform by the time the U.S. entered the war, as head of the Air Force Office of Statistical Control. He started out as a lieutenant but was promoted to full colonel within a matter of weeks, making him, at twenty-eight, the youngest man to hold that rank. He gave the military its first taste of systems management, developing a program that permitted the Air Force to obtain quick, complete information about its airplanes and their deployment. It showed, in Thornton's words: "what the hell we had by way of resources, and when and where it was going to be required." To beef up his organization he established a training program in statistical analysis at the Harvard Business School. At the peak of the war he had 2,800 officers spreading the gospel of modern management at Air Force installations throughout the world. Although he rode out the entire war at his desk, Thornton was laden down with decorations at war's end. The grateful top brass awarded him the Distinguished Service Medal, the Legion of Merit, and a Combination Ribbon with two oak-leaf clusters.

It occurred to Thornton that there might be a place in industry for his brand of management. He drew up a list of the brightest members of his staff—ten men including himself—and set out to see whether any company was interested in hiring them as a team. The group got an offer from Robert R. Young, the head of a holding company that controlled the New York Central Railroad. But some of the group didn't find that offer glamorous enough, so it was kept in abeyance while they continued to look.

One member of the group, George E. Moore, suggested that they try Ford. His father, who lived in Detroit, knew one of the officers of Ford and thought there might be an opportunity there. Young Henry Ford II had recently succeeded his grandfather and namesake, the founder of the firm, who was over eighty years old and in failing health. The new boss was said to be anxious to revitalize the company. Old Henry Ford might have been an automotive genius, but he was, as Thornton puts it, "one of the worst executives ever." Planning and controls had been anathema to him. He preferred to operate by intuition, and in fact he made a rule that anyone caught with an organization chart would be fired. His methods had long since backfired, and those whippersnappers at General Motors had surged ahead to stay during the 1930s.

Thornton and his colleagues drafted a telegram to Young Henry. "We have a matter of management importance to discuss with you," it read in part. The telegram offered Robert Lovett's name as a reference and was signed by Thornton. The next day Thornton got a telephone call from the Ford district sales manager in Washington, who reported that Henry Ford was interested in his proposition and wanted to meet him. Thornton flew to Detroit, where Ford told him that he had checked with Lovett, who had given Thornton unqualified approval. Ford hired the entire team at salaries ranging from $8,000 to $16,000, with the top salary going to Thornton.

Because they were unfamiliar with the automotive business, the new men spent several months interviewing managers throughout the company. Some of the old-timers resented these nosy intruders, who ranged in age from twenty-six to thirty-four, and started calling them the "Quiz Kids." That later got changed to "Whiz Kids," a name by which the group has become known to legend. Two of the Whiz Kids—Robert S. McNamara and Arjay Miller—went on to serve as president of Ford. McNamara held the position for only a few weeks before moving back to Washington to become secretary of defense in 1961. He was reputedly recommended for that job by Bob Lovett. Thornton today has the highest praise for McNamara—"probably the finest executive in America. Any assignment I ever gave him, he never complained. He never asked for a raise, promotion or reassignment. He had a reputation when he was head of the company: many would complain that Bob would not listen. I know some of those people who complained. He *would* listen. If it was a good idea he'd say, 'Let's go!' If a bad idea, he would say *no*. If you had new information that would indicate he was wrong, he did not have pride—he'd change it. His pride was secondary. If you were just rehashing, he would say, 'The decision has been made.' "

Thornton and McNamara remained fast friends throughout McNamara's long tenure in the Kennedy and Johnson administrations. They would meet for breakfast whenever Thornton was in Washington. Another government contractor was unkind enough to suggest that this cozy relationship might have helped Litton financially: "A clever man would merely let it be known that he was having breakfast with McNamara every morning. When talking to procurement officers and the like, he wouldn't even have to mention McNamara's name."

The leader of the Whiz Kids remained with Ford for only two years. "My wife and I didn't like the weather in Detroit," Thornton explained. If that were reason enough, then Detroit would have long since been depopulated. Thornton went on to concede that he also had some strong differences of opinion with one of his superiors and had felt that "the excitement was gone."

He moved over to Hughes Aircraft, where two of his Air Force comrades had preceded him. Harold L. George, a retired lieutenant general who had headed the Air Transport Command during the war, was vice president and general manager of Hughes Aircraft, which at the time was a division of the Hughes Tool Company. Another retired lieutenant general, Ira C. Eaker, was a vice president of Hughes Tool. Eaker invited Thornton to come out to California and meet Howard Hughes, who was not yet the total recluse. Thornton wasn't sure he wanted to work for Hughes, but he went anyway. "I was curious just to see him," he recalls. "I spent many hours with him." Hughes Aircraft had rather puny revenues in those days—only about $2 million—but Howard Hughes assured Thornton that he wanted to build it into a major defense contractor. "I would give my last dime to protect American freedom," Hughes declared. Thornton says he was charmed by this remark, and it induced him to sign on as assistant general manager.

Five years later, Hughes Aircraft's revenues had increased a hundredfold, but for Thornton the fun had ended once again. He departed Hughes Aircraft for reasons that remain mysterious to this day. Some sources contend that he was forced out, but Thornton himself insists that he resigned voluntarily—as did a number of other Hughes Aircraft executives—because of a series of policy disputes with Noah Dietrich, the executive vice president of Hughes Tool.

Thornton started Litton Industries with backing from Lehman Brothers, the investment bankers. He had to do some fancy talking to get the money, since one prominent Lehman partner, Paul Mazur, was dead set against the idea. Thornton told the partners that Litton would soon be bringing in tens of millions of dollars a year, much of it from contracts with the military. Mazur, underestimating Thornton's leverage with the defense establishment, couldn't believe that the government would be all that eager to

deal with Litton. He predicted that the $1.5 million in seed money
—to be raised from Lehman's clients—would be lost forever. But
he was overruled, and Litton proceeded to grow much faster than
Thornton had suggested. Thornton later confided that he deliberately understated Litton's prospects, because he didn't want to
seem an impractical visionary. If he had told the partners that
Litton would be doing more than a half-billion dollars' worth of
business at the end of its first decade—as in fact it did—they
would have laughed him out of Wall Street.

Litton got there by acquiring companies, companies and more
companies—eventually more than one hundred. After joining
Litton the companies remained essentially unchanged and were
run by operations experts who were given a great deal of autonomy. The headquarters staff monitored the financial results and
offered guidance when problems arose. For a remarkably long
time there were no *serious* problems. Thornton, who was Litton's
top deal-maker as well as its top executive, seemed to have an
unerring instinct for quality and value in making his acquisitions.
But at last some dubious companies and dubious managers
slipped into the fold, and in 1968, its fifteenth year, the company
began a decade of financial turmoil. At this writing, however,
Litton seems to have overcome its problems and to have re-
claimed much of its reputation for sagacity. Through it all Thornton has remained the one constant. After more than a quarter of
a century, and already well past his sixty-fifth birthday, he continues as chairman and chief executive.

For the tycoons the war was a time of acceleration. Whether
they served in the military or remained behind as businessmen,
they found themselves forced to perform faster and better than
they had ever done before.

It was also a time of learning. The tycoons learned how to
analyze, how to plan, how to organize, how to administer. They
emerged from the war with their skills refined and developed to
the highest degree.

It was a time of expanding horizons. The tycoons had a world
view thrust upon them, observing—often at close and dangerous
quarters—how the nations of the world interacted, for good or
ill.

They also discovered the wondrous workings of the military-industrial complex, long before it was accorded that name in public rhetoric. There were those among them, like Tex Thornton, who were to build mighty fortunes on that foundation.

With a maturity and judgment that belied their years, the young businessmen of the postwar world were to prove a formidable force indeed.

Chapter Four

Boy Wonders

AFTER THE war, companies competed frantically for young men with the potential to become executives. It had been a long time since business was able to hire young men in any quantity—what with the Depression and then the war itself—and there was a great scarcity of executive material. The executives of the Depression era were either gone or on their way out, and because there had been so little hiring during that era, there were few middle-aged employees qualified to move up. Anyone returning from the service in the weeks and months following V-J Day found the opportunities both abundant and attractive. The ease with which Tex Thornton and his Whiz Kids slipped into lucrative, responsible positions at Ford was only the most extravagant example of what was happening throughout American business.

The best and brightest young men were promoted rapidly, and as they matured into their thirties and forties they found themselves fighting it out, a generation ahead of schedule, for the chief executive's job. John Connor, for example, was a mere lad of forty when he became the head of Merck in 1955, having spent just eight years with the company. He also had several more years behind him in law and government, but as he frankly acknowledges: "I didn't have the broad experience over a period of time you'd usually expect of a chief executive officer." He was propelled to the top as much by circumstance as by merit.

The chances for rapid advancement were especially great in the banking business, which had been hit earliest and hardest by

the Depression. Walter Bigelow Wriston, a young Army lieutenant, applied for a job in 1946 at New York's First National City
Bank and discovered a huge generation gap in the executive
ranks. "There were a tremendous number of us who were twenty-
five years old," he recalls, "and a tremendous number who were
fifty years old, and there was absolutely zilch in between. We got
sucked into a vacuum in which the opportunity and the explosion
of our business, plus the lack of other bodies in the way, gave us
a tremendous opportunity at an age where prior generations in
the bank would not have had it." First National City was one of
the very largest banks in the nation, and Wriston was to become
the youngest man ever to lead it. He was named president in
1967, at the age of forty-seven, and ascended to the chairmanship
three years later.

Wriston today is unquestionably the nation's most respected
banker, and it can be argued that he also is the most powerful
and important businessman of all. Practically every major company is a client of his bank—and the hand that pulls the purse
strings rules the business world. Citibank, as First National City is
now known, is part of a one-bank holding company called Citicorp, which Wriston also heads. Citicorp recently forged ahead of
BankAmerica, of San Francisco, to become the largest commercial-banking company, measured by assets. It is also second to
none in aggressive, innovative management. Before Wriston became president, his bank wasn't even the largest in New York. It
trailed a respectful distance behind Chase Manhattan, the principal bank of the Rockefeller brothers, which was headed by David
Rockefeller himself during the sixties and seventies. Under Wriston, Citibank left the Chase far behind. Wriston had the notion
that banks should make money for their shareholders, not merely
preserve it for depositors. That might have seemed obvious—
especially to the shareholders—but in some banking circles it was
considered heretical. Wriston steered Citibank into several new
businesses. It is now probably the largest leasing company in the
world, for example, furnishing airliners, oil tankers and any other
capital equipment that its customers prefer not to buy.

The man who runs this mighty enterprise cuts an elegant figure. He is six feet three and slender and moves with athletic
grace. His face is narrow and his features are sharp, giving him a

passing resemblance to Joe DiMaggio. His game, however, is tennis, not baseball, and he manages to play a couple of times a week. He lives in an apartment in Manhattan, but spends weekends and vacations at his tree farm, which straddles the borders of Connecticut and New York. He reads a book almost every weekend —"I read reasonably rapidly"—and also performs a variety of farm chores: "I am a carpenter, electrician, plumber, backhoe operator, front-end-loader operator and chainsaw operator—you name it." His neighbors say that Wriston seems to enjoy riding the range on his tractor.

At the office Wriston is effectively insulated from unauthorized intrusions. The headquarters are in a block-square building on Park Avenue, and the vast lobby is swarming with security guards, fiercely dedicated to keeping the wrong people away from the elevators. On the fifteenth floor, where Wriston and the other top executives reside, anyone stepping off the elevator has to confront both a male guard and an equally formidable female guard. A thick, bulletproof sliding panel, controlled by a button at the reception desk, seals off the executive suite.

In conversation Wriston seems almost to be chanting aloud to himself, rather than addressing the other party. The words slide out slowly, in deep, melodious tones, with a steady rhythm. He likes to project an image of nonchalance, but it is marred by a facial tic. One former colleague has suggested that Wriston is "very much less assured in his gizzard than he gives the impression he is."

He does get high marks from practically everyone for his skills as a banker and administrator. A subordinate attests that Wriston has "an extremely alert, intellectually oriented mind" and "an ability to see through quickly to the consequences of any action." And one of Citibank's outside directors declared: "Wriston has a computer-analytical mind. He has more knowledge in detail than anybody I know. It's very hard to argue with him because he always comes to board meetings very well prepared, with all the information sorted out. I'd hate to be competing with Walter Wriston."

Wriston is a master of the sardonic quip, and when discussing even the most mundane matters he tries hard to be witty. As a result his version of events sometimes sounds a bit fanciful. But no one can fault an artist for improving on reality—and in any case it is fun to listen to him. Evidently it's less fun when you are working for him, and when your career and your life hang on his favor. As one former Citibanker put it: "He is arrogant, flip and runs the place with a needle. Every comment is a wise-ass remark." Some of his ex-employees have come to loathe him for that, but I think they do him an injustice. They seem to be confusing form with substance. Wriston has a useful message for those with the sense of humor and the self-assurance to hear him correctly.

He derives his sharp tongue and ready wit from his father, who happens to be quite an eminent man himself. Still alive and past ninety, Dr. Henry Merritt Wriston was for many years one of the nation's leading educators. Born in a log cabin in Wyoming, the son of a traveling Methodist preacher, he earned his bachelor's and master's degrees at Wesleyan University, in Middletown, Connecticut, then taught history there while simultaneously pursuing his doctorate at Harvard. At the age of thirty-six Dr. Wriston was appointed president of Lawrence College, in Wisconsin, and he later became president of Brown University, where he remained until his retirement in 1955. He wrote numerous books and articles, received the staggering total of thirty-four honorary degrees, and served as a valued adviser to the State Department. He drafted a plan for reorganizing the department at President Eisenhower's request.

Asked whether he found it challenging to follow such an act, Walter Wriston responded characteristically, with a wisecrack followed by a somewhat more serious statement. *"Psychology Today* had not yet been published," he said, "and I never gave it much thought. [Pause for audience reaction] There were only two instances. One was I got a lousy grade in something in high school, and my father said rather plaintively that it was destroying his argument against upgrading the educational system if his own son was getting such a lousy grade. I remember that as if it was yesterday. It made quite an impression on me. Then the other is that I decided early on that I would (a) not go into his profession, or (b) live in the same town when we were both working."

Life in the Wriston household was a heady, stimulating experience. The whole family was keenly devoted to intellect, and Walter recalls that "the dinner table, or the lunch table, or whatever was a floating conversation that wound up with books all over the floor." His mother, the late Ruth Bigelow Wriston, was one of the relatively few women of her generation to graduate from college —Vassar, in fact—and she taught high-school chemistry. His sister, Barbara Wriston, went to Oberlin College, took her master's degree at Brown and became an expert on art and architecture. She served until recently as the executive director of museum education at the Art Institute of Chicago and is now a writer and lecturer in New York. "She is a highly independent person, to put it mildly," says Walter. "To be a single person, and pre-eminent in her field as she is—just to stop working and decide 'I'm gonna go and make my living lecturing in the Big Apple and writing books'—I have nothing but admiration for her courage. Not only that—she's pulling it off." Daughter, father and son have three consecutive entries in the latest edition of *Who's Who in America.*

In discussing his youth, Wriston tends to lapse into homilies about self-reliance. He was born in Middletown in 1919, and he recalls that his family lived comfortably though not lavishly during the Depression. "There was never what you would call a dollar around the house," he says. "We ate. Nobody felt deprived, and nobody felt poor, and nobody felt that somebody ought to do something for you. Today we've transferred the individual responsibility to institutions. It's been the most remarkable thing that's happened in the last twenty-five years. We now speak of institutions as 'they ripped us off.' " He says his parents impressed him with the need to be independent, telling him, in essence: "We'll teach you what we can teach you, and we'll help you when we can help you—but it's sort of your problem." Wriston did seek his father's help many times over the years, sometimes in intimate, personal matters, but most often when he just needed to check historical references in his speeches. "I call him and say: 'There was a fellow in the eighteenth century in France who said so and so.' My father will say: 'You've got it wrong. I'll call you back when I check it.' He's a great help."

As a college student, Wriston had more than the usual amount of trouble deciding what to do for a living. "My life is a series of total accidents," he remarks. "People look back afterwards and make believe they had a rational plan." He enrolled at Wesleyan, planning to major in chemistry. "I had a big laboratory in the cellar, where I used to make useful things like smoke bombs and stink bombs." But when he discovered that basketball practice conflicted with the school's laboratory schedule, he switched to history and government. He was a local correspondent for some newspapers, and he applied to the graduate journalism school at Columbia University—but then backed down. "It was pointed out to me that I couldn't spell. That seemed to be an impediment." He was accepted at Yale Law School, and his immediate future seemed clear enough. But the year was 1941, and his father warned him that he was draftable and that he'd never make it through law school before the U.S. entered the war.

He decided to try the one-year course at the Fletcher School of International Law and Diplomacy, a part of Tufts University. To qualify he had to be fluent in a foreign language. "Since I had only two months to learn one," he recalls, "I called up my dad and said, 'Where do you go to learn a foreign language—like right away?' " His father suggested the Ecole Francaise, in Middlebury, Vermont. The dean of the school tried to interview him in French, but Wriston cut in. "Sir," he said, "I do not know what you are talking about." According to Wriston, the rest of the conversation went like this:

DEAN: "All the classes are in French."

WRISTON: "I understand that."

DEAN: "You'd better go home."

WRISTON: "I can't go home. I have to learn to speak this language."

DEAN: "You've got more courage than brains."

Wriston slogged through the course, passed the examination and entered the Fletcher School, where he earned his master's degree in 1942.

He joined the State Department as a foreign-service officer based in Washington. He spent a year there before joining the Army and came away doubting that he would return. At one point he had been assigned to help obtain the release of a captured hospital ship. Unfamiliar with the Hospital Convention, he stayed up most of the night reading it. "And so I wrote a note which I took up to the secretary of state, Mr. Cordell Hull—who read it and signed it—which instructed the American ambassador in London what to do." That gave him a feeling of power and accomplishment, but he couldn't help imagining himself in the ambassador's shoes. An ambassadorship was supposed to be the crowning reward for long and faithful service. "If I worked here thirty years," he remarked to his wife, the former Barbara Brengle, "I might get to be an ambassador. Then there'll be some kid from the Fletcher School who would write a note telling me what to do."

Wriston encountered the customary snafu in trying to join the armed forces. Only a step ahead of the draft, he applied for a commission in Naval Intelligence and was accepted. His papers mysteriously vanished from the files, however, and before he could be reprocessed he got his draft notice from the Army. "I said, 'I'm a lieutenant in the Navy.' They said, 'Show us.' And I couldn't."

On entering the Army he was assigned to the Medical Corps at Coney Island. "I sewed people up for a few minutes," he remarks, "and I applied for OCS in the Air Corps, and I was accepted." He was walking through Grand Central Station to board a train when he was accosted by some military policemen, who told him to report back to his original unit. It seems that the Officer Candidate School had just been closed to anyone not already in the Air Corps. Back at Coney Island his captain commiserated with him and suggested that he try the Signal Corps. "Do you know anything about codes and ciphers?" the captain asked. "Sure, I've read Poe's 'Gold Bug,' " said Wriston. He trained in codes and ciphers at Fort Monmouth, then was shipped to Cebu, in the Philippines, where he ran a signal center. He wasn't directly engaged in combat, but he recalls that "they took the odd shot at you."

After the war he hoped to find a job in New York, where his wife was teaching school. The family physician suggested that he try banking. Wriston thought the suggestion was "stupid" and that banking was "the dullest profession I ever heard of," but he was willing to endure it until the school year ended. "This is known as vocational planning," he says. He applied to First National City, was hired at a salary of $2,800 a year and was placed in a training program with some twenty other young men, most of them veterans like himself.

At first his instinctive loathing seemed justified. "They would try to send you home if you didn't wear a stiff collar and black shoes," he recalls. "A lot of us got told to go home and get properly dressed. Having worn a uniform for so long, there was a certain amount of resistance." Nor was he encouraged by the attitude of the old-timers around the bank. "There was a scurrilous book on Citibank called *The First Billion*," he says. "Particularly embittered elderly clerks would drag it out of the bottom drawer and let you take it home and read it in great secrecy."

But the more deeply he got involved in his job, the more he came to enjoy it. "In the banking business you're in daily contact with a rainbow full of diversity," he observes. "You meet a lot of entrepreneurs—who are a lot of fun. You get involved in every conceivable kind of enterprise. And you get fascinated with the diversity of the world. Banks sit at the center of all that." He became an inspector in the comptroller's division and took evening courses at the American Banking Institute to improve his understanding of the profession. He continued to challenge what he considered archaic practices at Citibank, and he claims that he was fired several times for insubordination when he tried to do things his own way. But on reflection his bosses found that his methods worked pretty well, and he never stayed fired very long.

After he had been with the bank for three years, he was taken under the wing of George Stevens Moore, who at the time was running the national division. Moore had reviewed the records of all the recent trainees and had lighted on Wriston as someone who showed promise. Wriston was promoted several times in the next few years, becoming a vice president—albeit one of many dozens—in 1954. Moore became head of the bank's overseas division in 1957, and when he moved up to president in 1959, Wriston succeeded him. As the overseas boss, Wriston held sway over 7,750 employees at 204 outlets in sixty different countries.

Moore, a balding man with large, friendly eyes, was known to his colleagues as "Uncle George." Although he was rather warmhearted, he did his best to conceal the fact. Energetic and volatile, he loved to talk—rapidly, repetitively and bluntly as well. "You got told about your general aptitude in rather stark terms," Wriston says. "He fired me more times than anyone else in the bank." On one occasion Wriston was working on a complicated loan— "involving twenty-five ships and twenty corporations and I don't know what all. I'd been working like hell on it." He spent an entire weekend sorting out the details and submitted a memorandum to Moore. Moore read it, called him in, and declared, "You're an absolute idiot!" Wriston figured that his days at Citibank were numbered, and when he got home he said to his wife, "Where would you like to live?"

"What did Uncle George say today?" she replied.

"Well, he called me an idiot."

Soon afterward, Citibank held a reception for its correspondent bankers, and Wriston attended. "Uncle called me over," he recalls. "He was holding court with a bunch of wheels. He said, 'Hey, fellas, I want you to meet Walt. He's gonna be one of my senior lending officers.' I just shook my head at him. He grabbed me and said, 'What's the matter? What's the matter?' I said, 'George, you called me an *idiot*.' He said, 'I did? I did? I did?' I said, 'Yeah, you did!' He said, 'If I didn't think I could teach you something, I wouldn't even talk to you.' "

Wriston also received special care and attention from James Stillman Rockefeller, who became chairman and chief executive of Citibank in 1959. A distant cousin of Nelson and David Rockefeller, he was an exceedingly reserved, private person who seemed the very image of the old-fashioned banker. But in fact he had a certain taste for the unorthodox and would often acquiesce when pushy upstarts like Moore and Wriston came forward with exciting ideas. Wriston particularly admired Rockefeller for giving the bank's bright young men jobs and authority beyond the scope of their experience. Wriston had been with the bank only thirteen years and was still shy of his fortieth birthday when Rockefeller made him head of the overseas division, which was one of the three or four highest-ranking positions. "He took enormous chances on people, which is the bravest thing you can ever do," says Wriston. "He took a hell of a chance on me and a lot of others. How people make personnel decisions is something that those who don't make them write books about. It's a very inexact science."

Once he became head of the overseas division, Wriston knew that he had an excellent chance to go all the way to the top at Citibank. "It never entered my mind when I came into this bank that I wanted this job at all," he insists. "It wasn't till I was in the overseas division running that that Stillman started to talk about it, and then my lights suddenly went on. Some people come in and decide, by God, they want this or that. My life has been a series of accidents, and pretty soon I was standing at a place where I could really get hurt with an accident. Getting there was not a planned thing."

Wriston claims that Citibank is relatively free of politicking and power struggles. "No doubt if you get two people together, you have a conversation," he observes. "You get three together and you have a contest. But there is less politics around this store than any one I've ever seen. It's basically a meritocracy. People on a high level do not engage in stuff out of the dime novels. Do people work their tails off trying to get things moving around here? The answer to that is *yes*. Do they compete with each other for all kinds of things? The answer to that is *yes*—I hope. Do they engage in Tammany Hall politics? The answer to that is some of them probably do. But do they do it at a Policy Committee level, the Group level? I think the answer to that is *no*."

One memorable achievement that pushed Wriston ahead of the pack at Citibank was his invention of negotiable certificates of deposit. Actually he shared credit for the invention with one or two other officers of the bank, but he evidently was the most ardent and persuasive in getting Rockefeller to try it. Negotiable certificates of deposit, or CDs, are short-term notes, typically maturing in ninety days and issued at high interest rates. Unlike bank deposits, they are readily transferable, with the proceeds payable to the bearer. They are designed to attract companies and rich individuals who might otherwise invest in treasury bills and other short-term instruments. Citibank introduced them in the early sixties, when the economy was heating up and the demand for loans was rising. The bank needed new sources of money to meet that demand, and the CDs worked out just fine. They have become an exceptionally popular investment and are now common at all the major banks.

Under Citibank's rules Rockefeller was to retire in 1967 when he reached the age of sixty-five. There seemed little doubt that George Moore would move up to the chairmanship, but everyone wondered who would succeed Moore as president. He himself was due to retire in 1970, so the next president could expect to become the top man quite soon. The betting favorites were Wriston and Thomas Robert Wilcox, executive vice president of the metropolitan division, which embraced 184 branches in New York City and its suburbs. Wilcox, a native of New York, had started at the bank as a page after getting out of high school, and had gone through Princeton on a bank-sponsored scholarship. He was three years older than Wriston, considerably shorter, and a "brisk man of action," according to one account. The two were good friends and showed no outward sign of rivalry. In later years it was suggested that Wilcox never stood a chance, that Chairman Rockefeller decided without hesitation to choose Wriston. "There was no contest," a director of the bank recalled. (Wilcox has since become the chief executive of Crocker National, based in San Francisco, which is one of the largest commercial-banking companies on the West Coast.)

When Rockefeller wandered into Wriston's office and told him the good news, the new president found it difficult to summon up much enthusiasm. His wife had died a few months earlier— he still chokes up in recounting the episode—and he felt weighed down rather than elated by his responsibilities. He went to his father's apartment to talk things over, and Dr. Wriston assured him that "it's really not the end of the world." He got married again in 1968 to Kathryn Dineen, a lawyer.

Wriston's rapid ascent was more remarkable than most. While it was likely that *somebody* from his generation would reach the top at a tender age, there was certainly no guarantee that the winner would be Wriston. Citibank was a huge, highly respected institution, and it had no trouble attracting top-grade people after the war. Wriston had to compete with hordes of talented, ambitious men in his own age group. But he matched or surpassed his competitors in all the ways that mattered. He was just as hard-working, enthusiastic and aggressive as anyone else, and he also was brighter, more knowledgeable and more imaginative. Above all, he knew how to ingratiate himself with the right people—

namely Stillman Rockefeller and George Moore. It's safe to assume that they seldom felt the sting of his rapier wit.

Unlike Wriston, Donald McIntosh Kendall, who became chief executive of PepsiCo, Inc., at the age of forty-two, did not have to worry about tough competition in climbing through the ranks. His company, known as Pepsi-Cola when he joined it straight out of the Navy, had a tradition of weak management and a dismal public image. As a distant second to Coca-Cola it could neither attract nor hold the more talented people in the soft-drink industry. Kendall, who was bright, hardworking and extremely eager to get ahead, thoroughly outclassed his contemporaries—and his seniors to boot. His rise was spectacular. Just sixteen years after walking in the door for the first time, he had become the top man.

After taking charge of Pepsi, Kendall worked hard at improving its image. Through a series of mergers he turned it from a single-product company into a diversified giant, and he moved the headquarters from leased space in Manhattan to a fabulous 112-acre spread in Purchase, New York, some thirty miles upstate. The site was formerly the Blind Brook Polo Club, and it adjoins the vast estates of Westchester County's landed gentry. The neighbors raised quite a ruckus when they heard about Pepsi's plan to build there. But Kendall carried off the project in high style, getting Edward Durell Stone to design the buildings and Edward, Jr., to do the landscaping. He also acquired two dozen works by some of the world's greatest sculptors, placed them about the grounds, and invited the public to come and look. Formerly disgruntled residents of the area can now be seen wandering awestruck from Calder to Lipchitz to Rodin. Kendall also has a nice art collection of his own at his mansion in Greenwich, Connecticut.

At headquarters he occupies a huge corner office, with eleven windows offering a fine panoramic view of the grounds. In the middle of the grounds is a large fountain, and Kendall can switch the fifty-foot jet on and off with a control panel at his desk. At the far end of the office is a mirror-fronted fireplace, which he will set ablaze at the slightest provocation. "This headquarters—I take tremendous pride in this," Kendall exclaims. "Look at it! I have a great sense of accomplishment. The same with building the company. Not many people can equal that feat." Kendall, as one of his fellow tycoons warned me, "likes to tell you how good he is."

Kendall is physically imposing, a burly six-footer with a crushing handshake. He is a fitness fanatic, who plays tennis, skis and runs, and he encourages his subordinates to work out too. It has been suggested that physical fitness is a prerequisite for advancement at PepsiCo, and some of the executives do their running on the company grounds, where the boss will be sure to see them. There is also a fully equipped gymnasium at headquarters. During our interview, when we took the inevitable break for soft drinks, I had a regular Pepsi, but Kendall, with a worried eye to his waistline, ordered a diet drink, Pepsi Light. Kendall never misses a chance to hoist a Pepsi in public, and he expects his employees to behave the same way. No matter what else they consume at restaurants or parties, a Pepsi must be part of the feast.

Kendall's fashionably long white hair curls upward at the collar and mercifully conceals a pair of large, jug-handle ears. He has bushy eyebrows and an elfin countenance, and one might even be tempted to liken him to Santa Claus—except that his generally gruff demeanor does not inspire cheer. He is tough, and he lets you know it. He does have a sense of humor, but it is on the heavy side. At a banquet where Kendall was receiving an award, a speaker suggested that his wife had a lot to do with his success. Kendall allowed as how that was true. She had acquired a couple of credit cards, he said, "and I've been working hard ever since." Another time he told some aides: "If you work twelve hours a day, you finally get to be boss so you can put in sixteen to eighteen hours a day." But he might not have been joking. It does take plenty of hard work to reach the top, and plenty more to stay there. Practically all the tycoons are certifiable workaholics.

One of Kendall's closest associates is Cartha D. DeLoach, who was a top-ranking FBI administrator during the reign of J. Edgar Hoover. A Georgian with a sugary accent, he serves as vice president of corporate affairs at PepsiCo, with jurisdiction over governmental and public relations. He also accompanies Kendall on most of his business trips. DeLoach reputedly supervised the FBI's electronic surveillance of Martin Luther King, Jr., during the 1964 Democratic National Convention. He has described Kendall as "a J. Edgar Hoover with heart."

Kendall was born in 1921 in Sequim, Washington, a small town about fifty miles northwest of Seattle, and grew up in a one-story frame house on his family's dairy farm. The demand for milk and cheese stayed relatively steady during the Depression, and the Kendalls were always prosperous enough. But Donald recalls that he and his two brothers "worked our tails off" at farm chores, such as milking the cows, sawing wood, and clearing the land—which they did with a team of mules. Their father, Carroll C. Kendall, was a stalwart opponent of Franklin D. Roosevelt and the New Deal. "He was sympathetic to other people's problems," Donald says, "but he felt that people should be self-sufficient."

At more than 200 pounds Kendall was naturally inclined to football, and he played tackle on two championship teams at high school. He also boxed in the Golden Gloves. For a while he seriously considered a football career—"Several of us on the team talked about playing professional"—and he was offered athletic scholarships to the University of Washington and Western Kentucky State. He chose Western Kentucky even though Washington had the better football team. His parents had divorced, and his mother was remarried and living in Kentucky, not far from the campus in Bowling Green. Kendall wasn't an exceptional student. "My marks were never spectacular," he says. "When I'd find something I had an interest in, and the teacher could turn a spark on, I did very well. It was the reverse when I didn't." The subjects that intrigued him most were the social sciences and history.

Whatever his academic shortcomings, Kendall certainly displayed a good head for business. He took a job in a women's clothing store that had just opened in Bowling Green. "They had what were then considered high prices," he recalls. "When they opened I offered to go on commission in the shoe department. They offered me a deal where I got paid extra if someone asked for me." To assure that someone would, he had a batch of business cards printed up and went through the town passing them out to the better-heeled residents. "I started making good money," he says. "I wouldn't take all the holidays. I helped in trimming windows. I was able to buy my own car—an old Buick convertible—and I had money in the bank."

He dropped out of college in 1942, after three semesters, to join the Navy. Both his brothers, one of them younger than Donald, had already enlisted ahead of him. He piloted a patrol bomber in the Philippines and New Guinea and was evidently quite a hero, though he is reticent about the details. He won two Distinguished Flying Crosses and three Air Medals and rose to the rank of lieutenant (junior grade). While attending flight school at a base in Corpus Christi, he met Ann McDonnell, whose father was the chief of staff. They were married in 1945 but divorced twenty years later, and Kendall soon got married again —to a German baroness, Sigrid Ruedt von Collenberg.

By the time he was discharged from the Navy in 1947, his dream of becoming a professional football player had faded, and at twenty-six he felt it was too late to return to school. At the urging of his father-in-law, whose home was on Long Island, he began looking for a job in New York. "He kept putting the needle in," Kendall recalls, "telling me 'this is where the action is.' I had no intention of staying in the East. I was very fond of hunting and fishing. But he told me there was wonderful salmon fishing available in the East." A Navy friend, John R. Fell, who was a partner with Lehman Brothers, suggested that he try the Pepsi-Cola Company. He said the company had a good product, but the management was largely inept, and a swift ascent through the ranks seemed possible. Pepsi trailed so far behind its rival that the people at Coca-Cola were scarcely aware that a rivalry existed. Coke's revenues in 1947 were more than three times as great as Pepsi's.

Kendall walked in unheralded and was interviewed by Edward Loughlin, who was in charge of Pepsi's fountain-syrup sales. Loughlin agreed to hire him as a salesman, and since it was a Friday he asked Kendall to report the following Monday. That placed Kendall in a quandary, since he was just about to leave for a week-long fishing trip to Nova Scotia. He was afraid that it might cost him the job if he requested a delay, but he took a chance. Loughlin was a fishing enthusiast himself, and he was glad to give Kendall the extra time. Kendall started out at a salary of $400 a month—quite a comedown from the $700 he was receiving in terminal pay from the Navy. "At that time I was looking more for opportunity than money," he says. "Ed Loughlin convinced me the opportunity was there."

He wanted the top job at Pepsi, and he worked like a fiend to get it, often getting by on just four hours of sleep per night. "I always wanted to be Number One," he says. "When I went out selling, I would work later and longer than anyone else because I wanted to have the best sales. Later, when I ran a sales group, that group was Number One. How else are you going to be Number One if you don't outperform the others? I wanted to be the head man. Some people are competitive, some not. I like to win on the tennis court. Even as a kid, I was in the 4-H Club. J. C. Penney used to put up the money for the champion Guernsey. I wanted to be the one who raised it. Even then I was competitive."

Kendall's ambitions were fed by Loughlin, who was delighted by his young protégé's drive and determination. "He thought I had the qualities to be head of the company," Kendall recalls. "He was very good at motivating people. He was a super human being. He gave me a lot of time and a lot of attention." Kendall repeatedly raced past competing executives, receiving four promotions in five years. Still only thirty-one, he became a vice president of the company, in charge of national accounts. Four years later he was placed in charge of Pepsi's marketing, and before another year was out he was named the president of Pepsi-Cola International, a wholly owned subsidiary of the Pepsi-Cola Company. That gave him authority over all operations outside the U.S. and Canada.

Early in Kendall's career Pepsi-Cola came under the leadership of a flamboyant marketing man, Alfred Nu Steele. (That middle name is not a typographical error. Steele's father had been an unusually dedicated member of the Sigma Nu fraternity.) Steele was greatly impressed with Kendall's record and took a direct hand in most of his promotions. The two worked closely on a number of projects, and when Steele decided to fire the man who was running the international company he immediately turned to Kendall as the logical replacement. Kendall speculates that he might not have gotten the job so soon if Steele had bothered to check his age. He had gone gray in his youth and looked considerably older than his thirty-six years. After the appointment went into effect the subject of ages came up in casual conversation, and Steele indicated that he thought Kendall was in his mid-forties.

Kendall admired Steele at first, but as he got to know the chairman better he began to have grave doubts. "Steele was a very good marketing man," Kendall remarks, "but if he made one dollar he'd spend two." Kendall says that Steele's extravagant habits carried over into his private life, and that when he became strapped for cash he indulged in business practices that "didn't exactly fit my standard of morals." He won't elaborate for the record, except to say that "there were things Steele was doing with franchised bottlers he just shouldn't have been doing. Let's just say I question some of his business tactics."

Steele became well known outside the business world when he married one of the leading American actresses, Joan Crawford, in 1955. He was her fourth husband, and they stayed married until he suddenly died of a heart attack in 1959. As everyone knows by now, Miss Crawford was an extremely difficult woman, and the executives of Pepsi-Cola dolefully accepted her as the cross they had to bear. There is a story, which came out some years ago in *Esquire*, about an occasion when Kendall was escorting Miss Crawford at the Stork Club. Noticing Ernest Hemingway at another table, she sent Kendall over to ask him to join their party. Papa bellowed in reply: "Tell her to bring her ass over here if she wants to meet me." Kendall has other woeful tales about Miss Crawford—but he won't tell them. "Somebody who's gone like that, I don't think it's fair," he says. "She did a lot of bad things," he adds tantalizingly. "She could stir up trouble. She was a strange one. She really was two different people. She had a public image and a private image, a Jekyll and Hyde. I saw Hyde plenty of times." Kendall said he hadn't read *Mommie Dearest*, the condemnatory book about Miss Crawford by her daughter Christina; for him, the book would not be a revelation.

Miss Crawford was elected a director of Pepsi-Cola after her husband died, and went on promotional tours throughout the world, opening new bottling plants and speaking at conventions. After Kendall became chief executive he curtailed her activities. When Pepsi-Cola and Frito-Lay merged to form PepsiCo, Inc.,

Miss Crawford was left off the board of the parent company, though she remained a director of the Pepsi-Cola division. Her promotional appearances, for which she was handsomely paid, became few and far between, and eventually they stopped. According to one account she began referring to Kendall as "Fang." After she died in 1977 her friend Doris Lilly, the show-business correspondent, wrote an article for *People* suggesting that the death might have been a suicide and that estrangement from her late husband's company had helped make her despondent.

In the wake of Steele's death, Kendall became embroiled in a bitter struggle with another high-ranking Pepsi executive. His rival was Emmett R. O'Connell, the executive vice president, who dominated the new—and nominal—head of the company, Herbert L. Barnet. Barnet had joined Pepsi in 1949, after performing the company's legal chores for fifteen years, and had served as president under Steele. He succeeded Steele as chief executive, but in that role he turned out to be hopelessly weak. Pepsi's inability either to attract good managers from outside or to develop them within had finally produced a power vacuum at the very top. Emmett O'Connell rushed to fill it.

"Barnet was a lawyer who should have stayed a lawyer," says Kendall. "He was over his head." Barnet also had been crushed by the prolonged illness and death of his wife. "He was very close to his wife," Kendall remarks, "and he was never the same afterward. He never had many friends. He lived pretty much alone." Kendall says that O'Connell was constantly working behind the scenes, prodding Barnet to interfere with the international operation. "He was trying to take over total control," Kendall says. "He had always wanted to get his hands on International, which I was running. I would never let him into the international operation. I guess I was a threat to his position. If I was out of the way, in effect he'd be running the company."

Kendall was approached in 1959 by an officer of the U.S. State Department, who suggested that Pepsi-Cola set up a booth at the American National Exhibition in Moscow scheduled for that July. The man confessed that the State Department had tried Coca-Cola first but had been rebuffed. He said Coke's officers evidently were concerned about how the American public would react if they consorted with the Russians. Kendall, however, saw the exhibition as an opportunity to get some unique publicity for Pepsi and perhaps even a foothold in the Russian soft-drink market. He arranged for a display booth, complete with Russian-speaking hostesses recruited from American universities, at a cost of a quarter-million dollars.

O'Connell thought he had a real issue this time. He nagged Barnet relentlessly, arguing that the booth would be a waste of money. Kendall, who had his spies at headquarters, was convinced that he would lose his job unless the Pepsi exhibit turned out to be a big hit. The night before the exhibition opened he attended a party where Vice President Richard M. Nixon was the guest of honor. Nixon was scheduled to escort Soviet Premier Nikita Khrushchev through the exhibition grounds in Sokolniki Park the next day. Kendall knew Nixon slightly, having worked with him on President Eisenhower's "People to People" program. When he reached Nixon on the receiving line, he explained his plight.

"I'm in a lot of trouble. You've got to help me out," he implored.

"Don't worry," Nixon replied. "I'll bring Khrushchev by for a Pepsi."

Nixon kept his promise. He and Khrushchev stopped at the Pepsi booth on their way—as it turned out—to the immortal "kitchen debate" on the relative merits of capitalism and communism. Tagging along were reporters and photographers from all over the world. Kendall had stocked the booth with bottled Pepsi from the U.S. and with syrup which could be mixed with water and carbon dioxide to produce fountain drinks. "I told Khrushchev I wanted him to try a Pepsi made in New York and one made in Moscow," Kendall recalls, "knowing full well which one he'd like best." As the cameras clicked, the roly-poly Premier gulped the bottled product first, then tried a cup of the "Russian" Pepsi and pronounced it superior. In fact he drank seven or eight cups as he walked around and chatted amiably with the hostesses. "He couldn't believe these were American girls," says Kendall. The newspapers gave the episode a big play, many of them running pictures of Kendall, Khrushchev and Nixon beaming at one another—while Kendall carefully gripped a Pepsi bottle with the label facing the cameras. Kendall recalls that at least one paper carried the headline "Khrushchev Learns to Be Sociable"—a takeoff on "Be Sociable, Have a Pepsi," the company's advertising slogan in those days. "And that," Kendall exclaims with grim satisfaction, "was the end of O'Connell's mission." Almost exactly a year later, O'Connell dropped dead of a heart attack at his desk.

The meeting with Khrushchev had more than passing significance for Pepsi. As he had hoped, Kendall used it to establish contacts with a number of key Soviet officials. Pepsi opened a soft-drink plant in Russia in May 1974, becoming the first American company to manufacture a consumer product there.

Pepsi-Cola International was in shabby condition at the time Kendall took it over. "It was poorly organized," he recalls. "It was totally centralized, with all the decision making in New York. A guy in New York would decide whether a truck in Bangkok would have six wheels—or whatever. One of the first things I did, I decentralized it and put the decision making in the field." He divided Pepsi's international territory into six regions—or "profit centers"—and appointed a boss for each region, responsible for making a profit the best way he knew how. After submitting a budget for the year, each region would conduct its own marketing program and would have a free hand with all the other details involved in running a business. In return for autonomy, the regional boss lost a measure of security; if his region did poorly, it would presumably be his fault, and he would face dismissal. Four of the six original bosses were replaced during Kendall's six-year tenure as the head of International.

Kendall traveled extensively to keep abreast of the international operations, logging 175,000 miles a year—roughly the equivalent of a transatlantic flight every week. He also remained an irrepressible salesman, unable to resist the urge to peddle Pepsi's wares in person. That urge nearly proved fatal twice during July 1958. He left Iraq just two days before King Faisal II was overthrown and assassinated by Army rebels—and later learned that other Americans staying at his hotel had been murdered by rioters. He arrived in Lebanon just before President Eisenhower sent in the U.S. Marines to prevent revolution from spreading to that country. When Kendall tried to take a swim in the Mediterranean, he was chased from the surf by fighter planes, their guns blazing.

Under Kendall's direction Pepsi-Cola International expanded at a phenomenal rate. In six years it nearly doubled the number of countries in which it did business—from 53 to 102—and increased the number of franchised bottling plants from 160 to 283. Revenues tripled, profits quintupled, and the growth made Pepsi-Cola International a major force in the company. International had accounted for only 31 percent of the Pepsi bottles sold in 1957, but by 1963 its share had climbed to 41 percent. Most important was International's contribution to the bottom line: nearly all of Pepsi-Cola's $6.5 million gain in net income during the six-year period came from the international business. Domestically, Pepsi's share of the cola market shrank slightly, but thanks to International the company managed to narrow the gap between itself and Coca-Cola.

It was just a question of *when* Kendall would become the top man in the company. He was appointed president and chief executive officer in September 1963, while Herbert Barnet, still in his fifties, was kicked upstairs with nothing but the title of chairman to console him. The change was precipitated by a rebellion among Pepsi's domestic bottlers. Pepsi had substantially raised the price of its concentrate in the U.S.—a dubious move considering that domestic sales were weak. The bottlers angrily protested, and the management then backed down somewhat, cutting the increase in half. But discontent remained, and the bottlers took their case to the board of directors, charging that the company lacked leadership.

Kendall wasted no time in straightening out Pepsi's domestic business. Within days after his appointment he set out on a tour of the U.S., visiting the bottlers and listening to their complaints. He traveled in Pepsi's Lockheed Lodestar, accompanied only by a secretary and the head of the company's executive-health unit, who functioned pretty much as a manservant. "I would get a group of bottlers together during a travel break," Kendall recalls, "then fly to another place for lunch and another for dinner. I dictated between towns. I did that for two or three weeks. By that time I had written two books on the subject." The problems of the domestic business, he found, were much like those he had encountered at International. Decision making was concentrated almost exclusively among the top people at headquarters. "You could take a bottler in Miami or Seattle or San Diego who had a problem—he had to go through four district and regional managers for a decision," Kendall observes. "By the time the decision came back, the poor bottler no longer had a problem. There was a great deal of animosity." The animosity was so intense, he decided, that it was necessary to sacrifice some of the Old Guard, and on his return he got rid of three marketing vice-presidents.

As the domestic business began to show sprightly gains in sales and earnings, Kendall launched a search for a merger partner. "Pepsi-Cola was a reasonably small company then," he says. "A lot of companies were starting to merge. If we didn't have a big enough base, we wouldn't be able to compete. Did you want to have someone take you over, or build your own company? That was the choice." In fact he was approached in 1964 by CBS, Inc., which was interested in taking Pepsi over. Kendall rejected the proposition out of hand. He says he was peeved because the offer wasn't proffered by the CBS chairman, William Samuel Paley. "He sent a messenger boy—Mike Burke. If Paley himself had called initially, it could have been an entirely different story. Paley knows that—I've told him." CBS didn't care to attempt a hostile takeover, and the matter died. The next year Pepsi-Cola merged with Frito-Lay, a manufacturer of corn chips, potato chips and other snack foods. Based in Dallas, Frito-Lay was still headed by its founder, Herman Warden Lay, and some people predicted that there would ultimately be a collision between two large egos. But Kendall and Lay got along beautifully. "We had one of the best personal relationships I ever had with anybody," Kendall says. Lay became chairman of the merged company, PepsiCo, Inc., replacing Herbert Barnet, who stayed on for about four years as chairman of the Pepsi-Cola division. Kendall continued to serve as president and chief executive officer and became chairman of PepsiCo in 1971, when Lay stepped aside to become chairman of the Executive Committee.

Kendall wasn't about to stop with just one merger. PepsiCo annexed Wilson, the sporting-goods company, Pizza Hut and Taco Bell, the fast-food chains, and North American Van Lines and Lee Way Motor Freight, the truckers. It was an indirect way to do it, but PepsiCo finally overtook Coca-Cola. During 1979, Pepsi reported revenues of $5.09 billion, while Coke, which made some acquisitions itself over the years, had revenues of $4.96 billion.

On the day Kendall was appointed chief executive, one of the people who telephoned to congratulate him was Richard Nixon. Kendall and Nixon had become the best of friends after their triumphant collaboration in Sokolniki Park. They dined together, golfed together and attended football games together, and their families became friendly too. When Kendall remarried in 1965, Nixon played piano at the reception in the Hotel Pierre.

It sometimes seemed as though Kendall couldn't do enough to repay the man who had saved his job. After Nixon lost the 1960 Presidential election to John F. Kennedy, Kendall proposed that he join Pepsi-Cola International as chairman. Nixon decided instead to return to California, where he lost another election in 1962, to Governor Edmund G. Brown, Sr. In 1963, when Nixon joined the Mudge, Rose law firm in New York, Kendall gave him International's account, and when Kendall became chief executive of the parent company later in the year, Mudge, Rose got *all* of Pepsi's business. Nixon toured the world twice at Pepsi's expense, ostensibly to visit the company's foreign franchises and to spread goodwill. The tours also kept him in the political limelight, and his meetings with various statesmen along the way enhanced his reputation as an expert on foreign affairs.

When Nixon made his comeback, Kendall proved a dedicated helper. He rounded up support from other business leaders in both the 1968 and 1972 Presidential campaigns, and during Nixon's term in office, according to one account, he served as the President's "leading adviser on corporate affairs." He held only one *official* position, spending a year as chairman of the National Alliance of Businessmen, a federally subsidized organization set up to find jobs for the hardcore unemployed. "It was a great experience," he says. In an interview at the end of his tenure in 1970, Kendall offered this strange insight into what he thought the Alliance was accomplishing:

> There's a company with offices in midtown New York that hired five young people from Harlem as messengers. They were about as far out as you could find—wild clothes, wild hairdos, beards. The company assigned one of its supervisors to work with these young

men. He took one of them to lunch at a restaurant where everyone was pretty conservatively dressed. The young boy was obviously embarrassed, because he was just wearing an open shirt and no tie. After lunch he asked the supervisor, "Could I come here with my girl friend and have lunch?" And the supervisor replied, "Why, of course." And he arranged for the boy to have lunch there on a Saturday with his girl. The boy underwent a remarkable change. He showed up for work in a suit and tie. His long hair was gone. He was a different person, because he saw that he was accepted like everyone else. That sort of thing is happening all over the country, and it doesn't take many such experiences to give you a lot of encouragement.

Kendall also helped Nixon with foreign policy, serving as an unofficial ambassador at large. On his business trips abroad he would convey messages to foreign leaders or gather economic and political information in notebooks and disgorge the contents to the Chief back at the White House. On one occasion he conferred with Japanese leaders, seeking to reduce the flow of low-priced textile imports. Another time he gave Nixon a report on conditions in the Middle East. He also is said to have taken a hand in stirring up the Nixon Administration against the Allende faction in Chile. When it looked as though Dr. Salvador Allende Gossens, a Marxist, would be elected president in 1970, Kendall set up discussions between key U.S. officials and an anti-Allende newspaper editor, Augustin Edwards, who happened to run a Pepsi bottling plant in Chile. The Central Intelligence Agency later made an unsuccessful attempt to prevent Allende from taking office.

During our interview, Kendall forcefully defended his political activism. In fact, he views political activism as a duty of any conscientious chief executive. "A chief executive officer has got four responsibilities," he remarked. "One, to pick a good board of directors, so if he is not giving direction to the company, they'll protect the shareholders. Two, he has to find the talent to operate the company. Three, he has to be sure the business has momentum, so it continues, and you haven't milked the last nickel out of it. Four, he must create the political and economic environment in which that company can survive. That's why I'm involved in political and other outside activities." Most chief executives, he says, are too timid to take a stand. "They don't want to rock the boat, upset the customers or anyone else, so they become political neuters. One thing I don't like is an independent. I think 'independent' is a cop-out."

Kendall's friendship with Nixon has continued undiminished since Watergate. After the former President went into seclusion in San Clemente, he and Kendall still kept in touch, getting together for dinner or a game of golf when Kendall was on the West Coast. Kendall concedes that he was disappointed at the way Nixon handled the Watergate matter. "*Naturally* I was disappointed! How could you help but be?" He thinks Nixon should simply have placed all the facts on the table at the beginning. As Kendall perceives the situation, Nixon met his downfall not out of an urge to protect his own hide, but because of his "great loyalty to his friends."

Nixonologists might dispute that interpretation, but it is understandable that Kendall sees things that way. He places a high premium on loyalty, and he and Nixon in particular have remained loyal to each other for more than two decades.

The boy wonders of the postwar period undermined one of the most sacred traditions of American business. Propelled to the top by a rare combination of circumstances, they proceeded to demonstrate that younger men could lead just as effectively—and often more effectively—than older men. In the past it was widely believed that a man acquired the necessary maturity and wisdom for corporate leadership only as he approached the age of sixty. This was a devout belief, to be sure, but a convenient one as well. Since the customary retirement age was sixty-five, no man would hold the top job in a company for very long. In the course of just twenty years, three or four men, each presumably younger than the last, could savor the ultimate reward. This made *them* happy, of course, and it also served as an incentive for executives on the rise, keeping them on their toes and hopeful.

Before the war the suggestion that a professional manager might serve as chief executive of a major company for more than twenty years—as Donald Kendall seems likely to do—would have been dismissed as preposterous. Only the people who founded their own companies, or who inherited the leadership, enjoyed such longevity. But the performances of the Kendalls, the Wristons, the Connors—and others like them—demonstrated that the old ways were not necessarily the best. What the younger men lacked in experience they more than made up for in imagination, in aggressiveness, in a willingness to take risks that produced rewards for the shareholders. The lesson sunk in, and business became more receptive to youthful leadership. In 1976 *Fortune* found that the median age of top business executives had dropped from sixty-one to fifty-seven during the previous quarter-century.

Chapter Five

Marathon Men

SOME COMPANIES continue to discourage any rapid climbs through the executive ranks. They prefer to put their most promising managers through an extremely long and painstaking selection process, shifting them from one job to the next every few years over a period of three decades and more. It is their policy—indeed, their faith—that no man is qualified to become chief executive until he has learned practically everything there is to know about the company, and has demonstrated his proficiency in a great variety of assignments. "What you're looking for," the head of one such company explains, "is the people that are going to be constant contributors, rather than shooting stars." Young men in a hurry, impatient with the authority of others and eager to run things themselves, are encouraged to look elsewhere.

It takes a special kind of person to run the corporate marathon. He must have tolerance and a dedication that can be described as either superhuman or neurotic, depending on your point of view. He must perform consistently and impeccably in every one of his many assignments and be able to tolerate the effects of rootlessness while constantly moving from city to city. He must do whatever his bosses tell him to do, year after year and decade after decade, without qualms—or at least without complaints. It is an enervating ordeal, and ordinary mortals fall by the wayside long before the race is finished. Some tycoons who have been through the marathon claim that they never felt as though they *were* in a race, that they simply plugged away at each job until they found themselves magically transported to the chief executive's chambers. But it is difficult to believe that someone who wasn't aiming to win the marathon could in fact win it.

The corporate marathon has reached its highest state of refinement at the American Telephone and Telegraph Company. There are a million AT&T employees—more than in any other company—and the task of determining which few will rise to the top is pursued with great reverence. One sometimes gets the impression that AT&T devotes as much attention to training and testing managers as it does to operating the nation's telephone system. Every supervisor in the Bell System—they number in the tens of thousands—is required to keep constant vigil over his subordinates in an effort to identify those who belong on a faster track. By the time a man becomes the chief executive of AT&T, he will have been tested in at least a score of assignments.

This method of choosing chief executives has not produced perfect results at AT&T. The method is founded on the assumption that each generation of executives will include at least one person who is in fact capable of serving adequately as the chief executive. But there is no logical reason to make this assumption, and in practice it has proved unsound. In 1967 the company's board of directors elected a chief executive, Haakon Ingolf Romnes, who wasn't equal to the demands of the office. In fairness to Romnes, it should be pointed out that those demands were particularly harsh during his tenure. It was a period when severe service breakdowns afflicted the telephone systems in a number of large cities, among them Boston, Denver, Houston, Miami and New York. The operating companies serving those cities had underestimated the growth in demand, and they didn't have the equipment to handle the calls their customers were making—or at least trying to make, since many customers found themselves waiting endlessly for dial tones or unable to complete their calls when they were lucky enough to dial. To meet the demand, the operating companies were forced to embark on major new construction programs that cut heavily into their profits, already squeezed by inflation. The operating companies needed the permission of their state regulatory bodies to raise rates, and they weren't getting permission fast enough to keep pace with rising costs. Romnes simply lacked the imagination to extricate AT&T from its difficulties, and the company floundered until he reached retirement age in 1972.

He was succeeded by John Dulany deButts, who turned out to be one of the ablest chief executives in the company's history. A tall, heavyset, courtly Virginian, deButts snapped the company out of its slump, and he did it largely on the strength of his considerable charisma. He and two other top executives went on a grand tour of the U.S., giving pep talks to thousands of Bell System managers. "We talked to people at mass meetings to give them confidence," he recalled, "and also to let them know what this new management team looked like, and what we sounded like. We let them ask anything they wanted to ask, and we'd answer them." Within a few years the Bell System had not only overcome its service problems, but had surpassed all previous records for trouble-free service. The company's earnings, which went nowhere during the Romnes regime, surged to new heights under deButts.

In retrospect it seems clear that deButts should have been appointed the head of AT&T five years earlier and that Romnes should have been skipped entirely. Even at that early date it was understood that deButts eventually would become the top man. When Romnes was elevated to the chairmanship, deButts became the vice chairman, leaving him with absolutely no competition. In fact, it has been reliably suggested that Romnes was appointed as a caretaker chairman so that deButts could get more seasoning. Not that deButts was either young or inexperienced by ordinary business standards; he was already fifty-one years old at the time Romnes took over, had been with AT&T for thirty years, and had served for nearly a year as the company's executive vice president, which placed him third in the hierarchy. But by Bell System standards he was little more than a callow youth. The company got trapped—and mangled—by tradition.

In February 1979, deButts was succeeded as chief executive by Charles Lee Brown, Jr. True to the company's tradition, Brown had spent nearly thirty-three years shuttling through two dozen positions, and he was past his fifty-seventh birthday when he finally reached the top. AT&T has been so much a part of his life for so long that he refers to it as "The Business," a phrase eloquent in its simplicity—and exclusivity. (Executives at General

Motors, it should be noted, speak of *their* employer in much the same spirit—as "The Corporation.") Like his predecessors, Brown regards the chairmanship of The Business as a public trust, a "unique responsibility to maintain and enhance the telephone service to this nation."

Brown insists that he never worried much about how far he was going at AT&T, that he simply accepted each assignment as it came along and did the best he could. He says he enjoyed his work most of the time. "I've always felt you can't get paid enough if you don't like what you're doing," he remarks. "The intrinsic enjoyment of my jobs has been the highest motivating factor." He confesses, however, that there were a couple of jobs that aggravated him, because they involved "detailed or routine work extensively." He won't say which ones, because he doesn't want to demoralize the people who hold them now.

I interviewed Brown in Basking Ridge, New Jersey, at the Bell Laboratories, a vast, sprawling complex that owes its architectural inspiration to the hanging gardens of Babylon. I found him in an enormous top-floor office, with a plainclothes bodyguard—an ex-policeman—posted just outside. A handsome, graying man of medium height, Brown has a somber mien, and his voice, which belongs more to the Midwest than to his native Richmond, carries a sepulchral overtone.

Brown was a good athlete in high school and college, and he keeps in fine trim by playing golf and tennis. He also finds time to read a book a week—mainly history. He lives with his second wife—the first died—in Princeton, New Jersey, and they also own a cottage near Palm Beach, Florida. Brown travels to and from AT&T's Manhattan headquarters in a chauffeured company-owned limousine, and he also enjoys the luxury of a corporate jet when he travels farther afield. But he is not particularly free with his own funds. He recently bought a new Oldsmobile, but only because his 1965 model was ruined in an accident. "I've had a lot more money than I thought I needed for a long time now," he says.

He rarely jokes, though he does respond to humor with a quick smile. He obviously doesn't enjoy talking to journalists, but he accepts it as part of his job and remains unfailingly courteous. He digests each question with a deadpan expression, staring into the middle distance for some time before coming up with an answer. He is usually stingy with words, though he is capable of eloquence when extolling the virtues of the Bell System or when discussing some knotty business problem.

All in all he presents a strong contrast to John deButts, whose outgoing manner and genial warmth make him the very model of the southern gentleman. Nor is he much like William Maurice Ellinghaus, the bluff, hearty charmer who lost out to Brown in the contest for chairman and now serves as president.

Brown's subordinates describe him respectfully—if not affectionately. He is said to be quick-witted, decisive, flexible and disciplined, but nobody accuses him of being colorful. The words that crop up most often are "tough" and "demanding." As one colleague remarked: "He's a man who brings out the best because people know they have to be prepared." Brown flinches at the suggestion that he is "tough." He insists that he is not tough on people, though he allows that he is tough in confronting *problems*. "A corporate executive would be foolish to exercise power autocratically," he says. Still, it is not stretching the imagination to suppose that it takes a very tough man to reach the top at AT&T, where executive performance is measured both precisely and impersonally. The ambitious executive must rely heavily on his subordinates to produce the kind of performance that attracts favorable attention from above, and it would be only natural for him to crack the whip now and again. The trick is to remain fair, to avoid descending into mere brutality—which is usually counterproductive. Self-control is extremely important to the aspiring tycoon.

After getting out of the Navy in 1946, Brown briefly considered going into the airline business on the maintenance side. He had finished in the upper third of his engineering class at the University of Virginia and had gotten plenty of practical experience maintaining equipment aboard the U.S.S. *Mississippi*. He did receive a job offer from an airline—he doesn't recall which one— but rejected it because he would have been forced to start work immediately in a remote location.

He applied instead to the telephone company, where he already felt very much at home. His father had been a traffic manager there for many years; his mother had served as an operator and supervisor; and he himself had spent two summers before the war digging holes for telephone poles in Cleveland, at a salary of $13 a week. (His younger sister got into the act later on, working as a service representative for New Jersey Bell, one of the AT&T operating companies.) Brown says his parents "gave me an idea what The Business was like, what the satisfactions are, and what feelings people in The Business have toward it."

Brown felt that he had a good chance to surpass his father's record at AT&T. The elder Brown's attainments were respectable, but like so many others of his generation, he had been held back by the Depression. Charles, Jr., however, stepped into the telephone company during a period of exploding growth and opportunity. He also came to the job with considerably more drive than his father. "My father," he recalls, "was a hardworking person who had a broad view of life and business experience, and surely was anxious to do a good job in what he was doing—anxious to be able to provide well for his wife and children. But I don't recall him as being a driving person in the sense of ambition pushing him." On the other hand his mother, the former Mary McNamara, was "a strong person who was anxious that my sister and I do the right thing and excel at what we tried to do." He diplomatically suggests that "the combination and examples of both parents contributed to what I am."

His first permanent job with the company was less than glamorous. He was sent to Hartford, Connecticut, as a maintenance man in the Long Lines Department and frequently found himself crawling in and out of manholes, to check and repair underground cables. The job was intended strictly as basic training, however. "You have to understand how the apparatus works," he explains. After six months he was transferred to New York City, where he was given an engineering job.

Brown began receiving special attention from the head of the Long Lines Department, Henry Thomas Killingsworth. Even more than most Bell System bosses, Killingsworth was concerned about the young men in his organization and did all he could to move the brightest ones along. He liked to slice through layers of bureaucracy and telephone his young charges directly, to grill them about their jobs. He might ask why a long-distance cable had been broken, or he might request some information about a customer who had filed a complaint. Brown, who received his share of these calls, sensed that Killingsworth already knew the answers and was using the questions to test him. Killingsworth would place his subordinates in what Brown describes as "difficult, testing" assignments, to determine the scope of their abilities. Brown was repeatedly asked to join task forces formed to investigate extraordinary problems and recommend solutions. "They ranged all over the map," Brown recalls. "A task force might be involved in the accuracy of customer billing or the maintenance of equipment or productivity improvement." The task forces were made up of people from several different departments, and Brown was exposed to the scrutiny of high-level managers who might not otherwise have had an opportunity to meet him.

By 1952, Brown had become the Long Lines district-plant superintendent in Birmingham, Alabama, a job he finds particularly memorable because it seemed like such a huge responsibility for a thirty-year-old. He had authority over the maintenance and installation of long-distance facilities not only in Alabama, but also in Louisiana and Mississippi. He says the assignment "opened my eyes and helped me grow." He was appointed to his first nontechnical job in 1954, becoming the Long Lines commercial manager in Atlanta. It was a clear sign that he was considered a prospect for top management at AT&T. He was being tested to see how well he could cope with tasks that required more than an engineering background. Having passed the test, he received still more assignments of a general nature. In 1961 he was appointed the first dean of AT&T's Data Communications School in Cooperstown, New York. The school was established to teach Bell System employees about the data-processing market, in which the company hoped to take a strong position. After less than a year as an academician, Brown became general manager of the Long Lines Central Area, based in Cincinnati, and he later returned to Atlanta as general manager of the Southeastern Area.

In July 1963, Brown went to work for Illinois Bell Telephone, one of the better performers among AT&T's operating companies. It turned out to be the most important transfer of his career, for it brought him into the orbit of John deButts, who was serving at the time as president of Illinois Bell. DeButts had a sudden need for someone to fill the job of vice president and general manager, the incumbent having retired early when his wife became seriously ill. DeButts had never met Brown, but he sought him out at the recommendation of another Bell executive. The two hit it off well—"the chemistry between him and myself has always been good," Brown says—and Brown became deButts's protégé. In 1965, deButts promoted Brown to vice president for operations, and four years later, while serving as vice chairman of AT&T, deButts got Brown appointed president of Illinois Bell. That was when Brown recognized that he had a good chance to go all the way to the top of AT&T. He was still in his forties, relatively young for the head of a Bell System operating company. And as he surveyed the competition—the high-ranking executives in his age group—he concluded that "I had as good a shot as the others."

As head of Illinois Bell, Brown impressed everyone with his swift, decisive response to one of AT&T's greatest crises. The Federal Communications Commission had ruled that the company couldn't compel its subscribers to restrict themselves to telephones and switchboards supplied by its manufacturing arm, Western Electric. The ruling came in response to a complaint from a company called Carterfone, which wanted to manufacture telephone equipment for use in the Bell System. Brown created a separate marketing department at Illinois Bell so that the company could devote special attention to the needs of its commercial customers, and he himself met with some of the customers to tout the virtues of Western Electric's equipment. He might not have agreed with the FCC's decision, but he felt comfortable with it. He considered himself a competitive person, and he relished the opportunity to compete with Carterfone or any other company that thought it could outshine AT&T.

DeButts brought Brown to headquarters in July 1974 as executive vice president, and a month later he appointed him chief financial officer as well. Brown proved to be a talented and innovative financier. When interest rates declined during 1976, he got the holders of $630 million worth of AT&T bonds to sell them to the company at premium prices. He then issued new bonds carrying lower interest rates, saving the company some $60 million. He also offered a 5 percent discount to shareholders who reinvested their dividends in the company's stock. The move proved so popular that it added $800 million to the company's equity in a single year.

In April 1976, both Brown and Bill Ellinghaus were appointed vice chairmen of AT&T. The race to succeed deButts—who would reach the age of sixty-five in 1980—seemed to have boiled down to just two contestants. Ellinghaus, who had started with the company in 1940 climbing poles as a repairman, had reached the penultimate rung of the corporate ladder despite the lack of a college education. He had been named president of New York Telephone in 1970 with a mandate to straighten out the service mess, and he succeeded faster than anyone had hoped. (His record as a troubleshooter later got him appointed to the board of the Municipal Assistance Corporation, the body formed to put New York City's finances in order.) In April 1977, deButts shuffled his top managers some more, naming Brown president of the company, and making another executive, William Sutherland Cashel, Jr., vice chairman along with Ellinghaus. At AT&T a president and a vice chairman are considered equals, so it was impossible to be sure what deButts had in mind. But the move seemed to indicate that Brown had been singled out as more equal than the others.

By the summer of 1978, deButts had decided to retire early. One of the first people he told was Brown, pulling him aside after a meeting of high-level Bell System executives. Brown was startled to hear the news and was still struggling to absorb it when deButts added that he would recommend Brown as his successor. Brown asked deButts whether there was anything wrong with his health, and deButts assured him that there wasn't, that he simply wanted to step aside early. As he later explained: "For forty-two years I've been eating, thinking and dreaming the telephone business. I thought it was time to give my wife and family some attention." Brown told deButts he was flattered by the appointment. "I thanked him for his confidence and promised to give my best efforts. And I thanked him for all the opportunities he had given me."

At one point during our conversation, Brown offered a lengthy summary of the qualities and circumstances that were most important in getting him to the top. "There's a certain element of good fortune involved," he observed. "I happened to have been at the right place at the right time. I don't think there's any blinking that fact. I found myself in charge of an organization in Illinois that's an exceptionally high-quality one. Possibly it's easier to excel there than it is in certain other circumstances. And I had the fortunate situation of an early identification by an individual, Henry Killingsworth, who thought about such matters and worked hard to pursue his methodology. Had I been in other parts of the organization, I might not have been helped by circumstances.

"I don't know whether others have had as intense an enjoyment of their work at all levels as I did—the sense that the work was intensely worthwhile and thus deserved extraordinary effort.

"Also, I'm convinced that broadly the ability to write—specifically, the ability to capsulize important points in an articulate way that gives those around you an ability to understand you, without beating around the bushes—that's a factor, has been an important factor in the ability to move.

"Then there is the ability to recognize an opportunity when it shows up. Some people have this ability, others don't. The jobs I was offered involved a tremendous amount of moving around, getting involved in different kinds of work. They were difficult, uncomfortable transitions, but I recognized them as opportunities, rather than feeling abused. There are those who complain and those who will not move. There are plenty of illustrations where people will not recognize an opportunity or are not willing to take it enough to endure the discomfort that goes with it. Certainly you have to be willing to take disadvantages in order to move up."

Brown insisted that there was no place in his company for political infighting, backstabbing or any of the other heavy-handed tactics that laymen associate with business success. "One of the quickest ways to ruin yourself in this Business is to exhibit characteristics of trying to step on people's necks in order to get ahead," he remarked. "It's almost a sure method of hurting yourself. That sort of thing doesn't appear at very high levels here. Either that or I've been very naive in my observation." Brown doesn't strike me as naive—nor do I think that he was being disingenuous. High-level power struggles do occur in business, and sometimes they turn into veritable donnybrooks. But it is difficult to picture that sort of thing happening at AT&T. AT&T is different from other companies—by virtue of its immense size, its century-long tradition and its special, ubiquitous role in American life. In a word, it is *stodgy*, like a gentlemen's club in London. The people who go to work there, and especially those who rise there, are straight arrows, squares and, above all, civilized.

The companies that favor the marathon method tend to be the really huge ones—the vast bureaucracies, of which AT&T is the grandest example. This is understandable, for in a company with hundreds of thousands of employees, most of them with narrow, specialized functions, it does take quite a while to determine who is capable and who isn't. That it should take thirty years and more, however, is certainly open to dispute.

The marathon method usually produces steady, dependable leaders, with all their buttons in place. Any outrageous personality quirks are bound to emerge sooner or later, and their owners will be shunted aside. At General Motors, for example, it is a well-established fact that oddballs and mavericks don't make it to the top. And in a way, that is just as well. As one commentator has suggested, GM functions as a flywheel for the rest of the economy. If the man who runs GM happens to be out of kilter, "the business world wobbles."

The selection process at GM does not entirely suppress individuality. All the recent chief executives have been clearly distinguishable from one another, each with a personality he could call his own. Frederic Garrett Donner, who led the company from 1958 to 1967, was a tight-lipped curmudgeon who shunned publicity. James Michael Roche, who succeeded Donner, was a gentle, conciliatory man, GM's version of Pope John XXIII. Richard Charles Gerstenberg, who became chairman in 1972, had a crustier disposition than Roche, but unlike Donner, he was willing to engage in frank exchanges with the press and critics.

The most mirthful of the lot is Gerstenberg's successor, Thomas Aquinas Murphy, who recently retired after six years in the top job. Murphy projected an image that was even slightly buffoonish. Legend has it that he once pilfered a plastic model of the Wankel rotary engine from the desk of another top executive and replaced it with an unassembled kit. He kept little signs around his office with messages like "Bless this mess" and "Please don't straighten the mess on my desk! You'll goof up my system," and at one time he displayed a cartoon with the caption: "I don't do anything, but I do it very efficiently." He made a point of telling interviewers that he read the funny papers and detective stories—"but not the highbrow ones like Agatha Christie." In fact, he read plenty of heavy material too, and his colleagues confided that he was thoroughly informed on world affairs as well as business. They also said that this friendly, folksy fellow, who encouraged his subordinates to call him "Murph," could be a very tough and demanding boss. "I have some fine associates around here who have offices close to mine," he told an interviewer. "To work off my frustrations, I often go in and kick them in the shins." It was a joke, of course, but not totally without foundation in fact.

If Murphy sometimes came off sounding like a court jester rather than the king, perhaps it was because he recognized how menacing the head of General Motors seems to people in the outside world. "Large numbers of Americans," he once observed, "apparently believe that businessmen are not reasonable, that businessmen are willing and able to sacrifice most moral or humanitarian considerations in the blind pursuit of profit." He wanted to make it plain that he wasn't a bogeyman.

Although his personal ownership in General Motors amounted to a microscopic fraction of 1 percent, Murphy was just as dedicated to his company, just as emotionally entwined, as any proprietor could be. "He cannot understand why everyone does not love GM as much as he does," *Nation's Business* reported. After an hour-long interview with a representative of that magazine, Murphy "chased the visitor down the hallway to show him a letter that had just arrived. Mr. Murphy was ecstatic. The letter was from the owner of a 1956 Chevrolet who told how well his old heap was still running."

In 1975, as he approached the age of sixty, Murphy let his employees know that it would be nice if they could honor the occasion by pushing the company's share of the auto market to 60 percent and the price of its stock to $60. "He was kidding," wrote a columnist for *Motor Trend*, "in a deadly serious way." Kidding or not, it was an unusually imperious suggestion for a professional manager to make. One is vaguely reminded of those old newsreels showing the Aga Khan sitting on one end of a huge scale, while his subjects, in tribute, heaped their most precious belongings onto the other end. However, GM's employees fell short of both their goals. Sadder still, they gave Murphy a truly wretched send-off when he retired. His last year as head of GM —1980—was a financial debacle for the company and indeed for the entire American auto industry.

I interviewed Murphy at the General Motors skyscraper on Fifth Avenue in Manhattan. As I arrived in his office, which was somewhat larger than certain hotel lobbies around town, he was sitting behind his desk, intently perusing a stack of documents. Not one to squander time, he kept his head in his work until his public-relations man had plugged in the tape recorder that would preserve this interview for posterity. Later on, I was furnished with a neatly typed, and largely accurate, transcript. The GM public-relations machine is justly renowned for its efficiency.

Murphy has a tendency to answer some questions much more thoroughly than his interviewer expects. Unfortunately, they tend to be the innocuous questions. When I asked him how he got the middle name "Aquinas," he responded with a thousand-word monologue. It seems that there was a nurse named Sister Mary Aquinas at the hospital where he was born in Hornell, New York. His older brother, born at the same hospital, had needed a blood transfusion, and the Sister was the donor. Murphy's father then gave her the privilege of naming his succeeding children. She had a twin sister named Sister Thomasina—hence, Thomas Aquinas.

But having said that, Murphy went on to tell me, without the slightest prompting, all about "Tom Murphy Day," staged in his honor by the city fathers of Hornell in September 1978. Hornell, once a bustling town on the Erie Railroad, has lost much of its industry in recent decades and is trying to get some back. "Tom Murphy Day" was part of "Industry Week," and Murphy, accompanied by several of his relatives, was happy to oblige everyone with his presence, even though he and his family had moved out of Hornell when he was six years old. Murphy's picture appeared in windows all over town, even at the Ford dealership, and he participated in several public ceremonies and a motorcade, riding in an open Chevrolet convertible. He adored every moment of it.

Murphy was hired by GM as a trainee during the summer of 1937, following his junior year at the University of Illinois. He served as a clerk in the financial department in New York City and was told that the company would like to hire him permanently after he graduated. Murphy says he got the summer job by luck. Ordinarily, GM didn't hire juniors, preferring to recruit from the graduating class. But the company had been hit by a long sitdown strike, and by the time it ended most of the seniors had made other commitments. Murphy almost turned the job down, figuring that it wouldn't be worthwhile financially. He was to receive $100 a month, and after paying for his meals, laundry and a room at the YMCA, he would have scarcely anything left. But his parents felt that this was a fine opportunity, and they helped him with his expenses.

After his graduation, Murphy was assigned for a couple of weeks to the GM headquarters in Detroit, then was transferred back to New York. He rose from clerk to accountant and felt secure enough to get married in 1941 to Catherine Maguire, the youngest of seven children of a deceased postal worker. But in 1943 he was drafted into the Navy, and after earning a commission he sailed aboard a light cruiser in the Pacific. During the Okinawa campaign Murphy's ship was assigned to protect aircraft carriers. When the war ended, the ship called at Japanese and Chinese ports, and early in 1946 it reached New York, where Murphy was discharged.

Murphy had felt unhappy at GM in the days before he entered the Navy. His chores had increased tremendously as the draft spirited away the young men in his department. His supervisors extended the work week to five and one-half days, then to six. "It just got into a grind," he recalls. "There was always more than you could get done. I guess this earth at one time was intended to be something of a paradise, and our first parents blew it. And I'd say probably ever since then, why there have been some things about any environment in which you live, whether it's a work environment, whether it's a home environment, or whatever, that kind of gets to you." He considered looking for a job that was "less pressure-prone," but got drafted himself before he could make his move. While in the service he talked things over with some of the other men and discovered that GM was no worse than other companies. Even so, he looked around a bit after returning to civilian life and carefully considered an offer from a company operated by the family of a Navy buddy. But the job was in the Midwest, while Murphy's wife and children were comfortably ensconced in New York—and his wife was a devout New Yorker from way back. He returned to GM "with a feeling of satisfaction that this was what I wanted to do."

For the next two decades Murphy moved through a succession of lowly assignments, gradually becoming an expert on statistics and finance. In 1954 he was placed in charge of a group that analyzed GM's pricing policies, and in 1956 he became the director of financial analysis in the treasurer's office. How did he win those promotions? "I guess the only thing that I can think of was that I was willing to work," he says. "I think the educational background that I had was a sound one. It gave me the opportunity to demonstrate that I did have some capability and that I was willing to work at whatever came along. I guess I always felt that whatever they had, or asked me to do, if my bosses felt it was important, it made it important to me, and I tried to do as good a job as I could at it." His patience, dedication and consistent application won him a promotion in 1959 to the grandiose position of assistant treasurer. He was already forty-three, an age when many of his contemporaries were at or near the pinnacle in other, less ponderous companies. But Murphy was perfectly content to be an assistant treasurer of GM, though he was only one of four. "I had never aspired to necessarily go that far in the organization," he claims. "I guess the major aspiration, I always felt, was to hold on to the job that I had and be sure that I did a job that would result in my being compensated fairly. I don't think I've worried too much about my career path.

"I remember one of the two people that interviewed me when I was hired at General Motors—at the time he was assistant director of the tax section in Detroit. One of the things he told me is that you ought to ask yourself the question at least once a year: 'Am I making progress?' And he said that doesn't necessarily have to be physical progress. But are you making progress in the sense of expanding your range of knowledge and vision and perspective? And if you can't say that you have, then maybe you'd better take a look either at yourself or the environment in which you find yourself, and decide whether or not something should be done. And I guess I've tried to follow that philosophy. I guess I always felt with each passing year I was expanding my horizons, my range of knowledge, my contribution.

"I'd say that the biggest problem that talented people have is to sit down and do a job that's before them, and not worry about what the promotional opportunities might be—or, for that matter, what another career path might have meant for them. . . . I remember being disappointed one time when one of my associates in the organization was transferred to what looked like a job that I could have certainly handled. It was just a case of sorting people out, and as it turned out, I'd say it was probably to the benefit of both of us."

Especially to Murphy, since he ultimately became chairman of the board.

After being named assistant treasurer, he waited eight years for his next promotion, and he says that even then it came as a surprise. The company's comptroller, Ralph Campbell Mark, was scheduled to retire at the end of April 1967. Murphy was aware of this, but it hadn't occurred to him that he might be considered for the position. There were four or five men on the comptroller's staff who seemed to have a better shot than he did. He was vacationing in Florida when he received a phone call from George Russell, an executive vice president of GM. "I wanted to tell you," Russell said, "we decided about the comptroller." Although temporarily deprived of the Florida sunshine, Murphy did his best to sound enthusiastic. "That's great!" he replied. He remembers thinking that it was nice of Russell to call him, but it wasn't necessary. He would have caught up with the news soon enough. "It's you," Russell went on, "if you'll take it." Murphy was visibly shaken, causing his wife some alarm until he explained that it was good news, not bad.

Murphy figured that the comptroller's job might be his last. His predecessor had held it for eighteen years, and Murphy, already past his fifty-first birthday, would be forced to retire in less than fourteen. He even began pondering the merits of early retirement, since he preferred not to remain in the job for more than ten years. When it was offered, he told George Russell not to count on his staying to age sixty-five. Russell, who obviously had a clearer perspective than Murphy, replied soothingly, "Nobody can predict the future."

As comptroller, Murphy stood slightly below the treasurer, Franklin Hewett LaRowe, in the company's pecking order. La-Rowe was two years older than Murphy and had been his boss. Murphy felt that LaRowe had the better chance to reach top management. He was rooting for LaRowe, not only because he liked and admired him, but also because he thought he might succeed him as treasurer. Murphy did become treasurer, but under unexpected circumstances. LaRowe, plagued by poor health, retired in November 1968.

Early in 1970 General Motors started to make some important changes on the operations side of the business. As a financial man, Murphy didn't think the changes would affect him, and he says he was puzzled when Jim Roche, who was then chairman, called him in one day to meet with the members of the Executive Committee. "I'd like to discuss with you the organization changes that we're going to recommend to the board of directors," Roche said. Murphy says he felt honored that the boss would take the trouble to fill him in on the details before they were formally announced. Roche began reciting the plans in his low-key manner, and eventually he got around to the position of vice president in charge of the car and truck group. "What we have in mind," he said, "is for you to go in and fill that job."

"You've got to be kidding!" Murphy blurted. "I'm a financial man, and I've grown up in the financial end of the business. I think I understand the business. But you know, hell, I practically could count the plants of General Motors that I've visited on the fingers of one hand. I don't know a lot about the day-to-day operations of the plant. Yes, I know the financial side of it, but I've heard a lot of people say that—particularly a group job such as that—that it's extremely important that an individual has had some background and training and evolution in that area." Roche and the other executives listened in amused silence. "We've sorted all that out," Roche told him, "and we think that this would be a good thing for you and for General Motors." Murphy didn't need any further prompting. "Well, okay," he replied, "if that's the way you look at it, I'm your boy."

Murphy's promotion to a high-ranking job in operations seemed to indicate that he was being groomed as a candidate for chief executive. Indeed, that could be the only plausible reason for plucking him out of the financial staff, where he had served so capably for more than thirty years, and plunging him into a position for which, on the surface at least, he seemed unqualified. The new job would test his versatility, broaden his perspective, and perhaps make him a more effective manager once he reached the top. GM traditionally had been headed by men who rose through the financial side of the business, so it shouldn't have been difficult to draw the appropriate conclusions when Murphy, a prominent financial man, was selected for the assignment with the car and truck group. And yet Murphy himself claims that he did not regard himself as a likely contender for the chairmanship. "There had been other cases," he says, "where people had been given operating assignments and came back into their straight career path."

He says he didn't feel secure about his prospects even after he moved up to vice chairman of General Motors in January 1972. He was vaulted into that position over the heads of several senior vice presidents, succeeding Dick Gerstenberg, who became chairman at that time. As vice chairman Murphy ranked second in the hierarchy, just ahead of Edward Nicholas Cole, the president, who was a few months older than Gerstenberg. Murphy says his election to chairman was not a sure thing, pointing out that two earlier vice chairmen of General Motors, Donaldson Brown and George Russell, retired without making it to the top. Russell, however, had been older than his chairman, Jim Roche, so there was never any suggestion that he would move up. Murphy, on the other hand, was six years younger than Gerstenberg. While Murphy might have had his doubts, the business press confidently predicted that he would become the head of GM in December 1974, when Gerstenberg had to retire—and of course they were right. If Murphy was truly surprised, then he was the only one.

Murphy says he never did adjust completely to the enormous public demands that go with the top job at General Motors. "I guess if you'd asked me forty years ago, when I was in my infancy with General Motors, would I have the capability of performing a job, and gave me a job description of a typical day or week in the life of a chief executive officer as it is now, I'd have told you, 'No way.' If you told me I would have to make as many speeches as I have made, as many public appearances as I've made, as many interviews as I have had, I'd have said, 'Well, you know, you'd better get somebody else. You'd better get somebody that is comfortable, who has some capabilities and talents, whatever you want to call it, that's oriented in that direction. Because I'm basically a bookkeeper, a financial guy, and where I feel comfortable is behind my desk with a work sheet in front of me, kinda sorting out the facts and the figures, and in my own comfortable way doing my thing.'

"Then there is always a certain—call it a hazard if you will— in being in the public eye and being on the record, because you— we all—can put our foot in the mouth. And I guess I can do it as well as anybody. It doesn't worry me greatly, and if I do—well, I do. And I'll try to extricate it the best way that I can."

Prudential, largest of the insurance companies, also favors the marathon method in selecting its top managers. It has not, however, been inflexible. Men have been known to rise to the top at Prudential even though they started their business careers elsewhere. Robert Arthur Beck, who has been the chief executive since 1978, worked at Ford before joining the Pru. It was only for a year, but that would still be considered an inexcusable heresy at either AT&T or General Motors. Beck's immediate predecessor, Donald Sinclair MacNaughton, was even more heretical. He didn't arrive at Prudential until he was thirty-seven years old, having previously practiced law in upstate New York and served as deputy superintendent of insurance in the state government. MacNaughton was named chief executive of Prudential in 1969, after just fourteen years with the company—which doesn't qualify as a marathon at all. On the other hand, MacNaughton's own predecessor, Orville Ellsworth Beal, was the quintessential marathon man, joining the company fresh out of high school and working his way up the ladder for the next thirty-six years.

Bob Beck started with Prudential as a sales agent and moved

through nearly a dozen assignments over a period of twenty-seven years before becoming chief executive shortly before his fifty-third birthday. Under normal circumstances he would have waited even longer, but MacNaughton retired four years early. Although he got off to a bumpy start, Beck became convinced quite early that he could make it to the top. "Nowhere in my mind had I ever thought that I wasn't gonna go all the way at Prudential," he remarks. "I had this feeling about always going one step further, always aspiring to the top. It never occurred to me to think in any other manner. I always enjoyed being given the responsibility and opportunity to run things. Usually there was a vacuum to be filled. I felt the need to have influence over the organization. I started believing that's what I wanted—the top—that hopefully one day I would be qualifying for it."

His colleagues from the early days remember him as a young man with "a crusading zeal" for the life-insurance business. He was "self-contained, smooth, sweeping everyone along with his air of confidence," and he had "an unusual ability to inspire other men to extraordinary levels of performance." As Don Mac-Naughton put it at the time he handed over the reins, "Bob maybe has more drive and enthusiasm than any person I've ever met, including myself." And Beck himself countered, "I love being chairman and chief executive officer of Prudential. There's not another job anywhere I'd rather have."

Beck says his success was due largely to his versatility. He was equally at home in line functions, such as managing a sales office, or staff functions, such as supervising a group of agencies. This gave him a considerable advantage over most of his competitors. "There are not many people who both like and are able to do both staff and line work," he remarks. "Most like staff or line, but are not comfortable moving between them." Beck endeared himself to his superiors with his knack for solving problems. Whether by chance or design, he often found himself assigned to jobs that had been handled ineptly by his predecessors, requiring "a great deal of reconstruction work." The reconstruction work invariably succeeded, and more promotions would follow.

Like Donald Kendall, he is a fitness fanatic, which seems particularly appropriate for the head of a life-insurance company. He jogs, scuba dives and plays paddle tennis, squash and golf. He also likes to hunt, and keeps a 24-foot, 115-horsepower fishing boat at his colonial-style home on the New Jersey shore, more than an hour's drive by chauffeured car from the Prudential headquarters in Newark. His study at home is crammed with mounted fish and other sporting trophies. Until some years ago he did a lot of hang gliding, but he gave it up after his own company refused to underwrite a new policy on his life. "I really didn't mind," he says. "I got awfully bruised." Beck stands five feet eleven, weighs 175 solid pounds, wears shell-rim glasses, and has reddish-brown hair and a tough, weathered appearance. He is articulate and speaks with a gravelly voice.

He is friendly and informal. He was in shirt-sleeves when I interviewed him in a small temporary office on the second floor of Prudential's white-marble headquarters building. The company's top executives had been displaced from their normal habitat on the twenty-fourth floor, which was being remodeled. After the interview a public-relations man conducted me on a tour of that floor, where everything is tailored to Brobdingnagian proportions. The offices could be used as ballrooms, the ceilings rise beyond the sight of man, and in the boardroom stands the largest table I have ever seen, where thirty-two people can sit on their leather chairs in absolute comfort, without bumping elbows.

Beck was born in the Bronx and attended the Bronx High School of Science, which then as now accepted only honor students. "It was a super school," he recalls. "The people in it were competing constantly." He savors the memory of "being removed from the crowd and having a chance to compete with people so much better than average." To assure a respectable showing, he would wake up several hours before schooltime and grind away at his studies. Later on, in the military service and in the business world, he was satisfied only if he could belong to "the top outfits."

He came from a long line of military men. His earliest ancestors had arrived in America during colonial times, and some of them had fought in the Revolution. Beck's father, Arthur, was a career Army man who served in General Pershing's expedition against Pancho Villa and rose to the rank of major during World War I with the Army's celebrated "Rainbow" Division. After the war he remained active in the National Guard, while becoming quite prosperous in real estate. But his holdings were wiped out in the

Depression, and he eventually wound up as the warden of Castle Williams, a military prison on Governor's Island, just off Manhattan. He was noted for his enlightened policies and made a special effort to keep hardened criminals separated from youngsters who had been picked up for light offenses.

Bob Beck was eager to join the military himself. "I was raised with military heroes," he remarks. He got a kick out of reading about men like Francis Marion, the "Swamp Fox," who had confounded the British during the Revolutionary War, or Teddy Roosevelt and the Rough Riders. "I still read a lot of biographies and autobiographies," he says. "I feel I get something out of each one. This country would be well off if it had a few heroes. The nation would like to have people it feels are of heroic quality. It would help get past this tendency to tear people down all the time."

He dreamed of attending the Military Academy at West Point, but it was to remain a dream, for he couldn't pass the eye test. At the age of seventeen he joined the Army Special Training Reserves. The U.S. had already entered World War II, and he was supposed to be called for basic training when he reached his eighteenth birthday in October 1943, although in fact the call came a couple of months earlier. In the meantime he studied during the evenings at Fordham University, and through a friend of his father's he got a daytime job with Metropolitan Life Insurance, which happens to be Prudential's greatest rival. Kids just out of high school normally were assigned to the Met's mailroom, but the draft had caused so many vacancies that Beck was given a more responsible job. He worked at the company headquarters in Manhattan as an audit clerk, figuring out the payroll for commissioned sales agents in Pennsylvania.

After finishing his basic training at Fort Benning, Beck was assigned to the infantry with the Eighty-sixth Division at Camp Livingston, Louisiana. "The outfit was filled with sergeants transferred from other outfits," he says, "so the opportunity for any promotion was tough. I felt that one way to get rid of that problem was to respond to a call for volunteers for the paratroops." He attended jump school and Officer Candidate School, and by the time his training had ended, so had the war.

Nevertheless, he remained in the Army, joining one of the

greatest fighting units in the armed services, the Eighty-second Airborne Division. He describes the Eighty-second—commanded by General James M. Gavin, with Colonel William C. Westmoreland as chief of staff—in almost ecstatic terms. "It was a great outfit with great officers and great training. It was a great thrill hearing the men say that a paratrooper was better than five men in any other outfit. You learned you could do anything if you made your mind up. I saw in the service so many illustrations of things men could do because they believed they could. You never say you've arrived. You say, 'How can I do more, learn more?' This is a mental set that's been present for me all these years— the experience of learning early that if something went wrong, you should examine what *you* have done wrong before looking outside yourself. There's the old Army response: 'No excuse, sir.' The lesson of being compelled to examine my own actions has been of tremendous value to me through the years."

He calls the Eighty-second Airborne "a true follow-me outfit." "A young officer would just have to wave his hands for troops to follow him," he explains. "On a forced march an officer would carry as much gear as enlisted men. The officers wouldn't eat until the enlisted men had eaten. Gavin was a fantastic leader, great in that follow-me approach. Whatever he would have others do *he* would do. That had a very strong influence on me. I have believed in that all my life." At first Beck regretted missing combat. "But later, as I got a little older—and wiser, I hope—I realized how fortunate I was. There were very heavy losses for people in the paratroops."

Beck was appointed the division's insurance officer. It seems that his humble association with Metropolitan Life was mentioned in his Army papers, and his superiors concluded that he was qualified for the job. Under the National Service Life Insurance Program, servicemen were entitled to buy up to $10,000 worth of insurance at a low cost, but few of them had bothered to take advantage of the opportunity. It was Beck's task to persuade them that they were missing a great bargain. He got Westmoreland's permission to organize a series of group meetings so that he could explain the life-insurance program to all 15,000 men in the division. It was an insurance salesman's dream. Westmoreland produced the huge captive audience a battalion at a time. "They were called into a theater," Beck recalls, "with a big presentation with charts, to tell them why it was so good. When they would leave, they'd fill out papers. Those who still didn't take it were asked to stay a little longer so we could explain it further. Any time anybody got the full story, they *had* to buy it. It was only when they misunderstood that they wouldn't. National Service Life Insurance was just like any other. It takes a good demonstration of its value to induce people to buy it." By the time he had finished demonstrating, 99 percent of the outfit had signed up.

His performance as an insurance salesman landed him other assignments requiring the gift of persuasion. He solicited contributions for charities such as the March of Dimes and the Red Cross. "I would collect from Westmoreland and Gavin," Beck recalls. "Westmoreland was a guy who wasn't fast with his checkbook. I would report seven mornings in a row. 'Colonel, Lieutenant Beck reporting for the Colonel's contribution.' " Westmoreland finally suggested, none too graciously, that Beck ought to make the insurance business his career after leaving the service. "You're so damned persistent!" he growled.

"There were tremendous opportunities for learning in the military," Beck observes. "There were numerous opportunities to speak. For a young man or woman getting started in business, the ability to speak is a tremendous advantage. It gives people a chance to see what you can do. Increasingly, people who are the heads of companies like mine are gonna have to be articulate, to stand up and be counted, and make their presence felt."

Before he embarked on any sort of career, Beck wanted to complete his education. He had subscribed to a correspondence course in speed writing while in the Army, and after he got out in June 1948 he studied at Syracuse University on the GI Bill, majoring in business administration with an emphasis on marketing and insurance. He did so well at school that he amazed even himself. "I'd always been pretty good, but never right up at the very top," he says. He believes that his tour of duty with the elite Eighty-second Airborne inspired him to new heights academically. He was invited to join the business honor fraternity, Beta Gamma Sigma, and he realized that he had a good chance to graduate *summa cum laude*. "I really put on the pressure—and made it."

While at college Beck sold insurance for Prudential in his spare time. He had met a Prudential agent in the service who was impressed enough with his salesmanship to refer him to the Pru's director of agencies, Sayre MacLeod, and MacLeod in turn recommended him to the Syracuse office. But after his graduation in 1950, Beck temporarily forsook the insurance business in favor of a job as a financial analyst with Ford. He was hired in a group of sixty bright young men, the company's second generation of Whiz Kids. Beck was one of only two who didn't have a master's degree, but his undergraduate record had been dazzling enough to get him the job. He was delighted to be in such outstanding company, but he eventually decided that the job didn't suit him. He couldn't persuade himself that he was making a significant contribution to the company. "Purely and simply, I was too far from the action." Although his stay at Ford was brief, he managed to profit from the experience. "Bob McNamara, the comptroller, was very strong about what he wanted in staff reports prepared for Henry Ford and Ernest Breech," he remarks. "All these financial reports went through McNamara. If McNamara didn't like the way they were written, he threw them back. Very few people know how to write a good staff report—or to write, period. By the time I came to Prudential, I was able to write. Our schools today do a just terrible job of teaching to write properly."

He returned to Prudential in 1951 as a full-time sales agent operating out of the Syracuse office. He drove from Detroit to Syracuse in a blizzard, accompanied by his wife and the first of their five children. They had $46 to their name plus $500 that they had borrowed. "The only thing I considered was Prudential," Beck says. "There was a quality I respected. It was a known quantity and a leader in its field, respected and liked. Through the years I've been offered all kinds of chances to go with other insurance companies. The feeling I had about the Prudential ruled that out—its accomplishment and size and significance. I was proud of the people here. And the thought of someday getting a shot at being the top officer in a company like this was a pretty nice carrot—the brass ring in an organization as big and powerful as this."

Some people have made much of the fact that Beck is the first sales agent to become chief executive of the Pru since John Fairfield Dryden, who founded the company in 1875. Life-insurance agents traditionally were the butt of rude jokes and were tolerated as necessary evils by their colleagues on the headquarters staff. Beck's rise to the top was hailed as a sign that this sort of prejudice had been squelched and that agents could now raise their heads and stand proudly alongside anyone else in the business. In fact, the selection of Beck wasn't all that startling, since he had been an agent for only fourteen months before being promoted to the first in a succession of managerial positions.

Beck was promoted to assistant manager of the Syracuse office in April 1952. "The people in Newark decided that my background in the service and my academic credentials from Syracuse combined to make me a good candidate for management," he says. "I ate that up. It was a great experience!" The Syracuse office wasn't performing very well, so Beck hired nine new salesmen. All of them turned out to be successful—an astounding stroke of good fortune (or good judgment). Within eighteen months the office was outselling all the others in its region.

His record at Syracuse earned Beck another promotion in November 1953. He was summoned to the Newark headquarters to serve as a training consultant. He taught classes for new agents and assistant managers and also toured the Prudential offices offering tips on how to improve their performance. "I was a good trainer," he remarks. "I'd done a lot of training in the service. Military training experiences are really outstanding." In March 1955 he became the supervisor of training in the South Central Home Office. Based in Jacksonville, the office had jurisdiction over Prudential activities in six states. Later that year Beck was named assistant director of the agencies in the region. The office had been organized by Charles W. Campbell, a man who was to become legendary at Prudential for his skill in developing young managers. Beck turned out to be his most successful protégé, but dozens of others moved along to positions in middle and upper management after learning at Campbell's knee. Campbell's leadership also produced solid financial results. During his regime, South Central quickly moved from last to first in sales among all the regional offices.

Beck's immediate goal was to manage his own agency, and he achieved it in 1956. He was sent to Cincinnati, where a good agency had fallen on hard times. "It needed a building job from the ground up," he says. There were seven agents operating out of the office when Beck arrived, and in little more than a year he beefed the force up to thirty. He took a decidedly paternal approach to his salesmen. Remembering his own days as an agent, when he faced hostility and rejection over and over again in his quest for customers, he vowed that nobody under his supervision would suffer the same fate. "I knew how it ripped people apart," Beck says. Too often, he found, agents were sent into the field without being told how to select the best prospects, or to make the most effective sales pitch once they were selected. "We used to say that a man would be given a rate book and a mirror. The mirror was so he could watch himself starve to death. Very few people are such complete self-starters that they can make it without any help."

He was sent back to Jacksonville in 1957, this time as director of all agencies in the South Central region, and he remained there for six years. The assignment was noteworthy if only because he stayed in one city for so long. "We moved fourteen times in twenty years," Beck recalls. "This was the first time I made a move where my wife and I were able to make as many as fourteen mortgage payments. We had a block party to celebrate. Three of our children were born in Jacksonville." Like any successful marathon man, however, he was a good soldier. "We've enjoyed living in each and every location we've been assigned," he said.

He actually became a bit bored with stability and started working on a book about success and failure. He had outlined twenty chapters and was bracing himself for the onerous task of writing, when he was transferred back to Newark. He never went any further with the book, but he still has it "on the back burner." In his new job he served as chief of staff of the Prudential sales operation, with authority over research, personnel planning and sales promotion. His title was executive general manager, and in 1965, after two years in the position, he became a vice president of the company as well.

Beck was transferred once again in 1966, this time to Chicago, as a senior vice president in charge of the Mid-America Home Office. It already was a healthy operation, and Beck's skills as a troubleshooter rarely came into play. Beck enjoyed living in Chicago, and he was distressed when he was asked, after just a year, to return to Newark as senior vice president in charge of agencies. It was a lateral transfer, not a promotion, and he tried to beg off. His bosses told him he could stay in Chicago if he named someone else who was qualified for the job at headquarters. In the past, Beck had always encountered strong competition as he moved from job to job, but this time things were different. He racked his brain, but he couldn't honestly think of anyone else who was suitable, and so he made the unhappy trek to Newark.

In 1970, Don MacNaughton, who had been serving as president and chief executive, was promoted to chairman. Kenneth Colley Foster replaced MacNaughton as president, while Beck succeeded Foster as executive vice president in charge of marketing. There were two other executive vice presidents—Fredrick E. Rathgeber, who was in charge of administration, and Frank J. Hoenemeyer, whose specialty was investments. Since Foster was older than MacNaughton, it seemed likely that one of the executive vice presidents would eventually become the next chairman of Prudential. Rathgeber himself was slightly older than Mac-Naughton, so the plausible candidates were Beck and Hoenemeyer.

Foster took early retirement in 1974, and MacNaughton tapped Beck as the new president of the company. From then on it was virtually certain that Beck would become chairman and chief executive when MacNaughton stepped down. That appeared to be quite a while off, however, since MacNaughton would not reach the mandatory retirement age until 1982. But MacNaughton abruptly left Prudential in 1978, and Beck, as anticipated, became the boss.

MacNaughton's departure seemed rather mysterious, and some observers wondered whether he was fired. MacNaughton explained that he had always intended to leave Prudential before he reached the age of sixty-five. After eight or ten years at the same job, he said, "the things you do become routine, and frankly, they get boring." He announced that he was looking for another job, and the offers soon began pouring in. He became chairman and chief executive of the Hospital Corporation of America. Based in Nashville, HCA operates more than one hundred hospitals in some two dozen states, and its revenues in 1979 were a respectable $1.04 billion. But the company doesn't carry a fraction of the mighty Prudential's clout.

Beck maintains that MacNaughton's resignation was completely voluntary and that his predecessor did "a fine job" as head of Prudential. The company's financial record certainly seems to bear that out. When MacNaughton became chief executive, Prudential had only the slimmest edge over Metropolitan Life in total assets, the gauge by which life-insurance companies are customarily measured. By the time MacNaughton left, Prudential had become the largest life-insurance company by a comfortable margin, with assets of $50 billion against Metropolitan's $42 billion. Beck says he was perfectly happy working as president under MacNaughton and had no significant disagreements with him. When a reporter asked what he would do differently after he took over, he couldn't think of anything. He had worked so closely with MacNaughton that he would have felt "an absolute hypocrite" to suddenly turn around and make changes. He does intend to depart from MacNaughton's agenda in at least one respect, however. Barring ill health—and the board of directors willing—he will remain chief executive of Prudential until he reaches his sixty-fifth birthday in 1990.

Nowadays it seems anachronistic to put executives through the corporate marathon. The boy wonders proved that advanced age is not a prerequisite for sound leadership, and it also has been repeatedly demonstrated that sound leadership is transferable from one company to another: most tycoons moved about a bit before settling down in the companies they now lead. It obviously isn't necessary to start at the bottom of a company to qualify for the top. In fact, it isn't necessary to start in a *company* at all. Some of today's tycoons spent the greater part of their careers outside the business world. The companies that persist in the marathon method have effectively shut themselves off from great numbers of managers who are extremely gifted, but who refuse to devote half a lifetime or more in pursuit of their goal.

Still, the marathon will undoubtedly survive for quite a while. Men who have run the marathon themselves are very much in charge at certain companies, and they are not inclined to change things. They naturally believe that the marathon is the best of all possible ways to select a chief executive.

Chapter Six

Job Jumpers

THE MOST common method of getting to the top in business is to jump from one employer to another. This represents a significant change from the pre-war period, when the aspiring tycoon would pledge himself irrevocably to a single company, then pray for the best. In those primitive times, it was widely believed that an executive could not successfully transfer his skills from industry to industry, or even from company to company. But a survey of 419 modern-day chief executives, published in *Fortune* in 1976, shows just how far things have evolved since that kind of wisdom prevailed. Of the executives covered by the survey, only about one-third had begun their business careers at the companies they headed.

That figure is slightly misleading, since the survey included individuals who had founded their companies, or had reached the top through inheritance—and could therefore be expected to stay put. If the entrepreneurs and heirs had been excluded from the tabulations, the proportion of tycoons with experience in only one company would have been even lower, something like one in five. By *any* reckoning, the job jumpers now greatly outnumber all the other tycoons put together.

The job jumpers come in two varieties—Also-rans and Opportunists. The Also-rans usually start out running in the corporate marathon, chugging along faithfully in a single company for a couple of decades, until some other executive sprints ahead and wins the race. Most businessmen will accept such a defeat with equanimity and straggle on to retirement in a comfortable, sub-ordinate role. But a few, driven by an ungovernable urge for supremacy, will jump to some other company where they have a chance for the top job. More often than not, it will be a company that is smaller and less prestigious than the one they left behind.

The Opportunists, by contrast, are simply too impatient to even attempt the marathon. When the promotions don't come fast enough to suit them, and when a more exalted (and better-paying) job opens up elsewhere, they will abandon their current employer without much qualm or hesitation. With good judgment and proper timing, the Opportunist can make it to the top a lot faster than any marathon man.

Among the Also-rans the most emphatically successful has been Robert Anderson, today the chairman and chief executive officer of Rockwell International, a diversified industrial company based in Pittsburgh. For twenty-two years Anderson had been a stellar performer with Chrysler, joining the auto company in 1946, after getting out of the Army, and moving through nine different positions. His appointment as head of the Chrysler-Plymouth division in 1965 left him just three rungs from the top of the ladder. He didn't expect to become chairman and chief executive of Chrysler; a claim to that job had already been staked by Lynn Alfred Townsend, who was just about Anderson's own age. But he did think he had a shot at the presidency. "That was kind of the word around the industry, and the word from my supervisors," he recalls. "Nobody else in the company had the kind of experience I did in production, planning, sales, marketing and engineering. I felt why would they put me through all those jobs if they didn't have plans to make me president. I probably should have known better." In 1967, John Joseph Riccardo, four years younger than Anderson and a protégé of Townsend, suddenly became a group vice president and thus Anderson's boss. The next year Anderson left to join Rockwell International. At the time, it was called North American Rockwell, having recently been formed by a merger between North American Aviation, an aerospace and electronics company, and Rockwell-Standard, a producer of auto parts and other industrial products. Anderson became president of the company in two years, and after four more years he was named chief executive as well.

Although barely half the size of Chrysler, Rockwell International is a giant in its own right, with revenues of some $6 billion annually. It has done well under Anderson, with both its revenues and earnings soaring to record heights in recent years. Certainly it has fared better than Chrysler, where first Townsend and later Riccardo were forced to resign prematurely, having failed to staunch the flow of red ink. Anderson can't suppress a malicious grin when he discusses the present plight of Chrysler, which was at its zenith when he left. It is interesting to speculate whether Chrysler's fate might have been different if Anderson had been given a chance to run the company.

Anderson is considered a cautious, conservative manager, but his personal style inclines to the flamboyant. He arrived for a golfing date in Orlando, Florida, a few years ago in a police helicopter, its sirens howling and bells clanging. "Our dealer or manager there was a friend of F. Lee Bailey," he recalls. "He wanted me to have a ride in a new helicopter Bailey had invested in. It was a demonstration copter for the city police." Anderson likes to hobnob with celebrities in and out of the business world. One of his golfing partners that morning in Orlando was Arnold Palmer, a friend from the days when Anderson was at Chrysler and Palmer was endorsing the company's cars. Another friend is John Zachary DeLorean, whose long hair, flashy clothes and dashing lifestyle made him an anomaly during his days as a high-ranking General Motors executive. Both Anderson and DeLorean are known as expert appraisers of female beauty. Anderson, whose second wife is a former actress and model, appreciatively describes the third Mrs. DeLorean, Cristina Ferrare, as "one of the most beautiful models in the world."

Although hardly in Arnold Palmer's class as a golfer, Anderson plays a good game, usually shooting around eighty. A six-footer and built like a grizzly bear, he can drive the ball exceptionally far. He also plays tennis and is an aficionado of bullfighting—as a spectator, not a participant. He has been known to drag friends to the bullring on visits to Mexico or Spain, but he can't get them to share his enthusiasm. "Too many times I'd hear, 'Gee, Bob, it's getting cold. I'm going back to the hotel.' " People close to Anderson say he is driven by an intense desire to win. "You've heard of winning through intimidation?" his wife once remarked. "He wrote the book on it."

Rockwell International has its headquarters in the U.S. Steel Building, which causes the public-relations staff some embarrassment. The executive suite is as sumptuous as anyone could wish, however, and Anderson's office is appropriately huge. The door to his office is fitted with an electronic locking device. Once it is shut, you have to push a button to get it open again. I found Anderson seated at a large, rather messy desk, wearing a gray suit, blue shirt and rep tie, and flashing an ultra-expensive gold wristwatch. He speaks briskly, in a mild accent that belongs vaguely west of the Mississippi.

He comes from a long line of Robert Andersons without middle names, dating back to a great-great-grandfather who was killed in the Civil War. He was born in 1920 in Columbus, Nebraska, a hundred miles west of Omaha, but he lived there only a few years. His father, a sales manager for Swift and Company, the meat-packers, was reassigned to Dallas and then to Los Angeles. The elder Anderson fell in love with California and steadfastly refused to leave, even when Swift offered him a promotion during the depths of the Depression. "He would have had to move to Chicago," his son recalls. "You couldn't have pulled him out of California with wild horses." He finally left Swift to work for the government during World War II, and later he went into business for himself as a food broker.

The family was always financially secure. "We never suffered, never had any hungry kids in the house," says Anderson. But their father insisted that Robert and his two younger brothers take jobs in their spare time. Robert started off delivering the morning newspaper—a boring, time-consuming task that netted him just $3 a month. When he reached his teens he got a job as a clerk in a supermarket. Fascinated with automobiles, he saved up enough to cover the down payment on a Model T Ford priced at $125, paying off the balance at a rate of $8 a month. Later he got a Model A. He would spend the sunny California weekends tinkering and polishing. He still enjoys mechanical work and has been described as "the kind of man who prefers to take the lawn mower apart rather than to cut the lawn."

After graduating from high school, Anderson planned to attend a commercial aeronautics school, and he paid $100 in advance for tuition. Before classes began, however, he was awarded a scholarship to Colorado A & M College—now known as Colorado State University. He had been a good student at high school, finishing in the upper quarter of his class, but he got the scholarship because of his proficiency as a football tackle. He enrolled at Colorado, and to his eternal dismay the aeronautics school never refunded his $100. His father chipped in $5 a week, but Anderson covered most of his college expenses by working for a Chevrolet dealer as a janitor and handyman at $9 a week. While the pay was hardly spectacular, the job did offer one glorious fringe benefit—the occasional use of a car, which helped him maintain an active social life.

In fact, his social life became so active that he got married during his senior year to a secretary, Constance Severy. They went on to have two children and were divorced in 1971. Anderson married his present wife, Diane Clark Lowe, in 1973. The divorce rate is much lower among corporate chief executives than it is among the public at large, but Anderson insists that this doesn't mean divorce hurts a man's chances of getting to the top. In fact, he suggests that divorces often are caused by the executive's dedication to his job—his willingness to move from town to town, his hectic work-load, his frequent business trips. "In the old days you might take your wife with you on a trip, even take a train. The pace was a little slower."

Anderson earned a degree in mechanical engineering in 1943 and went directly into the Army, where he became a captain in the field artillery. With his love for cars, he had taken every college course dealing with internal-combustion engines. He was assigned to teach automotive maintenance to other servicemen at Fort Sill and Fort Knox, and in Japan after the war ended. He didn't see combat.

He had no trouble finding a job after getting out of the service in 1946. With his degree in engineering, and his experience in the Army, he was the sort of fellow who was in great demand during the postwar industrial boom. He got a good offer from Procter and Gamble, but rejected it. "I decided that I liked cars more than soap." He discovered that he could earn $225 a month *and* a master's degree by participating in a two-year work and study program at Chrysler's Institute of Engineering, and this struck him as ideal. He spent two hours a day in classes and worked six hours a day at various Chrysler installations. The institute's program was not an unalloyed blessing, however. He recalls being ordered to move hundreds of cans of antifreeze from one end of a building to the other. "That was fairly humiliating for a former captain," he remarked, "but the next morning when my boss told me to move them all back, the Chrysler Corporation nearly lost an engineer." He finished first in a class of thirty students, and Chrysler eagerly offered him full-time employment in 1948.

He was soon running on the fast track. In 1950, after two years as a member of the Plymouth division's chassis-engineering staff, he was placed in charge of engineering liaison with the Briggs Manufacturing Company, which built auto bodies for Chrysler. In 1951 he was given a supervisory job at a plant in Detroit. In 1952 he was appointed assistant body engineer in the central engineering division. And beginning in 1953 he settled into a four-year stint as chief engineer of the Plymouth division. He moved back to the central engineering division in 1957 as executive engineer for chassis, electrical and truck design, and the next year he became Chrysler's director of product planning and cost estimating.

"I personally tried to do the best job I could in each job I had," he recalls. "As I did, I was promoted. If you grow and mature and do your best, you usually do pretty well. If you do a good job in your current assignment, with demonstrated interest in the assignment and loyalty and a little extra effort, in that way you'll move up. When I visit business schools, one thing the kids ask: 'How do you get to be president?' It's not a good question. The thing is how do you survive in a tough world. You do the best job you can. And if you have a fair amount of mental ability, you succeed. If you're either not bright enough, or don't take your responsibility seriously enough, you're not qualified to go to the top. A lot of people say, 'The hell with it, who wants to be president?' You've got to have an inner need. Maybe a part of it is the fear of failure, but you overshoot the course and wind up president."

While Anderson was running the corporate marathon, a couple of talented outsiders suddenly dropped in and turned the event into a fifty-yard dash. The first to appear was Lynn Townsend, a partner in the accounting firm of Touche, Niven, Bailey and Smart, which audited Chrysler's books. Townsend had a great financial mind and gargantuan ego. He joined Chrysler as comptroller in 1957 and proclaimed: "I'll be president in three years." He was wrong; it took four years. In 1959, John Riccardo, who had worked for Townsend at Touche, joined Chrysler as a financial staff executive for international operations. Townsend described Riccardo as the smartest man in the accounting firm and predicted that he too would become president one day. Although Anderson had set his own sights on the presidency, he wasn't bothered by the remark, since Riccardo was younger. "I thought it would be after *me*," he remarks ruefully.

Anderson got along quite well with Townsend at first and thrived under his leadership. After Townsend became president, Anderson was promoted to vice president, and in 1964 he was appointed a group vice president in charge of corporate automotive manufacturing. The next year he was placed in charge of the entire Chrysler-Plymouth division, which had been formed by a merger of two separate divisions a short time before. He really loved the job, and it brought out the exhibitionist in him. He would personally drive the Plymouth pace car at the Daytona and Indianapolis 500 races, hitting speeds of 130 miles an hour before pulling aside to let the racers go by. He also liked to drive Chrysler's experimental turbine car—a noiseless vehicle that ran on alcohol—while basking in the stares of pedestrians and fellow drivers. On one occasion the turbine car ran out of fuel as Anderson was cruising through midtown Manhattan. He kept his cool amid the blare of horns, jogging over to a drugstore and buying a large bottle of perfume, which he emptied into the tank. He got back in, and the car went purring on its way.

He made a great hit with the Chrysler-Plymouth dealers. "Bob was never an ivory tower executive," one of them recalled. "He spent a lot of time calling on us in our showrooms, listening to our problems and breaking bread with us. At conventions he was always the most popular Chrysler official." One of his most treasured possessions is a plaque presented him by the Dealer Council when he left Chrysler, citing him for his "leadership, insight, and cooperation." "They are probably the roughest, toughest, meanest bunch of guys I have ever dealt with," he remarked, "and winning their respect means an awful lot to me."

The division's sales really took off under his leadership, and Anderson thought he had a reasonable chance to become president as soon as Townsend succeeded the aging George Hutchinson Love as chairman. Riccardo was still below Anderson in the hierarchy—in fact, he was Anderson's assistant—so things seemed to be going according to plan. Anderson just couldn't imagine that Riccardo, still a novice in matters other than finance, could be considered better qualified. He wasn't overly fond of Riccardo either. He concedes that Riccardo was "a very hard worker, a very bright guy, doing his best to learn the business," but he also contends that Riccardo was "quite emotional, occasionally very rough on people." Anderson says he sometimes had to step in and smooth things over when Riccardo "got the guys too stirred up."

Riccardo was placed outside Anderson's jurisdiction in 1966, when he was appointed the company's vice president for marketing. Even then, Anderson didn't realize that it was Riccardo who was Chrysler's man of destiny. Naively debating the promotion with Townsend, he protested on the ground that Riccardo's talents were in finance, not marketing. In 1967, however, Riccardo's prospects became clear to even the most obtuse observer. Townsend succeeded Love as chairman, and he in turn was succeeded as president by Virgil E. Boyd. Riccardo got Boyd's old job as group vice president in charge of the domestic automotive business, making him Anderson's immediate superior. Anderson was appalled. "I just hate like hell to get shafted," he said, in recounting the episode. Two years later, after Anderson had already left the company, Boyd was kicked upstairs as vice chairman, and Riccardo succeeded him as president. When Townsend resigned under pressure in 1975, Riccardo became chairman and chief executive. He too resigned under pressure four years later, to be succeeded by Lido Anthony Iacocca, the erstwhile president of Ford.

In August 1967, after Riccardo had passed him, Anderson began receiving friendly overtures from Willard Frederick Rockwell, Jr., chief executive of the Rockwell-Standard Corporation. "Al" Rockwell, as he is called, was about to merge his company, based in Pittsburgh, with North American Aviation, which was based in El Segundo, California. He would become chairman of the merged company, and he needed someone to replace him as head of the Rockwell-Standard side of the business. Anderson had been recommended by a Detroit securities analyst who knew them both and was aware of Anderson's discontent at Chrysler.

Anderson didn't accept immediately. After twenty-two years he was reluctant to leave the auto industry. "I've personally enjoyed everything I've done," he explains. "Chrysler was pretty tough to leave. But it opened a whole new world. One thing about the auto industry, when you're in it you're convinced it's the only industry in the world. When you get out you find that automotive, while an important business, is not the whole world." The months slipped by, the merger between Rockwell and North American took effect, and still Anderson held back. Al Rockwell, convinced that Anderson was the best man for the job, didn't seriously consider anyone else. He would meet with Anderson almost weekly, cajoling him to make the jump. Anderson wanted assurances that he eventually would become president. It wouldn't make sense to change companies if his ambitions were going to be thwarted again—particularly since leaving Chrysler would cost him about a quarter-million dollars in pension benefits and deferred compensation. Rockwell couldn't guarantee the presidency, but Anderson would be starting out just one notch below and would have an excellent shot at the job. What's more, the presidency would open up reasonably soon. The incumbent, John Leland Atwood, who had previously headed North American Aviation, was in his early sixties.

By Christmas of 1967, Anderson was finding life at Chrysler unbearable. Townsend had just appointed him vice president for product planning and development, a classic job for bypassed executives. To his credit, Townsend offered the job in a considerate, and even flattering, manner. They were hunting quail in Georgia when Townsend told Anderson: "I want you to take over all product planning, because we'll get killed if you don't." Anderson had accepted the position on those terms, but he was still working under Riccardo, and frequently squabbling with him to boot. "I was having trouble with that guy, getting the proper budget for these products. He was a financial man—he didn't understand. I felt that whatever good I could do, I wouldn't be allowed to do it under the environment I was working in. They were issuing budget figures from on high." Anderson believes that a lopsided dependence on financial controls actually led Chrysler into its financial crisis during the seventies. "They had such strong financial controls," he says, "that the gut feel of the automobile business was left totally out of the equation. Historically, at General Motors, the chairman has a strong financial background, while the president is from production and marketing. They try to keep a balance in running the company. We didn't have that. We had a preponderance of weight on the financial end."

Anderson finally went over to Rockwell in January 1968. One of the first things he did after joining the company was to take flying lessons—at the ripe old age of forty-seven. Corporate jets and other aircraft were among North American Rockwell's products, and he wanted to know all about them. Flying soon became one of his great hobbies, and he got a plane of his own. He also took to wearing aviator-style eyeglasses, even when earthbound.

The old Rockwell-Standard Corporation had become the commercial products group of North American Rockwell, and Anderson was given the title of group president. His counterpart out in California, the head of the aerospace and systems group, was John Robert Moore, who had been a longtime employee of North American Aviation and a protégé of Lee Atwood. There was supposed to be a contest between Anderson and Moore to determine who would succeed Atwood as president of the company, but in fact it turned out to be no contest at all. Anderson, using the cost-cutting procedures he had learned so well in the auto business, continually improved the profit performance of the commercial products group. Moore's organization was caught in a profit squeeze, brought on in part by a slump in the entire aerospace industry, and he seemed unable to come up with the necessary solutions. "I think Moore was perceived as not a strong executive," Anderson recalls. "From the practical standpoint, I do not believe he had the confidence of Lee Atwood, who almost raised him and had put him in there. Lee remained to a large extent in charge of North American, his baby. Although Moore was in there nominally to head it, Lee was there at every meeting, answering questions. He was in on every major meeting, reviewing the data and deciding technically what should be done."

By the middle of 1969 there was no doubt that Anderson would move up to president. Lee Atwood took him to dinner at the Duquesne Club, the citadel of Pittsburgh's business elite, and offered a promotion to the newly created position of executive vice president. Anderson would be based in California and would be assigned to straighten out the mess in the company's aerospace business. It was a sad scene for Atwood, having to seek salvation from someone who had no experience in aerospace, and he undoubtedly did it at the urging of Al Rockwell. Anderson said he would be delighted to take the job, but he didn't want Atwood interfering in every detail of the operation. "If I go out there, I'm running it," he said, "but I'll appreciate your advice, and I'm sure I'll need it, since I know nothing about aerospace." Atwood accepted the ground rules, and as Anderson recalls, "I never had one problem with Lee from the time I got there." Atwood did occasionally slip him inspirational messages, in particular a quotation from Alfred Pritchard Sloan, Jr., the former General Motors chairman and management philosopher, stressing the importance of technical knowledge to the business executive.

Anderson had to convince North American's technical people that it was important not only to make good hardware, but to turn a decent profit as well. Like most aerospace companies of the time, this one was run without much regard to costs. "I just couldn't live in this environment, where nobody knew how much we were making and didn't seem to care about it," Anderson remarks. "People at meetings—scientists and engineers—would spend all afternoon arguing about how to solve some technical problem. It seemed crass to raise the question of what it would cost." But Anderson raised the question anyway, sometimes with angry emphasis, as when he broke a pencil by heaving it against a blackboard. "I recall some pretty violent meetings," he said. He subjected the aerospace operation to the kind of cost controls common in other businesses, and as the industry slump deepened, he cut back heavily on personnel as well. From a high of 35,000 employees, the aerospace force melted away to just

6,000 in a few years. "It was a ruthless thing to do," Anderson later recalled, "but it had to be done." And it had the desired result, keeping the operation afloat through troubled times. In 1971 the Air Force gave the company a $2.5 million incentive award for coming in $10.5 million under the estimate in building the guidance electronics system for the Minuteman III intercontinental ballistic missile. It was a pleasant—not to say profitable—contrast with the old days.

Atwood retired in February 1970, and Anderson became president and chief operating officer. The company's earnings started to soar, and his managerial talents caught the attention of the Nixon Administration. During 1972 he was asked to succeed David Packard as undersecretary of defense. "They felt," Anderson recalls, "that they would like to have someone with a strong background in business and manufacturing who understood the importance of controlling costs and getting the job done right, and also had a history of dealing with the government on contracts, with some experience in aerospace. I was also a Republican, though not a very prominent one." Anderson talked things over with Packard and Melvin R. Laird, the secretary of defense, and was told that he might eventually succeed Laird himself. "That's a lot of power," Anderson muses, "one of the most powerful jobs there is." But he decided not to join the government. His company had recently been selected as the prime contractor on two huge government projects, the space shuttle and the B-1 bomber, and he had promised the authorities that he would give the projects his closest personal attention. He also would have lost a lot of money by taking the job. "It paid only $40,000 a year. I'd just gone through a divorce. I had no retirement benefits." He says he is glad that Nixon didn't offer the job in person, because he would have found it "almost impossible" to turn the President down. "Fortunately, they never put me on that spot."

He has spent quite a bit of time in Washington as it is, because of his company's heavy involvement with government projects. "I was never much interested in politics," he once remarked, "until I learned that you had to know a lot of politicians who have some control over government contracts." During 1972 he met with Senator George S. McGovern, shortly before the South Dakota Democrat received his party's presidential nomination. Mc-

Govern, who was opposed to both the space shuttle and the B-1 bomber, suggested in effect that Rockwell International beat its swords into plowshares. He ran through a list of consumer products that Rockwell might make, using the expertise it had gained in aerospace and electronics. The list included automobiles, refrigerators, washing machines, radios and television sets. Anderson explained that Rockwell couldn't start manufacturing these products from scratch and expect to compete effectively with established manufacturers. Rockwell did get into the production both of television sets and of household appliances in 1974, when it acquired the Admiral Corporation. Admiral turned out to be a chronic money-loser, however, and Rockwell got rid of it. The only consumer products the company now makes are power tools, which were part of the old Rockwell-Standard line.

In February 1976, Anderson was called on the carpet by Senator William Proxmire, vice chairman of the Joint Congressional Committee on Defense Production. The committee was investigating reports that Rockwell International and other companies had entertained government officials at company-owned resorts. Proxmire contended that the entertainment was designed to improperly influence the officials and that it seemed "far beyond what is allowed by government policy and regulations." It was mentioned at the time that Robert E. Hampton, the chairman of the Civil Service Commission, had been a guest at Rockwell's hunting lodge on Wye Island, Maryland. Some weeks later it was also disclosed that J. William Middendorf II, secretary of the Navy, had visited the lodge, and that Dr. Malcolm R. Currie, director of research and engineering in the Department of Defense, had spent a couple of days at Rockwell's fishing lodge on Bimini Island in the Bahamas. In his testimony before the congressional committee, Anderson explained that the company simply wanted "an opportunity to know better the people who share mutual problems," but he added that Rockwell would no longer entertain government officials. Anderson says the company has since sold its resorts on Wye Island and Bimini, but still has one on Cat Cay, another island in the Bahamas. "We're goddamned careful about who we entertain *anywhere,*" he says. "If he's in the government, we don't. The rules have gone overboard. You can't have a drink with someone in the armed services and then pick up the check. I have a son in the Air Force. I almost wasn't sure I could have him home for Christmas dinner. He was concerned about it too and felt he had to get clearance from his commanding officer." Anderson says his company had entertained people from all branches of government in the years before Proxmire's hearing. "He didn't want any information about those members of the Senate and the House who had been entertained. He sure as hell wanted to know about Defense, the Executive and the armed services. I asked him about the congressmen, and he said, 'We don't need that.' You have to protect the fraternity, I guess. He's a little unfair. He can say anything—it's privileged—while witnesses are torn between perjury and contempt of Congress. And if you don't know the answer, you look a little dumb, and he gets a headline. And if you say the wrong thing, you get into a helluva lot of trouble."

Anderson was appointed chief executive of Rockwell International in 1974, while Al Rockwell remained as chairman of the board. Rockwell announced that he would retire in April 1979, after reaching his sixty-fifth birthday, and that Anderson would succeed him as chairman at that time. As the date of his retirement approached, however, Rockwell found it difficult to let go. During the summer of 1978, according to a report in *Business Week*, Rockwell tried to persuade the board of directors to keep him on as chairman, while Anderson would be named to the new position of vice chairman, without clear authority. As one director put it, Rockwell "was having some difficulty facing up to the fact that the calendar moves." But the problem might have been more complicated than that. The company had always been headed by a Rockwell—first by Willard F. Rockwell, Sr., who founded Rockwell-Standard after World War I, and then by Al. Al Rockwell had two sons of his own in the management, the older in his mid-thirties, and he might have hoped to keep the leadership of the company in the family rather than passing it along to an outsider. Whatever his motives, they are likely to remain mysterious, since Rockwell not only won't explain them, but even denies proposing the plan to make Anderson vice chairman.

The board did agree that Rockwell could stay on as chairman until February 1980, but it refused to downgrade Anderson and chose instead to strengthen his position. It retained him as president and chief executive and revised the bylaws to give him full responsibility for management. He was instructed to report directly to the board rather than to Chairman Rockwell. Rockwell took the hint and stepped down as chairman in February 1979, a year earlier than the board had suggested, and still short of his sixty-fifth birthday. "I don't want to ruin morale," he explained enigmatically.

For Anderson the dispute with Rockwell must have brought back memories of those traumatic days at Chrysler when the presidency was snatched from his grasp. Having triumphed this time, he is anxious to let bygones be bygones. "Al and I have a fine relationship," he remarks. "Things got blown way out of proportion. We've said about all we'd like to say on the matter." Like Rockwell, he denied that there had been any dispute at all, though he looked extremely uncomfortable in doing so. He squirmed in his chair, then picked up a document from his desk and began scanning it. It was a highly unusual gesture for someone in the midst of an interview, particularly since he had obviously asked his secretary to hold all calls and messages until the interview was finished.

Of the job jumpers who can be classed as Opportunists, few have been more shrewdly opportunistic—or have done more jumping—than David Mahoney of Norton Simon, Inc., the consumer-goods company. Between 1946, when he got out of the Army, and 1969, when he became chief executive of Norton Simon, he worked for six different companies. He started off with a New York advertising agency, then ran his own agency, then went to the Good Humor Corporation, then to Colgate-Palmolive, then to Canada Dry, which in turn became part of Norton Simon. Sometimes he jumped for more money, sometimes for more power, but always he made progress. His career qualifies as a masterpiece of planning. Jumping from job to job entails considerable risk and uncertainty, of course, but that never bothered Mahoney. As he once put it: "The difference between playing to win and playing not to lose is the difference between the successful executive and the security-hunting, mediocre man."

My interview with Mahoney was conducted in a large sitting

room adjoining his office at the Norton Simon headquarters on
Park Avenue. The sound of Muzak wafted up in the background.
Mahoney, six feet one and a bit hefty at more than 190 pounds,
wore a gray suit, a blue shirt and a plain blue tie. His hair, once
brown, is mostly gray now and considerably longer than it was in
the days before the Beatles became popular. He smokes a lot—
both cigarettes and a particularly pungent pipe. We were joined
not only by the obligatory public-relations aide, but also by one of
the company's senior vice presidents, Orhan I. Sadik-Khan.
Sadik-Khan had a lamentable tendency to interrupt every so
often to remind Mahoney how great he is. Sample: "You know,
you would make a fantastic chess player, because you do really
reassess the options every minute." The interruptions didn't seem
to bother Mahoney.

Mahoney has a flair for publicity that makes him highly unusual
among the chief executives of major companies. As one writer
put it: "In a time when most corporate chiefs are about as visible
as ozone and as distinguishable as Big Macs . . . Mahoney, and his
neck, stick out . . . like the World Trade Center." He is always
ready to speak out loudly and unabashedly on any topic: poverty,
government bureaucrats, the volunteer Army—you name it.

He is an irrepressible gadabout, who takes many a lunch and
dinner at the most fashionable bistros in Manhattan. He also
throws party after party at his eighteen-room duplex apartment
on Park Avenue at Seventy-second Street. He makes a particular
effort to cultivate what gossip columnists call the "beautiful people"—writers, artists, sportsmen, show-biz personalities, politicians and the rich and famous generally, including even the
gossip columnists themselves. On one noteworthy occasion he
gave a sitdown dinner for sixty people, among them the publisher
of *Forbes,* the publisher of *New York,* the commissioner of football,
the head of the Urban League, two ex-mayors of New York City,
a famous actor and two well-known investment bankers. Mahoney
suggests, however, that the term "beautiful people" is inappro-
priate for such a gathering. He stresses that the people he hangs
out with are "hard workers and achievers," not "cafe society."
"Walter Cronkite—is he a beautiful person?" Mahoney asks. "I
would say so, but would someone else?"

I asked him what it was that made him so successful. How did he happen to be commanding the fortunes of 37,000 employees as well as thousands of shareholders? Why was it Dave Mahoney, and not someone else, sitting there telling the story of his life? "I don't know how much of it is genes," he said. "I don't know how much is drive. I don't know how much was timing. I don't know how much of it is luck—and that certainly is an element in it. I often think if somewhere along the line I fell and separated a shoulder and couldn't go to school on that athletic scholarship, would that have made a material difference? It's not only the things I did, it's a lot of the things that didn't happen to me the other way." Later on he seemed to clear up the uncertainty to his satisfaction. "Instinct," he declared. "It's got me where I am. The whole creative process is *instinct*."

Evidently it also helps to be a bit of an SOB. Mahoney is affable enough toward outsiders, but by most accounts he is a holy terror in dealing with his subordinates. *Fortune* recently included him on a list of the "ten toughest bosses" in American business, noting that he is "more explosive than he seems" and that he has "made Norton Simon known for executive turnover." One of the company's many ex-employees has declared: "Dave operates by fear. He likes to put two or three people in conflict and let them fight it out."

There is a well-worn anecdote about Mahoney's operating style that bears repeating. It seems that Richard C. Beeson, head of the company's Canada Dry unit, approached Mahoney early one fiscal year and told him that Canada Dry was apt to fall short of its profit goal. But Mahoney insisted that he meet the goal. "What if I can't, Dave?" Beeson asked. "Then clean out your desk and go home," Mahoney replied. Beeson met the goal that time. But when Canada Dry's share of the soft-drink market began to slip in 1979, Beeson departed (presumably with the contents of his desk). "I don't think Dave's ever been unfair," Beeson has said, "but he's an absolutely crazy man if someone screws up." Yet there is an obvious method in this seeming madness. Mahoney's subordinates, afraid for their jobs, are driven to produce the kind of financial results that enable Mahoney to keep *his* job.

Mahoney had begun studying at the Wharton School of Finance before the U.S. entered the war, and he planned to go back after getting out of the Army. He had a few months to kill before the 1946-47 school year started, and he went looking for a temporary job. At first he couldn't find one, and he lived on the $20 a week allotted by the federal government to unemployed veterans. He hung out with other veterans at a bar on Third Avenue in Manhattan, which like many bars of that era was equipped with miniature shuffleboard courts. Mahoney organized a shuffleboard tournament at the bar, then tried to find a beer company to sponsor citywide tournaments. He approached Ruppert—"the big beer in New York," as he puts it—and the company suggested that he take the proposal to its advertising agency, Ruthrauff and Ryan. "There was a wonderful man there who thought it was a great idea," Mahoney says, "but he told me it was totally illegal, that you weren't allowed to encourage sporting events in bars." Instead, the agency offered Mahoney a job as a clerk in the mailroom at $25 a week—$5 more than his unemployment allowance. He grabbed it.

He stayed in the mailroom only briefly. He was promoted rapidly, moving first to the research department, then to an account group. By the time the school year opened he was making $50 a week as an assistant on the Lifebuoy, Rinso and Spry accounts. Mahoney wanted to continue his advertising career, but he also felt that he should complete his education. "I had to get that degree," he once remarked. "I was the first one in my family to go to college." He enrolled in Wharton's night school, and would hop a train down to Philadelphia after work, returning to New York after classes. He did practically all of his studying on trains and finally earned his degree in 1949. Mahoney became a full-fledged account executive, handling Virginia Dare Wine and Motorola, and in April 1949, a month before his twenty-sixth birthday, he was promoted to vice president, making him one of the youngest people of that rank in the advertising business. His salary soared to $25,000 a year, nearly twenty times what he had been getting as a mail clerk just three years earlier.

It was around this time that he became friendly with Robert C. Ruark, a syndicated columnist for the Scripps-Howard newspaper chain. They were both attending the opening ceremonies at the Shamrock Hotel in Houston, and they met in the bar. Ruark later recalled his first impression of Mahoney: "Already you could see the quality shine on him, over the aroma of bourbon." Ruark, the elder by seven years, took a big brother's interest in Mahoney and did all he could to nurture his career. Over the years he wrote four columns about Mahoney, depicting him as a living triumph of the free-enterprise system. He introduced Mahoney to people who could help him in business, and he was one of three men who endorsed a $10,000 bank loan when Mahoney started his own advertising agency in 1951. The two friends lived together for a while in a three-room suite at the Elysée Hotel in Manhattan after Ruark separated from his wife.

Mahoney called his new agency David J. Mahoney, Inc. It was housed in a tiny office in the Chanin Building, a skyscraper on Forty-second Street. Ruark recalled the agency's founding in one of his columns—and in his distinctive style: "He borrowed what he could and he sold his new car and he put his wife back to work, although she was but a bride and still feeling fluffy aprony. He worked all day and all night and aggravated his ulcer." In fact, the agency did pretty well from the start, thanks to the fact that Mahoney walked off with the Virginia Dare account—$850,000 in annual billings—when he left Ruthrauff and Ryan.

He did encounter some problems when he tried to get his agency accepted into a powerful trade association. If an agency didn't belong to the association, it was assumed to be a poor credit risk, and most publications and radio stations wouldn't accept its advertising. An agency could belong to the association only if it held cash equal to 25 percent of its monthly billings—a requirement that Mahoney considered both unfair and difficult to meet. The association was ostensibly trying to assure that its members would all be stable and viable, but Mahoney feels that the rule was designed to suppress competition. "It was a wonderful little setup," he snarls.

A gallant champion named Howard Black came to Mahoney's rescue. Black was the executive vice president of Time Inc., and they had met through Ruark. Black had even joined Ruark in endorsing the bank loan used to start Mahoney's agency (the other signer was William Gargan, the actor, also a friend of Ruark's). Black wrote a letter to the trade group declaring that Time Inc.'s publications would gladly accept advertising from Mahoney or anyone else who paid cash on delivery. "He didn't understand why anybody wouldn't," Mahoney recalls. "I was willing to pay cash, you know, because what the hell, I'd just bill my client." Time Inc.'s competitors, unwilling to be outflanked, declared that they too would accept C.O.D. advertising.

As a kid, Mahoney used to hang around Toots Shor's restaurant, ogling the sports heroes of the day and trying to meet them. As a young adult, running an advertising agency, he would spend many evenings hanging around the bar of the 21 Club, trying to meet people who could lead him to new accounts. "Wherever he moved, Mahoney had the knack of attracting people who could help him," *Fortune* observed. "He was bright, personable, clearly a comer; the term 'dynamic' is retrospectively always applied to him. His operating principle, as he frequently said at the time, was to get on well with everybody. It is still hard to find an enemy of David Mahoney." He remains a regular patron of the 21 Club, even though it is no longer essential to his career. "It's the place where I got started," he says. "They know me. It's something I've grown up with over the years. I'm not that much of a connoisseur of food."

In the days when there was still a Stork Club, Mahoney could often be found there as well. He would show up for dinner almost nightly with his first wife, a lovely Powers model named Barbara Ann Moore. (They eventually were divorced, and he is currently married to Hildegard Merrill, Miss Rheingold of 1956.) With another young couple, Mr. and Mrs. Roger Van Schoyck, they appeared in the background of a television interview show originating from the Stork, and occasionally they would be asked to substitute when a guest failed to show up. It amounted to a free ad for Mahoney's ad agency. By the end of its first year the agency had added six small accounts—among them Roger Van Schoyck's leather-goods business—and raised its billings to $1.2 million. In later years Mahoney got some sizable accounts as well, including White Rock, Noxema Chemical and the Good Humor Corporation. Total billings reached a peak of $5 million, his staff expanded to more than thirty, and he moved the agency to larger quarters on Madison Avenue.

On one occasion Mahoney became a vice president and significant shareholder in a client company. He was approached early in 1953 by Roger Brown, a friend and public-relations man, who had organized a company called Micro-Moisture Controls with

Alexander L. Guterma. The company would produce a device that raised the top of a convertible automatically when it rained. Mahoney received stock for the services of his agency, and in April 1953 the company went public. Several months later both Brown and Mahoney withdrew from the company, and Mahoney received about $12,000 when he returned his stock to Guterma. Mahoney later explained that he was unhappy with the financial arrangement and would have preferred fees instead. He also said he had been concerned about the tactics used by Guterma's brokerage house in promoting the stock. Guterma went to jail some years later on charges of stock manipulation and fraud. As Mahoney told *Fortune:* "I wish I had never met the ———. The whole thing was a lousy deal."

He sold his agency in 1956 for $650,000, and went to work for one of his clients. Joseph Ansbro Meehan, whose family owned the controlling interest in Good Humor Corporation, persuaded Mahoney to replace him as president and chief executive officer. Meehan explained that he wanted to devote more time to a brokerage firm also owned by his family. He offered Mahoney a salary of $75,000, a bonus deal, and options on 50,000 shares of stock. It was a great opportunity, and Mahoney accepted the offer readily enough. But he found it painful to withdraw from the business he had built. "The day I made the deal, I walked out of there and never went back into it, even though I still owned it for two more months," he remarks. "I just emotionally didn't want to do it. I didn't even clean my desk out. It was a part of my life that was gone. I didn't want to face that scene. Why didn't I physically want to go in there? Because it was, to a degree, giving up my independence."

Good Humor, based in Brooklyn, manufactured coated ice-cream bars at four plants and sold them primarily through street vendors. Mahoney introduced several new bars with fancy names like Baked Alaska and Texas Pecan Crunch. He doubled the advertising budget to $300,000 a year—something he would gladly have done when Good Humor was his client—and placed heavy emphasis on radio jingles, which he considered more effective than television spot ads. Mahoney personally promoted the company's products as well. He kept dozens of Good Humor bars in the freezers at his homes in Greenwich, Connecticut, and

Bridgehampton, Long Island, and distributed them to children. He also had a home on Sutton Place in Manhattan, but he made no special effort to hand out ice-cream bars in that deluxe neighborhood. In his first four years with the company its revenues rose smartly—from $11.5 million to $15.6 million. Mahoney today makes light of his accomplishments at Good Humor. "I was always a genius on a ninety-nine-degree day."

He took a leave of absence from Good Humor in 1960 to work for Richard M. Nixon in the Presidential campaign against John F. Kennedy. In his youth he had been an admirer of Roosevelt, but after becoming a businessman he discovered that the Republicans were "more sympathetic" with his goals. "I knew a lot of people that knew Nixon," he recalls, "including Chuck Percy and so forth, and talked to them about it, and went to work for them." He was based in Chicago and was assigned to coordinate activities among Nixon's staff, the Republican National Committee, and an organization called National Volunteers for Nixon-Lodge. Mahoney had dated JFK's sister Patricia when they were both at college, but he was strongly anti-Kennedy. "I was wrong on Kennedy," he now concedes. "I thought he was too demagogic. I thought he was too much of a playboy. I didn't like his attendance record in the Senate. He didn't have any of the Protestant virtues that I had been brought up on, even though I was a Catholic. What I didn't realize at the time was the fact that he could coalesce and bring people together, and that he had big ideas. He had a sense of relating to people."

After Nixon's defeat, Mahoney remained active in Republican politics. He served in 1962 as co-chairman of a committee to reelect Governor Nelson A. Rockefeller and U.S. Senator Jacob K. Javits of New York. Like Donald Kendall, he kept close ties with Nixon even after Nixon was supposed to be washed up, and they became quite friendly, attending football games together and visiting Goldie's bar in Manhattan to listen to the piano music. Mahoney also served as a conciliator between the hostile Nixon and Rockefeller factions of the party. When Nixon was elected President in 1968, he offered Mahoney a chance to become secretary of commerce. But at that point Mahoney had just become president of Norton Simon, Inc., and felt that he couldn't break away. By 1972, Mahoney was publicly declaring that he wanted to be secretary of state or secretary of defense, but evidently that didn't fit in with Nixon's plans. Nixon did appoint Mahoney in 1970 to a part-time position as chairman of the American Revolution Bicentennial Commission. Created by Congress, the commission was supposed to supervise and coordinate the multifarious plans for celebrating the nation's two hundredth birthday. But Congress eliminated it in 1973, charging that it was ineptly managed—Mahoney himself wasn't too pleased with his staff—and that it was being used as a political instrument by the Nixon Administration. It was replaced by a new body with a slightly different name—the American Revolution Bicentennial Administration—and a full-time administrator was hired.

Mahoney is clearly disenchanted with Nixon in the wake of Watergate. "I knew enough about Nixon to know that he was strong-willed and everything," he remarks. "But I couldn't conceive that anybody would be either that immoral or that stupid—and I don't know which order you want to put it. Plain nuts! The people didn't trust Nixon and he didn't trust the people. It really started, I think, when the Democrats made those big election inroads. If you remember, the polls showed Muskie running ahead of him. The fears that were in Nixon—he suffered like all of us from insecurities, but he suffered more from them than most. He had a great fear he was going to be a one-term President. Here he had been the first Republican President since Hoover—Eisenhower could have been a Democrat—and you know what they did to you in sixty; he felt he was screwed out of the sixty election. I could see how he got where he did. I don't justify it. People say, 'Why the hell did he have to do that against McGovern? McGovern was a sure knockout.' But he didn't have McGovern two years before that, so the Watergate really started, for me, in seventy." Mahoney says Norton Simon, Inc., like many other large companies, was urged to make illegal contributions to the Nixon reelection campaign, but that he refused to play along. "It's difficult to say no, particularly when you're in a regulated business," he remarks. "I sure as hell wasn't going to get into any kind of deal once somebody started talking 'launder' to me. I mean, that scared the living . . . It was too contrived, just too contrived. We haven't tried to break laws, haven't looked for edges. We've always made full disclosure. I'd rather take it head-on. I wouldn't take the risk. I don't have to and the company doesn't have to. This is my canvas—I'm proud of it. This is what I did. I see it as a creative process. It has become my identity as well as my family."

He is less of a Republican these days, having supported New York's Democratic governor, Hugh L. Carey, in 1978. In fact, Mahoney contributed $25,000 to Carey's reelection campaign, which certainly expiated his sin in voting against Carey the first time, in 1974. Mahoney and Carey have become good friends, and the Governor made a surprise appearance onstage at Norton Simon's 1978 annual meeting, which took place a couple of days after the election.

Mahoney's career with Good Humor had ended in 1961 when the Meehan family sold the company. The principal stockholder, Mrs. William Meehan, mother of Joe, was in her late sixties, and the family felt that it would be best to sell before she died. If they waited until after her death they might be forced to accept a lower price in satisfying the estate taxes. The buyer was Thomas J. Lipton, Inc., an American arm of the giant Unilever holding company, based in the Netherlands. Lipton paid $8.2 million in cash for all the stock, and Mahoney made a $700,000 profit on his own holdings. The people at Lipton planned to keep Good Humor separate and intact, and they wanted Mahoney to continue running the business, but he found the prospect discouraging. "I was going to be running a subsidiary, which was not in my better interests," he says. "It was just going to be a subsidiary of Lipton, which was a subsidiary of Lever Brothers, which was a subsidiary of Unilever. Also, they had no stock options. They had nothing else either." He decided to take six to eight months off and spend part of his growing fortune on a trip around the world.

It never happened. Along came George Henry Lesch, the president and chief executive of Colgate-Palmolive, and hired Mahoney as his second in command. Lesch had become the head of Colgate the year before, after spending sixteen years in the company's Mexican subsidiary. He was looking for someone with strong experience in domestic marketing and had read a highly favorable article about Mahoney in *Time* when Good Humor was sold. He made Mahoney the executive vice president, with authority over three divisions—household products, toilet articles and associated products. Lesch was in his early fifties, while Mahoney was still in his late thirties, and it was practically certain that Mahoney would be the next chief executive if he did a good job. Lesch and Mahoney reorganized Colgate, delegating more authority to middle-management people, especially the sales managers. Until then, authority had been heavily concentrated in the headquarters staff, and sales managers were simply taking orders about how to advertise and promote their products. Colgate's goal was—and still is—to catch up with the mighty Procter and Gamble Company, and under Lesch and Mahoney it at least stayed in the race. From 1961 to 1966, Colgate's revenues increased by 54 percent, to $931.6 million, while Procter and Gamble's went up 45 percent, to $2.2 billion.

By 1966, Mahoney was getting restless. Lesch seemed unlikely to relinquish the top job any time soon, and Mahoney wanted to run something on his own. Through a mutual friend, Gustave Lehmann Levy, one of the leading figures on Wall Street, he got together with Norton Winfred Simon, the multimillionaire West Coast industrialist. Simon was the founder of Hunt Foods and Industries; and through it he controlled three other companies —Canada Dry, McCall and Wheeling Steel. He wanted a new chief executive at Canada Dry and offered Mahoney the job. With revenues of $171 million, the company was less than one-fifth the size of Colgate, but Simon assured him he would have sole and total authority—and that proved irresistible. Mahoney broke the news to George Lesch, and Lesch implored him to think things over for a few months. Mahoney said he would give Lesch time to reorganize Colgate's management, but insisted that he wasn't going to change his mind. He took over at Canada Dry on December 1 and sent Norton Simon a telegram: "Just jumped in the water and it's going to be quite a swim."

Before Mahoney stepped in, Canada Dry was being operated by a father-and-son team. Roy Worsham Moore, Jr., in his late forties, had been president and chief executive officer for seven years, while Roy, Sr., in his mid-seventies, was chairman of the board of directors and had previously served for more than two decades as chief executive. The Moores had angered Simon by resisting when he sought a seat on Canada Dry's board, but Simon controlled 32 percent of the stock, and the resistance proved futile. Simon wanted to displace the Moores for business reasons as well, feeling that Canada Dry was not properly exploiting its opportunities. The company was performing sluggishly even though it was involved in two fast-growing industries—soft drinks and alcoholic beverages. Roy, Jr., was kicked upstairs to the chairmanship, while Roy, Sr., was given the preposterous title of "honorary chairman." They both resigned within a few months. Canada Dry's earnings plunged during the fiscal year ending March 31, 1967, the Moores' last in management, and in the annual report Mahoney offered a devastating assessment of the company they had left behind: "[Its] cost of manufacturing has increased at a more rapid rate than that of its competition; its marketing and distribution policies have not kept pace with the times; its share of the domestic soft-drink market has declined; its overseas opportunities have not been fully exploited; its administrative expense has become excessive."

Mahoney turned the company around in a matter of months. He got rid of the more antiquated bottling plants and equipment, cut $1 million from operating costs, replaced many of the upper and middle managers, and hired two new advertising agencies to promote the soft-drink line, which was much weaker than the alcoholic-beverage side of the business. During fiscal 1968 the company's revenues reached record heights, its profits rebounded, and its stock price soared. Norton Simon was delighted with the performance. "Dave has done sensationally considering the time he's been aboard," he remarked. "Canada Dry is a substantially rejuvenated company."

In July 1968, Norton Simon organized the company that now bears his name, merging Canada Dry and McCall into Hunt Foods and Industries. William Edward McKenna, who had been chairman of Hunt, was named chairman and chief executive of Norton Simon, Inc. Mahoney was appointed president and chief operating officer, while Harold Marvin Williams, the president of Hunt, became chairman of the new company's Finance Committee. Simon himself remained as a director and a member of the Finance Committee, but at the age of sixty-one he preferred not to take part in the day-to-day management.

Mahoney hated the arrangement. After being the top man at Canada Dry for a scant nineteen months, he was suddenly a subordinate again. "I likened it to three men on a horse," he says, "and Norton owned the horse. I couldn't live with the system. I either wanted to run it, or I wanted to go elsewhere, and I made that very definite. It was a mistake the way Norton set it up to begin with, from my point of view. But from his point of view it was good. It gave him all the options. But I wasn't going to stay around in another big bureaucracy where I wasn't running it. I didn't like the idea of a bureaucracy to begin with, but I certainly wasn't going to be working down the line."

He got into bitter disputes with McKenna, a financial man by training whose personality and approach to business were radically different from his own. "Bill and I had various differences on how the company should go," Mahoney recalls. "His skills and mine were strictly in conflict. With Harold it was less so. But I figured I was the best line operator, and that's what it was all about. I was involved in running those companies, the rest of them were all strategizing, which I always get a little bit worried about, because—like I can't get my hands around it, it's like mercury."

He challenged Simon to choose between him and McKenna. Simon responded by having the board of directors form a committee of five members—not including himself—to determine who should be the head of Norton Simon, Inc. The committee interviewed a number of Norton Simon executives and reported back to the full board. In August 1969 the board fired McKenna and appointed Mahoney chief executive. "He was the natural top man," Simon later recalled. Harold Williams stayed on, replacing McKenna as chairman. McKenna came away with an unusually generous financial settlement: He was to be paid $13,167 a month through February, 1970, then $8,333 a month until August 1984, then $2,083 a month for the rest of his life. After leaving Norton Simon, he became chairman of Technicolor, Inc., and in 1979 he was named chairman of Sambo's, the restaurant chain.

Within a year after McKenna was deposed, both Simon and Williams resigned, leaving the field to Mahoney. Simon departed in December 1969 and wholeheartedly endorsed Mahoney's leadership in his farewell remarks: "I trust him with more than my money. I trust him with my being." It was high praise indeed, if somewhat mitigated by the fact that Simon soon sold off the bulk of his holdings in Norton Simon, Inc. In 1970 he made an unsuccessful run for the U.S. Senate from California, and today he devotes himself to his magnificent art collection. Williams left the company in July 1970 to become the dean of the Graduate School of Business Administration at UCLA, and in 1977 he was appointed chairman of the Securities and Exchange Commission, making him the chief regulator of Norton Simon, Inc., and all other publicly held companies. Mahoney speaks very respectfully of Williams: "a damned good attorney, a fine individual, one of the most sensitive people I know, and bright." For seven years after Williams left, Mahoney kept the presidency as well as the chairmanship to himself. Joseph Gamache, an executive vice president and faithful retainer, provoked a quarrel with Mahoney when he asked to be appointed president. He wound up resigning instead. Finally, in 1977, Mahoney felt secure enough to award the presidency to someone else. It went to an outsider, Timm Crull, who had been senior vice president of the Carnation Company. But Crull departed two years later.

Although it is still known as Norton Simon, Inc., the company today might appropriately be called David Mahoney, Inc. Mahoney moved the headquarters from Fullerton, California, to his native New York, and in little more than a decade he has presided over some three dozen divestitures and acquisitions that have transformed the business. According to the company literature, he has stressed corporate growth by "enhancing existing leadership brands, new product development, moving out of capital-intensive businesses and acquiring consumer-oriented companies, and building a strong financial structure." Mahoney himself put it more directly and succinctly in an interview some years ago: "Building a company is a very satisfying way of expressing your ego." He got rid of all the shares in Wheeling Steel, as well as some canneries and a match company that had been part of the Hunt Foods holdings. And he scattered the McCall empire to the winds, selling off *McCall's Magazine, Saturday Review, Redbook,* a magazine-subscription agency, a trade-book publisher and several printing companies. All that remains is the McCall Pattern Company, which is patronized by home dressmakers. Meanwhile, Mahoney has added Max Factor, Orlane and Halston in cosmetics and fashion, and Reddi-Wip, Old Fitzgerald and Tanqueray—

among others—in foods and beverages. His largest acquisition was Avis, Inc., the vehicle-rental firm, which became part of Norton Simon, Inc., in 1977, and now accounts for about a fourth of the company's more than $2.5 billion in revenues.

Mahoney considers it a personal affront when people use products that compete with Norton Simon's. He has been known to send a caseful of Hunt's tomato ketchup to acquaintances who dared show a preference for Heinz. When people from his company attend a banquet, the only scotch allowed on the table is Johnnie Walker, another Norton Simon product. (Alas, Mahoney himself can't touch the stuff, because of his ulcer.) William Flanagan, writing in *New York*, recounted a visit Mahoney made to Manhattan's swank Four Seasons restaurant. After trying in vain to get a bottle of Canada Dry club soda—the waiter kept bringing White Rock—he had a bitter confrontation with one of the owners, who explained that they didn't carry Canada Dry. "One of us is making a serious mistake," Mahoney growled. The Four Seasons added Canada Dry to its bill of fare.

Eventually Mahoney hopes to build a consumer business that will be on a scale with Colgate, his old employer, and even Procter and Gamble, his old rival. But Colgate, with more than $4 billion in revenues, is still well ahead of Norton Simon, Inc., while Procter and Gamble, with revenues exceeding $9 billion, is beyond reach for the foreseeable future.

The founder of Norton Simon, Inc., has never complained to Mahoney about the overhaul of the company. "Once he got out, he really got out," Mahoney remarks. "It had to disturb him in some cases. But I think one of the reasons that Norton never took it personally—and this I shared with him—he upgraded his whole art collection by selling off and buying. And Norton's an existentialist. Norton's reaching out all of the time. Norton also knows that things are never the way they appear, and never the way they're said to be."

The popularity of job jumping has proved a tremendous boon for executive-recruiting firms. The recruiters—or "pirates" as they are known to those who suffer their depredations—have flourished in the postwar period by luring restless executives from one company to another in return for a finder's fee. In some cases the executives don't even realize that they are restless until the recruiter starts touting the salary, benefits and opportunities available elsewhere. The recruiters look for executives who are highly competent and well regarded, but who have no immediate prospects for advancement. They may be tipped off by the executives themselves, or by third parties, or simply by studying the business press to see who is being promoted and who isn't.

In fulfilling their mercenary function, the recruiters have served as go-betweens for some truly momentous job transfers. For example, it was a recruiting firm, Ward Howell Associates, that brought Charles Peter McColough to the Xerox Corporation, which he now serves as chairman and chief executive. McColough likes to talk about how carefully he planned his career, but in fact he nearly rejected the opportunity to join Xerox when it was offered to him in 1954.

At the time Xerox was still an obscure company called Haloid, and it hadn't yet perfected the process that was to transform it into the world's largest manufacturer of copiers and duplicators, with current revenues exceeding $7 billion. McColough put off visiting the company for months, mainly because he didn't like the idea of living in Rochester, New York, where the headquarters were located. He finally made the visit to appease the recruiter and gradually found himself dazzled by what Haloid's managers told him about xerography, a revolutionary process that used ordinary paper and produced dry copies. The visit made him so eager to join the company that he accepted a huge pay cut. Fourteen years later he became the chief executive, and one of his earliest acts was to move the headquarters to Stamford, Connecticut.

A sturdy, balding man of medium height, with a deep, crisp voice, McColough is pleasant and extremely accommodating with visitors, but he can sometimes be stern and even ruthless with subordinates. He went to the Harvard Graduate School of Business Administration, where they teach future tycoons everything but compassion, and he simply will not tolerate managers whose competence falls short of his standards. Once, after successfully wooing a high-ranking executive away from Ford Motor, he startled the man with this savage, if slightly muddled, greeting: "It's your head on the block, not mine. If I don't get the results I

expect, your head is in the noose, and I will be the hangman."
McColough says he has very strong feelings for Xerox and considers himself a proprietor, even though he joined the company
forty-eight years after it was founded. "The business is very personal to me," he remarks. "Every building—I had something to
do with it."

An incorrigible chain-smoker and insatiable coffee drinker,
McColough evidently has great difficulty relaxing. He makes a
concerted effort, however, taking five or six weeks of vacation a
year. He loves sailing, and his seven-bedroom house overlooks
Greenwich Harbor, a short drive from the office. He also sails in
Palm Beach, where he has a vacation home, and he has another
vacation home in the Catskill Mountains, where he skis. He can
indulge himself without straining his budget, for he has grown
rich over the years from his Xerox stock options. "Money is not
too important," he told me. "It's scorekeeping. You can't have a
successful business career and not make money. On the other
hand, I'm having a half-million-dollar sailboat, fifty-seven feet
long, built for me in Finland. I like not having to worry about the
price. The one I have now is fifty feet."

To the casual observer, McColough seems too tightly wound to
have a sense of humor; yet he is said to be quite a practical joker.
Some years ago he played a gag on a colleague and friend who
was running a Xerox seminar in Los Angeles for "a hundred very
important customers" from the federal government. McColough
was asked to videotape a message, since he couldn't attend in
person. He made a serious tape, but he also taped another message, in which he insulted the guests: "You guys waste so damned
much money. And you don't know how to develop your products
in the military." He arranged to have the bogus version screened
first for the man who was running the meeting and recalls that
"he nearly had a heart attack before they set him straight."

McColough was born in Halifax, Nova Scotia, in 1922, the first
of four children. His father, Reginald, was an engineer who became deputy prime minister of public works in the provincial
government and served during World War II as director of construction for the national government. As a civil servant, the elder
McColough remained employed through both Liberal and Conservative administrations, though he overtly favored the Liberal

party. Peter worked for the party as a youth and served as a precinct supervisor during one election. "The opposition voted three dead men on me," he recalls, "and I got hell for it."

Years later, as a U.S. citizen, he became active in the Democratic party and even served as treasurer of the National Committee in 1972 and 1973. He says people often ask him how the head of a large company can support the Democrats. It is partly his heritage as a Liberal, he says, but he also has a fondness for the Democrats dating back to the early days of World War II, when the Roosevelt Administration openly sympathized with the British. "In social programs I'm quite liberal," he remarks, "but as a businessman I'm for free enterprise. I don't put a label on myself. I would not want to be classified with the New York City liberal Democrat. They seem quite impractical—the so-called Limousine Liberals." He says he was "very active" in the Humphrey Presidential campaign of 1968 and feels he would have had a "reasonable opportunity" to serve in the cabinet if Humphrey had defeated Nixon. During 1972, however, he voted for Nixon over McGovern, though he worked hard in behalf of the Democratic congressional candidates. "I voted for what I thought was a competent semi-crook, rather than an idiot. It's the first time I ever voted for a Republican in my life. I thought McGovern was an idiot as a Presidential candidate, though he's a nice man in other ways. He would have been a different kind of disaster for the country." McColough voted for Jimmy Carter in 1976, though he would have preferred Senator Henry M. Jackson as the Democratic nominee.

McColough's family was "quite well off" during the Depression, since his father remained steadily employed and adequately paid. "Enormous numbers of people came to our door for food—people we didn't know," he recalls. "My mother kept chits for the YMCA, worth fifteen or twenty cents for a meal. Sometimes she would feed somebody, but usually she would say, 'Take this chit and go to the YMCA for a meal.'" Requests for straight cash were rejected, however, since "she couldn't know who wanted the money just for liquor."

After McColough graduated from high school in 1939, his father told him he would have to finance any further education himself. "I could pay your tuition," Reginald McColough said, "but I really feel it's important that you get used to being on your own." They agreed that Peter would borrow against his father's signature from the Royal Bank of Canada and would pay off the debt as soon as he could. As it happened, Peter had a large appetite for education. He got his bachelor's degree from Dalhousie University in 1943, and after serving briefly in the Navy, he earned his law degree from Dalhousie in 1947 and his MBA from Harvard in 1949. He covered part of his expenses by working during the summers on construction jobs, but by the time he left Harvard he owed the bank $7,500, and it took him more than five years to pay it all back. "I've always appreciated that lesson from my father," he says. He hasn't tried a similar procedure with his own children, however. "I think it's more difficult to finance your tuition now."

McColough was, by his own admission, "a very uneven student." Although he had been at the top of his class in high school, his performance at college was "terrible—almost at the bottom or failing." He spent a lot of time playing sports, especially hockey and rugby, and going to parties—"lots of parties." It wasn't too hard to get into law school in those days, and once he did, McColough became more serious about his studies. His record as a law student, he says, was "generally very good."

His class at the Harvard Business School was exceptionally talented and competitive, and McColough achieved only a mediocre record, finishing "somewhere in the middle third." The Forty-niners, as they like to call themselves, have since gone on to glories unmatched by any other business-school class. About a fifth of the 621 class members became top executives of major companies. McColough is considered the greatest success of them all, since Xerox is the largest company headed by any member of his class. "The record of accomplishment corresponds negatively with the standing of the class," McColough says, demonstrating that the statistical courses were not wasted on him. "The top people did not do that well. The middle third did. The guys who got the highest marks tended to be in the middle in accomplishment." McColough's roommate at Harvard, James Edward Burke, also a middling student, is considered the next most eminent graduate of the Class of '49. He is the head of Johnson and Johnson, which has revenues of more than $4 billion. McColough and Burke remain good friends to this day. Legend has it that Burke once poured a bottle of green ink over McColough's head as a joke, while McColough was showering in the dormitory. It wouldn't have been so funny if he had used *red* ink.

After graduating from Harvard, McColough abandoned any thought of a career in law. Though he had taken the trouble to go to law school, he never really thought that he would practice. "I kept the option open," he explains. He had clerked for a large law firm in Toronto, and in fact it was the head of the firm, a man named Henry Borden, who prompted him to go to business school. Borden pointed out that the firm's legal work usually required a knowledge of accounting and finance. Having gained that knowledge, McColough chose to devote himself to business.

He took a job as a salesman with Standard Chemical, Ltd., a small company based in Toronto, with revenues of around $15 million. "I really took it as a starting job," McColough says. "I really didn't plan to stay in the firm. I really wasn't very impressed with the firm, though it has subsequently done very well. I didn't think it had good training programs." McColough's father was upset with him for becoming a salesman. "He was chagrined, and perhaps embarrassed," McColough recalls. "He was typically Eastern Canadian, conservative in his ways. To be a salesman—it had no prestige. He called me a 'traveler.' His image of a salesman was the guy at a table next to him in a restaurant, trying to make a date with the waitress after the meal." McColough wanted a career in marketing and felt that it was important to get some firsthand selling experience. "It's very difficult to get a supervisory job over salesmen and have their respect if you weren't a salesman yourself," he observes.

During 1951, McColough paid a weekend visit to a Harvard classmate, Winslow Martin, who lived in Philadelphia. Martin was looking for a job, and he asked McColough for a copy of his résumé, to study the format. The next week Martin visited an executive recruiter, and as they were going over his résumé he pulled out McColough's for comparison. The recruiter, Bill Megary, scanned McColough's credentials, and suddenly a light went on. One of Megary's clients, Glenn Kidd, a vice president of the Lehigh Navigation Coal Sales Company, was interested in hiring someone with a background in sales and law. Megary got Mc-

Colough to return to Philadelphia for an interview at Lehigh, and McColough was hired as assistant to the sales manager at a salary of $6,000—$1,800 more than he had been getting at Standard Chemical. Megary never did find a job for Winslow Martin, but Martin made out all right anyhow, becoming a senior consultant with the Arthur D. Little Company.

Long before he took the job at Lehigh, McColough had concluded that he ought to leave Canada and pursue a career in the United States. Canadian industry simply didn't offer the opportunities available below the border. "I've always been driven by ambition to play a role," McColough says. "I've never liked to be on the sidelines. Unless you *play* in the major leagues, you can't be a *star* in the major leagues. I've had confidence in my own decisions and abilities, and I've never had any doubts about it. I felt I could run as well as someone else. I have something to contribute. I want to be at the center; I want my ideas to be adopted because they're better, or good. I want to be in the *thick* of it."

On making the move, he promptly filed for U.S. citizenship, and it was granted after the customary five-year waiting period. "I felt very strongly that since I came to the U.S. voluntarily and was taking my living here, I should be an American." He says that Americans who settled in Canada were resented because they "didn't feel it was good enough to take out Canadian citizenship." But he adds that he might have drawn the line himself "if I went to Chile." McColough also was anxious to get involved in U.S. politics, something he couldn't do as an alien.

Lehigh Navigation Coal Sales had been founded in 1792, making it one of the very oldest companies in the nation. By 1951 it was a subsidiary of the Lehigh Coal and Navigation Company, which also owned two railroads—the Lehigh and Susquehanna and the Lehigh and New England. Railroading and coal were not exactly glamour industries, even in the early fifties, but Glenn Kidd promised McColough that the company would expand and diversify. McColough rose rapidly, winding up as vice president in charge of sales. "It was a good job," he says. "I learned a lot. I was given the chance to try all sorts of new things in merchandising and marketing. I had lots of freedom. Those were fun years. We tried different financing plans for coal. We would try to sell in the summer at lower prices, take notes in payment, and discount the notes at the banks so we could keep the coal operation going. We offered trips to Bermuda if someone bought enough coal." The promised diversification never came about. In 1954, control of the parent company shifted to some European financiers who wanted to maintain and emphasize the coal business. McColough, along with several other managers, decided to look around for another job.

He put his résumé on file with Ward Howell Associates, and within a week one of the recruiters got in touch with him and reported that the Haloid Company was looking for someone who could train to succeed the vice president for sales. The man who held that position, Jack Hartnett, was still in his fifties, but intended to retire in a few years because of health problems. McColough didn't know the company, and he had come to dislike Rochester in his business trips to that area. He promised Ward Howell that he would visit Haloid, but he put it off for months, hoping that the recruiting firm would find something more attractive in the meantime. Finally he had to go to Rochester on business again, so he made an appointment at Haloid.

The company had been founded in 1906 by a dozen entrepreneurs who sought to capitalize on the boom in amateur photography stimulated by another Rochester company, Eastman Kodak. It produced photographic paper and chemicals at first and later expanded into copying equipment and supplies. In 1942 Joseph R. Wilson, a son of one of the founders, wrested control of the company from the chairman, Gilbert Mosher, and four years later he appointed his son, Joseph Chamberlain Wilson, as president and chief executive. Young Joe Wilson began casting about for some way to galvanize the company, whose revenues were a piddling $6.8 million in 1946. Haloid bought the rights to the xerographic photocopying process from the inventor, Chester F. Carlson, and the Battelle Memorial Institute, which had financed Carlson. Xerography was far from commercially practical, and in the next decade and one-half Haloid was to spend more than $90 million to develop a machine that would make xerographic copies dependably and efficiently at a reasonable price.

To McColough, blissfully unaware of the great hopes for xerography, the first sight of Haloid seemed dismal indeed. The company's head office appeared to be a sorry afterthought, attached to the front of an old plant in a rundown section of town. McColough entered the office of Jack Hartnett, the sales boss, and caught sight of an orange crate used as a bookcase. On Hartnett's desk was a black metal lunch pail. "I thought, 'My God, if this is the way officers have to live in this company, it's not for me,' " he recalls. Hartnett invited him to lunch, and to McColough's relief they went to a restaurant—Howard Johnson's. McColough found that he liked Hartnett, "a delightful man."

Hartnett suggested that they drive over and see Joe Wilson, who was home with a cold. "I still had very little or no interest," McColough recalls, but he went along anyway. He spent the afternoon with Wilson, who told him all about xerography and, despite his cold, waxed eloquent about the revolutionary change it would make in communications. McColough began to sense that the company had "a great future" if it could make an efficient copying machine. "I must confess that by the end of the afternoon it was clear to me that it would be a great opportunity. I had completely switched. I decided if they would make me an offer, I would take it." The offer came, and he was hired at $15,000 a year—$10,000 less than he was making as the head of sales at Lehigh. McColough swallowed the pay cut with good grace, recognizing that Haloid's budget was stretched to the limit by research expenses.

McColough soon discovered that he was not the only candidate for Hartnett's job. Two other young Harvard Business School graduates were hired around the same time. One of them, John W. Rutledge, had been a colleague of McColough's at Lehigh, serving as assistant comptroller and industrial sales manager. The other, Donald L. Clark, was manager of market research for radio and television products at General Electric. The three contestants started out in widely dispersed marketing assignments—McColough in Chicago, where he ran the company's first copying center, Rutledge in Los Angeles, as head of sales on the West Coast, and Clark in New York, as head of East Coast sales. It was tacitly understood that they were vying to succeed not only Hartnett, but also, ultimately, Joe Wilson himself. Each of them was in his early thirties, Wilson was in his mid-forties, and no one between had a reasonable chance of becoming chief executive.

And so McColough became the heir apparent in 1960, when Joe Wilson tapped him as vice president for sales. Wilson never explained how he arrived at his choice, and McColough can't honestly say that his financial record was any better than Rutledge's or Clark's. Evidently the decision boiled down to a question of personalities. "I was probably somewhat outwardly quieter," McColough observes. "They were more the typical sales and marketing types. I think Mr. Wilson thought my overall judgment was probably better. I was not emotional, not so excitable through thick and thin. I'm sure on an I.Q. basis I was not nearly as high as Rutledge—he's got to be 160 or 170—but he was somewhat emotional, somewhat inclined to fold under pressure. I think probably one of the edges I had—Mr. Wilson was very much involved and interested in not just being a businessman, but a great social conscience. I suspect I was more like that. I was working in chambers of commerce and the United Way, while the others were not so interested." McColough continues to immerse himself in countless social-welfare projects, and he encourages his employees to do the same, even granting some of them fully paid leaves of absence. Shareholders sometimes protest the company's heavy involvement in extracurricular affairs, but McColough won't relent. "We try to justify it on the logic of why it is good for the company," he says. "We feel that if society goes to hell, we're not going to do very well. We've got a stake in society. I tell shareholders, 'Either sell your shares or try to throw us out—we ain't gonna change.' "

For all his similarities to Wilson, McColough was hardly a carbon copy—or even a Xerox copy—of the boss. Wilson was a shy man, while McColough, to all appearances, is not. Some of the older women in the company recalled that Wilson used to blush and fidget when they greeted him in the halls. In later years he emerged from his shell somewhat and would make an effort to be friendly and open. But he was still uncomfortable dealing with his subordinates face-to-face and preferred to bombard them with memorandums. "It wasn't uncommon for him to dictate fifty memos from his bed each morning over the telephone," Mc-

Colough recalls. "He wanted me to respond in writing to his memos, but I wouldn't. I would take them into his office, where he could see me while I argued a point." Wilson was a scholarly man, who liked to quote Browning and Keats and eventually served as chairman of the board of trustees at the University of Rochester. "He was a very unusual businessman," McColough remarks. "If you went with Wilson on a visit to the English Department, you'd think he was the professor to hear the conversation. I'm a great reader too, but I like histories, biographies, very little fiction, and have practically no interest in poetry. I don't like Shakespeare at all."

Both Jack Rutledge and Don Clark stayed with Xerox long enough to see it prosper and to become prosperous themselves through stock options. Clark wound up as vice president in charge of sales and advertising and left in 1966 to go into business on his own. He invested heavily in Bernz-O-Matic, a manufacturer of propane-gas torches, and became the chairman. Rutledge rose even higher at Xerox, becoming executive vice president before leaving in 1971. He served as a senior vice president of Magnavox, then as president of Bulova, and finally settled down to managing his investments, which he has reportedly done quite well.

Although the company marketed some xerographic products during the fifties, not until 1960 did it introduce its first real moneymaker, the Model 914 copier. The 914 not only made dry copies on ordinary paper, but also worked faster than any other copier—at a rate of 400 copies an hour. Almost overnight it rendered the rest of the industry obsolete, and it became one of the most sensationally successful products in the history of American business. Despite its technical virtues, however, the 914 might not have succeeded so dramatically without McColough's marketing acumen. Most copying machines in those days sold for around $500 at retail, while the 914 cost over $2,000 just to build. It would have been extremely difficult to sell the 914 in any quantity, and if the company charged a substantial leasing fee it would have frightened off prospective customers who wanted to make relatively few copies. At McColough's urging, Joe Wilson decided to rent the machines at an easily affordable rate, while charging extra for each copy the customer made. It turned out to be just the right strategy, and the company's revenues surged—from $37.1 million in 1960, to $59.5 million in 1961, to $104.5 million in 1962, and on upward.

It was McColough's job to build a sales organization that could take full advantage of the phenomenal demand for the company's products. He just about doubled the size of the sales staff each year for several years and managed to do it without any noticeable deterioration in quality. He also had the delicate task of weeding out veteran supervisors who had functioned well enough during the sleepy Haloid era, but weren't competent to hold their positions in the booming company called Xerox. "I had to change every branch manager in a couple of years and convince them they were no longer capable of handling the job and should go back to being salesmen. I didn't do it casually. We would bring a guy to Rochester for a full day, starting the night before. We talked about the change in the business; we'd have him see Mr. Wilson and even Mr. Wilson's father, who was a very old man. Half agreed with us, half disagreed, but the half that didn't later came back and said, 'You did the right thing.' The people we were replacing had hired other people who were loyal to them. If they felt we were doing this in a cavalier way, they would have spread dissent throughout the organization."

Ironically, some of the senior officers began suggesting that McColough himself should be displaced because of the company's explosive growth. They told Joe Wilson that he ought to look *outside* Xerox for an heir, someone who was older, more experienced and better known than McColough. "There was some mention of this even in front of me," he recalls. "I was very loose about it. I made it clear I wanted to be head of the company. They knew that I would leave otherwise. It was not a situation where I was threatening them, but it was clear that I wanted to go to the top of something."

Wilson seriously pondered the advice about bringing in an outsider, but finally decided against it. McColough had displayed outstanding judgment and ability in a hundred different ways, and Wilson considered him much too valuable to lose. He appointed McColough executive vice president for operations in 1963 and gradually began turning over more and more authority to his chosen successor. Wilson had been serving as president and chief executive, while the chairmanship had been occupied by a succession of old-time employees. In 1966, Sol Myron Linowitz, then the chairman, was appointed by President Johnson as ambassador to the Organization of American States. Wilson succeeded Linowitz as chairman while remaining chief executive, and McColough moved up to president.

Once the prize was won, McColough wasn't sure he really wanted it. The finality of it bothered him. Having reached the presidency, he felt duty-bound to stay with the company for the remainder of his career—and at the age of forty-three that seemed a long time. "Up until 1966 I wasn't absolutely sure whether I wanted a business life all my life," he recalls. "I was interested in politics, and I was already quite wealthy. When I became president, with everybody congratulating me, I went into a funk. I found it very uncomfortable. I was morally committed to this company. Up till then I at least had options, but now I felt locked in for the first time in my life. But after thinking about it I said to myself, 'I'm doing what I really want to do. I'll be losing options, but they're options I really wouldn't have exercised anyway.'"

At the annual meeting in May 1968, Joe Wilson announced that he was stepping aside as chief executive officer. It came as a surprise to most people since Wilson was still only fifty-eight years old. But those who knew him well realized that he was in frail health, suffering from heart trouble. He had reached the point where he could comfortably spend only six hours a day at the office. McColough became the chief executive, but Wilson retained the title of chairman until his death in 1971.

Other companies eventually developed plain-paper copiers of their own, and McColough made some ambitious attempts to diversify Xerox so that it wouldn't be overly dependent on an increasingly competitive line of business. The attempts have met with indifferent success, and the most ambitious of all turned out to be the greatest failure. In 1969 Xerox traded more than $900 million worth of its common stock for Scientific Data Systems, a manufacturer of computer hardware based in California. The new subsidiary, renamed Xerox Data Systems, just couldn't compete in the computer-mainframe market, and in 1975 Xerox was forced to take an $83 million write-off on its investment. That write-off, along with such external problems as inflation and recession, caused Xerox to register the first decline in its annual earnings since the spectacular debut of the Model 914 fifteen years earlier. The company has since rebounded nicely, reaching new highs in sales and earnings in each of the succeeding years. Today, as in the early sixties, Xerox dominates the copier business—and vice versa.

There are still some people who would debate the proposition that managerial talents can be transferred from company to company, or from industry to industry. But so many job jumpers have now reached the top—and have done so well in the top jobs— that for practical purposes the debate has been settled. To be sure, only a special kind of man can succeed in so perilous a venture as job jumping. He must have, first of all, extraordinary confidence and daring. It takes guts to leave the comfort of a good job and familiar surroundings for the uncertainty of a new job and a new company. And it takes an exceptional amount of versatility, dedication and ability not only to adjust successfully to the new environment, but to reach the top, and to stay on top as well. Nevertheless, there seems to be no shortage of men who have done just that.

A few decades ago, when job jumping was relatively rare, executives would go through life identifying themselves with particular industries. There were automen and steelmen and oilmen and foodmen and insurance men and bankers, and so on along the line. But today, with executives passing freely across industry borders, the labels don't seem to stick. Today's automan may become tomorrow's aerospaceman, as in the case of Robert Anderson. Or a coal salesman may wind up peddling photocopiers, as in the case of Peter McColough. The situation has been confused still further by the tendency of companies to diversify well beyond their traditional lines of business, usually through acquisitions. The great majority of tycoons can no longer be conveniently pigeonholed. The postwar business world has given rise to a vast new breed, which can be described only by one all-embracing term: the professional manager.

Chapter Seven

Outsiders

FOR NEARLY two decades Donald H. Rumsfeld was a dedicated, ambitious and highly successful politician. After serving as staff assistant to a couple of Republican congressmen, he decided to run for the House himself, and he made it on his first try, winning in a safely Republican district of Illinois in 1962. Having served three terms, he was chosen by President Nixon to head the federal Office of Economic Opportunity—the antipoverty agency. When Nixon imposed wage and price controls in 1971 he appointed Rumsfeld director of the newly established Cost of Living Council, and two years later Rumsfeld was named ambassador to the North Atlantic Treaty Organization. He stayed around during the Administration of Gerald Ford, his friend and close ally from their days together in Congress. Under Ford he rose to new heights of power and prestige, first as the White House chief of staff, later as the secretary of defense.

With Ford's election defeat in 1976, Rumsfeld found his career temporarily stalled. He dabbled in the academic world for a while, delivering lectures at the Woodrow Wilson School of Public and International Affairs, and at the Northwestern University Graduate School of Management. But what he really wanted was to go into business, feeling that it was time to make some money. "Living on a government salary was a strain," as he explained to *Fortune*. It wasn't long before he received some interesting and lucrative offers. The one he considered most appealing was to serve as president and chief executive officer of G. D. Searle and

Company, a major manufacturer of pharmaceuticals and other health-care products based in Skokie, Illinois. He took over at Searle in June 1977, at a salary of $250,000 a year. Under a special provision in his contract, he was permitted to buy 70,000 shares of Searle stock for a total of $23,333—at a time when the market value of those shares was greater than $750,000.

Becoming chief executive of Searle was quite a coup for Rumsfeld—and not only in financial terms. He had never been a corporate executive before, and, in fact, his sole business experience had been a year or two spent as a customer's man with a brokerage house in Chicago, just before he ran for Congress. It is highly unusual for a major company to give its top job to someone who hasn't proven himself in business. Indeed, it is the rare company that will appoint *any* man as chief executive without first testing him, if only briefly, in a subordinate role. Taking an outsider at face value, no matter how attractive that face might be, is generally considered too risky. It is the sort of thing that a company in desperate trouble might be forced to do.

Searle, as it happens, was in desperate trouble, and it couldn't find a proper savior either within its own ranks or elsewhere in the business world. The company, which now has revenues of some $900 million, had been declining rapidly for two years before Rumsfeld arrived. From an $80 million profit in 1975 it slumped to a $28 million loss for all of 1977. Its problems were manifold. It hadn't been developing enough new products, it was plagued by some dubious acquisitions, and it was engaged with the Food and Drug Administration in some bitter disputes that hurt its reputation and cut into its sales. The FDA had accused the company of "sloppy" procedures in testing certain drugs, and of falsifying some test data. The Justice Department had been asked to investigate Searle, and a grand jury had been convened. Under the circumstances Rumsfeld, with his savvy in dealing with government agencies and his reputation as a troubleshooter, seemed a logical choice to save the company, and he certainly wasn't hurt by the fact that Searle's chairman, Daniel Crow Searle, was an old friend and political backer.

Rumsfeld has turned out to be everything that Daniel Searle and the board of directors could have wished. Under his leadership the company rebounded in 1978 to show a $72 million profit, and the profit shot up again in 1979, to $88 million. Rumsfeld got rid of some twenty businesses that he considered "marginal," while expanding Searle's participation in promising fields, such as optical goods. He shook up the company's management, replacing many high-level executives with his own candidates. He brought in a new man to head the all-important research department and sharply increased the research budget. He cut millions of dollars off the company's expenses with firings and layoffs; the headquarters staff, for example, was reduced from 850 to 350. Rumsfeld also managed to establish a partial truce with the federal authorities. He persuaded the FDA to end a ban it had placed on a drug called Norpace, which is used to regulate heartbeats, and the Justice Department concluded its investigation of Searle without pressing criminal charges. All in all, Rumsfeld's performance at Searle just might give politicians a good name in the business world—something they haven't always enjoyed.

More to the point, Rumsfeld's record calls into question certain traditional methods of grooming and selecting chief executives. If someone like Rumsfeld, only forty-four when he took the job, can step out of an alien environment into a large business and perform exceedingly well, then where is the logic in compelling people to spend the better part of their lives struggling up the corporate ladder, rewarding them only after they have gone completely gray? It may be too much to hope, but the example of Rumsfeld conceivably could convince some other companies to accelerate the opportunities for their younger managers and to give talented outsiders a chance as well.

Before Rumsfeld began working his magic at Searle, there was no good reason to suppose that politicians would fare particularly well as tycoons. Few had ever been given the opportunity, and fewer still had succeeded in any dramatic way. One of the most prominent examples of a politician in tycoon's clothing was Charles Luce of Consolidated Edison, the utility which supplies electricity, gas and steam to New York City and Westchester County. Luce had spent a total of ten years in the federal government, and he was serving as undersecretary of the interior when he was asked to take charge of Con Edison in 1967. It was another case of a troubled company appealing to an outsider to nurse it to health. But despite Luce's earnest efforts, Con Ed's record has remained spotty. In 1974, for example, the company got into a severe profit squeeze and was forced to suspend its dividend—an action tantamount to sacrilege in the financial community. Utility stocks usually are bought primarily for their dividends, and the mere failure to *raise* the dividend each year is enough to cause angry mutterings on Wall Street. Impeachment was in the air in 1974, and some stockholders were inspired to carry "Impeach Luce" posters into that year's annual meeting. The dividend was eventually restored, but Con Ed's financial record continued to be something less than vibrant.

One of the events that led to the overthrow of Luce's predecessor was the Great Blackout of November 9, 1965, which left New Yorkers without electricity for twelve hours and more. On the eve of Bastille Day 1977, not long after Luce had confidently declared that New York was practically immune to another such calamity, the lights went out again, this time for twice as long. The second Great Blackout prompted looting and rioting in some parts of the city, and it had a ruinous effect on Con Ed's public relations, which Luce had labored for so long to improve. At first the company described the blackout as "an act of God," attributing it to lightning storms that knocked out vital links in the power grid. But it was later learned that operating errors by Con Ed plant supervisors had contributed to the problem, and might have made the difference.

Luce maintains a listed telephone at his home in suburban Bronxville, and he gets the inevitable angry calls. On good nights the callers will simply want to argue about their bills or complain about localized blackouts. But he also is occasionally bothered by the kind of people who ring at two in the morning and then hang up. When the cranks become too persistent, he leaves the phone off the hook. He can still receive emergency calls from Con Edison on a separate, unlisted line.

Although he seems to have inherited an impossible situation, Luce is taking it reasonably well. "I always sleep at night no matter what the miseries of the day," he says. But while he has no trouble falling asleep, he is sometimes bedeviled by what he calls "anxious" dreams. "In the current one, I'm in a school taking a test and I haven't been to class all semester." Luce was unaware that this "examination dream," as it is called, is a Freudian classic that afflicts many other people as well. It is especially common among those who were actually good students at college and did well on their exams. Freud explained the paradox in his book *The Interpretation of Dreams,* observing that the examination dream occurs "when the dreamer is anticipating a responsible task on the following day, with the possibility of disgrace." The dreamer will then recall "an occasion in the past on which a great anxiety proved to have been without real justification, having, indeed, been refuted by the outcome." In other words, when Luce has problems at the office, his mind turns, in self-defense, to the good old days at the University of Wisconsin.

Luce was certainly a good student. He nearly earned straight A's as an undergraduate at Wisconsin, and he also went to law school there, finishing third out of 120 in the Class of 1941. He won a Sterling Fellowship for further graduate work at the Yale Law School and completed his studies for a doctorate within a year, though he never bothered to write a thesis.

He was classified 4-F by his draft board, because of his history of polio, so in June 1942 he went to work as a lawyer with the Board of Economic Warfare in Washington. He left that job in July 1943, after he was offered one of the most exciting assignments any young lawyer could wish—a year as clerk to the great Hugo L. Black, associate justice of the Supreme Court. He got the assignment because he knew the right people. John P. Frank, the clerk who preceded him, had been a year ahead of Luce at Wisconsin's law school, and he too was a Sterling Fellow at Yale. Luce "liked and admired" Frank, and evidently the feeling was mutual. When Frank's term as clerk drew to a close, Justice Black asked him to suggest some possible replacements, and Luce's name stood high on the list. Black got in touch with the University of Wisconsin to check Luce's record, and Luce received a hearty recommendation from the dean of the law school, Lloyd K. Garrison, who like Black was a Democrat and an ardent civil libertarian. That evidently clinched it.

At this point Luce was all of twenty-five years old, and he figured he had a hammerlock on success. "I was a little overcocky," he concedes. But he was soon to be deflated. "Black's *modus operandi* was that he would dictate an opinion, then give you a crack at editing it," Luce recalls. "The first opinion I handled was a small, technical case. I came back with some changes. We had a conference, and he took my suggested changes and politely showed me where they were ridiculous. By the time I was through I wondered why I was wasting this great man's time. On the next couple of opinions I lost my confidence and didn't do well." Black sensed that Luce was performing below his potential and suggested that he take a week off. "I was really up against it, close to failing with that wonderful opportunity," Luce remarks. He spent the week taking long naps and long walks. "I walked up the old C. and O. Canal—up to the Chain Bridge and through Georgetown. Somehow it was good therapy. I got my confidence back, I came back to the job, and I feel I made some contributions to his office that year. We ended up great friends."

Black had a boarder who was a colonel in the Army, and Luce tried to use the colonel's influence to get into the war. But the colonel said that the best Luce could hope for was a job as a file clerk. So Luce turned again to John Frank, who had become an assistant to Abe Fortas, then the undersecretary of the interior. He told Frank he would like to work for a government agency after his term with Black expired and that he preferred to be located in the Northwest; he had come to love the region during a summer hitchhiking tour. Frank put in a word for Luce with the Bonneville Power Administration and the Bureau of Reclamation, agencies within the Interior Department, and Luce received job offers from both. He chose Bonneville—which marketed power from the Grand Coulee Dam and other federal hydroelectric plants in the Columbia River Basin—because he would be based in Portland, Oregon, a city he particularly liked. He spent slightly more than two years as an attorney on the agency's staff and also managed to obtain a military assignment of sorts, serving as a seaman first class in the temporary Coast Guard Reserve at Portland.

Luce had always wanted to go into private practice, and in September 1946 he hung out his shingle in the town of Walla Walla, Washington. At first he maintained an office above a drugstore, working entirely alone, unable to afford a secretary. "I guess I knew about ten people in town, all of whom worked for Bonneville Power," he recalls. "My office had no waiting room, but that didn't matter because there were no clients either." In his effort to attract clients he joined practically every organization in sight—Kiwanis, the Elks, the Masons, the Toastmasters, the Chamber of Commerce—and he made countless speeches. "I would talk on *any* subject to get known."

After four months he became partners with another local lawyer, John C. Tuttle, and moved to more commodious quarters in a conventional office building. They were to remain together for thirteen years, until Tuttle went to another law firm and on from there to become a judge. Luce handled mostly civil cases during his years in private practice, but he had a fair number of criminal cases at the start. One of his earliest clients was an organization called the Committee of Habitual Criminals, consisting of thirty inmates at the Washington State Penitentiary in Walla Walla who were serving mandatory life sentences. The sentences had been meted out under a state law applying to three-time offenders. Luce prepared a brief for presentation to the state legislature and successfully lobbied for an amendment to the criminal code that made his clients eligible for parole after their tenth year in prison. In the wake of this success Luce was asked to handle several individual cases involving inmates of the penitentiary.

Among his many civil cases, there were several that Luce considered particularly noteworthy. He successfully defended the Walla Walla school system against a suit by a taxpayer who sought to block the issuance of $1.8 million worth of bonds to build a new high school. He won an insurance award for a woman whose husband had been killed by a train, the insurers having claimed that the man committed suicide. And he represented some consumers before the Washington Public Service Commission, helping to prevent the Pacific Light and Power Company from obtaining a 10 percent rate increase. As the head of Con Edison, however, he has never been shy about demanding higher rates.

In perhaps his greatest triumph as a lawyer, Luce won several large cash settlements for an Indian tribe, the Confederated Umatillas, Walla Wallas and Cayuse. He was hired as the tribe's general counsel, getting the job only after it had been turned down by several other lawyers. In one case he helped the Indians quintuple the rents received from white ranchers who farmed their lands. In another, he won a $4.2 million settlement from the federal government for destruction of the tribe's fishing grounds on the Columbia River, caused by construction of a dam. And he won $2 million in damages by establishing that the government had improperly taken more than 4 million acres of land from the tribe during the nineteenth century.

Luce became a co-chairman of the Democratic party in Walla Walla County—a dubious distinction, since the county was overwhelmingly Republican. The Democrats fared reasonably well elsewhere in the state, however, and Luce got to know such leading lights of the party as Governor Albert D. Rosellini and Senators Warren G. Magnuson and Henry M. Jackson. "Scoop" Jackson was still in the House of Representatives when he and Luce first met during the early fifties. President Truman had sent Congress a bill to create the Columbia Valley Administration, a public power company that would be comparable in scope and purpose to the Tennessee Valley Authority. One of Luce's former superiors in the Interior Department asked him to come back to Washington at a fee of $50 a day to help the Administration prepare the case for the CVA. "Henry Jackson was pushing the bill, and I was getting facts and material from his office," Luce recalls. "I became *so* impressed with this young congressman. Unfortunately, the bill never got out of committee." Luce and Jackson became good friends, and when Jackson decided to run for the Senate in 1952 he asked Luce to serve as his campaign manager in Walla Walla County. Jackson decisively defeated the Republican incumbent, Harry P. Cain, even though the Republican Presidential candidate—Eisenhower—swept the state by more than 100,000 votes over Stevenson. When Jackson ran for reelection in 1958, Luce joined the ticket as a candidate for the state legislature—but he was trounced, while Jackson won.

Jackson proved a great help to Luce's career. He pulled strings to get Luce two important jobs in the federal government during the sixties, after the Democrats recaptured the White House. Jackson had hoped to run for Vice President on the Kennedy ticket in 1960, but he settled for the chairmanship of the Democratic National Committee instead. That gave him plenty of leverage when it came time to distribute the patronage. He recommended Luce—who had served as a Kennedy delegate at the national convention and had coordinated Kennedy's campaign in Walla Walla County—as the head of the Bonneville Power Administration. "I told Scoop that I'd rather be a federal judge," Luce recalls. His longing for a judgeship could be traced back to his childhood, when he idolized his Uncle Roscoe Luce, a county judge in Wisconsin. But Jackson told him that a judgeship wasn't available and pressed him to take the Bonneville job, insisting that it would advance his political career and gain him wide recognition.

Luce spent two weeks agonizing over the offer. He had been netting an average of more than $40,000 a year from his law practice, while the Bonneville administrator's job paid just $17,500. What's more, he would be forced to relinquish his legal fee—later determined to be $100,000—in the case involving the federal seizure of Indian land. To accept the fee would be considered a conflict of interest under the law, since the Interior Department's Indian Claims Commission had not yet fixed the amount of damages. Luce had already spent 2,500 hours on the case—a lot of time for volunteer work.

He took the job anyhow. "My mother thought I was crazy," he says. "We'd been through the Depression. But I told her I could always go back to practicing law. I think like all decisions it was not made for just one reason. Partly I was interested in what the agency was doing. The Republicans hadn't been doing anything on the Columbia River throughout the Eisenhower Administration. Further, I had to ask myself, 'Are you not going to do anything but practice law the rest of your life?' You know that song: 'Is That All There Is?' It was a self-testing, experimental new experience—an Act Two for me. I'd had Act One and here was Act Two. And I thought it might help me if a judgeship came along." In January 1961, a month before taking office, he merged his law practice with another firm, Gose, Williams and Gose—to form Gose, Williams, Luce and Gose. He didn't care to dissolve the practice because he wanted an escape in case he suddenly left the government. He also made special arrangements for handling the $100,000 fee from the Indian land case. Although he couldn't receive it directly, he did have the right to assign it to charity. He transferred the money to a trust in memory of a daughter who had been killed in an accident and stipulated that it be used to pay college expenses for Indian children. In 1962, finding that he was happy in his new job, he withdrew entirely from the Walla Walla law firm. He had spent fifteen years in private practice— and he never went back.

By all accounts Luce did an excellent job as head of the Bonneville Power Administration. He demonstrated exceptional talents as a negotiator, helping to push through a treaty with Canada for the joint development of the Columbia River and persuading the various public agencies and private companies that operated a total of forty dams on the river to agree to a program of coordinated, synchronized operation. He also planned the vast Pacific Intertie program, with extra-high-voltage lines linking the power systems of the Northwest and Southwest, and won approval for the program from Congress. In less than six years he completed or began projects that doubled the capacity of Bonneville—including a conventional power plant at the Grand Coulee Dam with a capacity of more than 7.2 million kilowatts, and an 800,000-kilowatt nuclear plant at Hanford, Washington. Above all, he restored financial health to what had been a shaky enterprise. His efforts earned him the Interior Department's highest honor, the Distinguished Service Award.

Luce continued to yearn for a judgeship. He almost got one in 1963, after he had been running Bonneville for a couple of years. There was a vacancy in the U.S. District Court for the State of Washington, and he was one of two candidates considered. Although it was President Kennedy who would make the appointment, Senator Magnuson made the choice, deciding against Luce because he was the younger candidate. Luce was still in his mid-forties, and Magnuson assured him that another opportunity would come along. But in fact Luce didn't come close to his goal again until 1979, while he was serving as chief executive of Con Edison. He was one of nine persons nominated that year for two openings on the U.S. Court of Appeals for the District of Columbia, and his name had been suggested by one of the incumbent judges, J. Skelly Wright, whom he had met during the days with Justice Black. With his long and varied experience, Luce seemed to have a good chance, and he was certainly eager enough, filling thirty-five single-spaced pages with his answers to an official questionnaire circulated to nominees. He evidently felt quite confident and went so far as to inform Con Ed's board that he would like it to name Arthur Hauspurg, the company president, as his successor. As he told the press: "I've been at Con Edison for nearly twelve years, and I've done about all I can do here. Here's another career opportunity." But then President Carter decided not to appoint him.

In September 1966, Luce was promoted from chief administrator at Bonneville to undersecretary of the interior. Once again Scoop Jackson paved the way for him, persuading Interior Secretary Stewart L. Udall to make Luce his second in command. Udall was quite familiar with Luce's work and agreed readily enough. "Scoop didn't have any difficulty twisting Stew's arm," Luce says. Luce's appointment had to be confirmed by the Senate Committee on Interior and Insular Affairs. Senate confirmation proceedings can sometimes be an ordeal, but Luce breezed right through. He received effusive praise from the committee chairman, who happened to be Scoop Jackson, and a friendly doff of the cap from Senator Gaylord A. Nelson of Wisconsin, with whom he had attended law school. As undersecretary, Luce was in charge of the Interior Department's budget and day-to-day operations, and he attended President Johnson's Cabinet meetings when Udall couldn't be present. In an episode that seems laughable by today's standards, Luce served as the Johnson Administration's spokesman in attacking the major oil companies for raising their gasoline prices by *one cent* a gallon during February 1967. After considerable jawboning, the increase was rescinded.

Luce had served as undersecretary for only six months when he was offered the chairmanship of Con Edison. The company was a shambles. Its management was old, intransigent and notoriously inept at public relations. The Con Ed plants and equipment were decrepit, and service was undependable. Although the company's rates were among the highest in the nation, its profit margin was low and its earnings were bumpy. During 1966, a good year for utilities generally, Con Ed had suffered a $1.5 million decline in earnings despite a $30 million gain in revenues. Con Ed's problems came to a head with the 1965 Blackout, which was shortly followed by an attention-grabbing article in *Fortune* entitled "Con Edison: The Company You Love to Hate." The Con Ed board hired a consulting firm to study the company, and the consultants filed a report that was highly critical of the management. When asked by the board to comment on the study, management reacted angrily and defensively, insisting that the consultants didn't know what they were talking about. And so the board decided it was time to look for new leadership, and it formed a committee to search for a chief executive—preferably one who was young and imaginative. Luce was not the top choice. Several other candidates were approached, some of them in the utility business, but they understandably refused.

Three visitors called on Luce without an appointment one day in March 1967, giving only their names—Frederick Eaton, Richard Perkins and J. Wilson Newman. Luce, who was in the midst of his hassle with the oil companies, assumed that the men were reporters, and he had his secretary show them in. They didn't waste time on idle chatter. The first words were: "Mr. Luce, we're here to offer you the job of chairman and chief executive officer of Con Edison." As Luce stood there gaping, they explained that they were members of the board and of the committee appointed to find a new top man. Luce said he would think it over.

He carefully assessed his situation. He stood an excellent chance of becoming secretary of the interior if Udall were to leave —but Udall didn't seem in any great hurry. The chairmanship of Con Edison provided a salary of $150,000 a year, plus $50,000 in deferred compensation, substantially more than the $28,500 he was earning in his government job. "Here was really an exciting new possibility of an Act Three," Luce recalls. "The corporate world—it would be totally new to me." He talked to Udall, who didn't try to dissuade him, and in fact said that it sounded like a great opportunity. "He said the problems of our generation are going to be in the cities," Luce recalls, "and you're going to be in the biggest city, where the action is." After three weeks, during which he dickered with the Con Ed board to be certain he would have all the authority he needed, Luce agreed to take the job. He figured that he could solve Con Ed's problems in five years, then return to law. "Of course, after five years that wasn't the case," he remarks with laudable understatement. Many of Con Ed's problems turned out to be chronic, and Luce didn't want to be accused of being "a quitter, a guy who runs away from trouble."

Senator Jackson approached Luce not long after he had accepted Con Ed's offer and twitted him about the decision. "What

kind of Democrat are you, heading a utility?" he said. "There are
all kinds of Democrats, Scoop," Luce replied. "I'm a responsible
Democrat." They both got a laugh out of this exchange, but in
fact Jackson, as Luce's patron senator, can take a lot of credit for
putting him in a position to get the job with Con Ed. It's unclear
who has the *last* laugh.

While Big Business only rarely chooses its leaders from among
the politicians, it *has* displayed a certain partiality toward military
men. This is readily understandable, since business and the military have much in common. Both are vitally concerned with strategy, tactics and the effective deployment of large quantities of
men, materials and equipment. Both are run along authoritarian
lines, demanding obedience according to rank, and subordinating
individual interests to the pursuit of overriding objectives. Business has all the form and spirit of war, if somewhat less blood-
shed, and the tycoons feel a natural affinity for the people who
head the armed services. As a result, a fair number of Old Sol-
diers, despite the lack of any practical business experience, have
been welcomed into the ranks of the tycoons after completing
their tours of duty. There was a time when the leadership of Big
Business might have been mistaken for a Who's Who of World
War II. General Douglas MacArthur became chairman of Rem-
ington Rand and its successor, Sperry Rand. General Omar N.
Bradley became chairman of Bulova Watch. General Lucius D.
Clay became the head of Continental Can. General Brehon Burke
Somervell ran the Koppers Company. Among the younger generation, General James M. Gavin served as chairman of the Arthur D. Little consulting firm, while General Lauris Norstad
became chairman of Owens-Corning Fiberglas.

All these men have either died or retired, but the current crop
of tycoons also includes a few who pursued long and distinguished military careers before getting into business. Colonel
Frank Borman, of the Air Force, who circled the moon as commander of the Apollo VIII mission in 1968, became a vice president of Eastern Airlines just two years later, and in 1975 he
moved up to chief executive. General Alexander M. Haig, Jr.,
who served as supreme allied commander in Europe—not to
mention White House chief of staff during Nixon's final days—

became the president of United Technologies in 1979. Haig appears to be in line to head the company, a diversified industrial with more than $9 billion in annual revenues, since he is five years younger than the incumbent chief executive, Harry Jack Gray. Haig's previous business experience was as a teenaged floorwalker in a Philadelphia department store.

The chairman and chief executive of Pan American World Airways, William Thomas Seawell, started out as a career officer in the Air Force. Because he never captured the kind of headlines that Haig and Borman did, his background remains unfamiliar to the general public. But it so happens that he was a *bona fide* hero and something of a boy wonder during World War II, and he attained the rank of brigadier general at the tender age of forty-one. Born in 1918 in Pine Bluff, Arkansas, he graduated from the U.S. Military Academy at West Point in 1941, and served with the Air Force for twenty-two years before succumbing to the attractions of business. Despite his military background, he doesn't seem particularly intimidating on casual acquaintance. He is a relaxed, quiet-spoken man, with large eyes, soft features and a neatly groomed headful of silvery hair. When I interviewed him at the Pan Am Building in Manhattan, he was pointedly casual, arriving in the conference room in shirt-sleeves. Very few chief executives display themselves that way to outsiders. Appearances notwithstanding, some people who have worked with Seawell, and particularly those who have vied with him for power and position, attest that a tough, extremely ambitious man lurks behind the mild facade. In fact the *Wall Street Journal* reports that Seawell is "famed for his fierce temper." Once, after arriving late on a Pan Am flight and losing his luggage to boot, he "blasted the hell out of everybody," in the words of one of his executives. "We spent weeks trying to make fixes in the system," the man added. I, for one, can attest that Seawell's public-relations men seem deathly afraid of him.

The son of a railroad switchman, Seawell decided quite early that he had to go to West Point. "It was the usual youthful bit," he explains. "I saw a West Point cadet come home and that sparked my interest. It also represented a good educational opportunity. I didn't go in with any real understanding of what the Air Corps and Army involved. Like any other career, you go step by step." He missed out on his first try for admission, so he spent a year studying at the University of Arkansas. But the next time around he got the appointment, thanks to a recommendation from his congressman, John L. McClellan, who was to become one of the leading figures in the Senate. In later years Seawell made a point of visiting McClellan's office whenever he was on Capitol Hill—"just to pay my respects. We would talk for a few minutes, or I'd leave word that I called. He showed an interest in my career all the way through."

Within a few months after his graduation from West Point, Seawell was putting his training to practical use in the European Theater of War, as the commander of a B-17 squadron with the Eighth Air Force. He was quickly promoted to commander of the 401st bombardment group, making him one of the youngest men in the Air Force with an assignment of that magnitude. From a base at Peterborough, in England, he completed thirty bombing missions without a single fatality among his crew, although the antiaircraft fire did cause some injuries. His performance won him a chestful of decorations, including the Silver Star, the Distinguished Flying Cross with three oak-leaf clusters, the Air Medal with three oak-leaf clusters, and the Croix de Guerre with palm.

The war failed to dampen Seawell's enthusiasm for the military, and he settled into what he assumed would be a lifelong career. He found himself in what he calls "a series of interesting assignments," serving as commander of the Strategic Air Command Eleventh Bomb Wing, then as deputy commander of the Seventh Air Division, then as a functionary in the office of the Air Force deputy chief of staff for operations. Along the way he managed to earn a degree from the Harvard Law School. In 1958, as a colonel, he was appointed military assistant to James H. Douglas, Jr., the secretary of the Air Force, and when Douglas was promoted to deputy secretary of defense the next year, Seawell—himself promoted to brigadier general—went along.

His alliance with Douglas brought him into frequent contact with Cyrus Rowlett Smith, the longtime head of American Airlines. Smith was a good friend of Douglas, having served as deputy commander of the Air Transport Command during the war while Douglas was the chief of staff. But friendship didn't prevent Smith from trying to pirate Seawell away, and he offered him a job in the American Airlines management. Seawell thanked Smith for the offer and said he was flattered, but at that point he wanted to stay in the service. Smith continued to hover in the background, however, and he was to prove helpful to Seawell on several occasions.

Douglas lost his job after the Kennedy Administration took over in 1961, and Seawell also had to look elsewhere. He joined the new Air Force Academy at Colorado Springs as its first commandant of cadets. The academy's mascot was the falcon, and Seawell became fascinated with this relentless predator. Today his office at Pan Am contains a collection of falcon statuettes, as well as a genuine, stuffed falcon.

In 1963, Seawell was offered a job by Stuart G. Tipton, president of the Air Transport Association of America, the trade group representing the domestic scheduled airlines. Tipton wanted Seawell to become his vice president for operations and engineering, and he made a special trip to Colorado Springs to talk it over. It turned out that C. R. Smith had recommended Seawell for the job. Seawell was sorely tempted, even though it would mean abandoning his military career. "I was forty-five years old," he remarks, "a last crossing-over point. I either stayed in the military and did the best I could, or got out and did something else." He and Tipton had several more conversations, and Seawell agreed to take the job.

His retirement caused a mild uproar in the Air Force hierarchy. Although he was eligible to retire with a full pension after twenty-two years in the service, there was a tradition in the Air Force that officers of general rank would serve for at least twenty-eight years unless disabled. The Air Force vice chief of staff, General William F. McKee, visited Seawell at the academy to express his displeasure. "He told me I oughta rethink it," as Seawell recalls. "I did. I came to the same conclusion. It was the right time to move on."

C. R. Smith made Seawell another offer in 1965, and this time he couldn't refuse. Seawell joined American Airlines as vice president for operations planning. "It looked as though it would be an interesting further aspect of aviation activity," he remarks, "and obviously the money had something to do with it too." He worked under Forwood Cloud Wiser, Jr., the vice president in charge of operations, and when Wiser was recruited to run

Northeast Airlines in 1966, Seawell got his job. Their paths were to cross again. "Bud" Wiser was approached about taking the presidency of Pan American in 1971, but he turned it down and the job went to Seawell. Five years later, Wiser *did* become president of Pan Am—serving under Seawell, his former subordinate, who by then had become chairman and chief executive. Wiser left the company in 1978 for reasons that have never been fully explained—though it was reported at the time that he had had some policy disputes with the boss.

Seawell was promoted to senior vice president of American in 1967, and today he claims that this was as far as he expected to go with that airline. At the time, however, there was speculation in the press that he would go considerably farther. He was forty-nine years old while Smith, the chairman and chief executive officer, was in his late sixties, and the president, George Marion Sadler, was in his mid-fifties. Early in 1968, Sadler resigned because of ill health and was replaced by George Alexander Spater, the vice chairman, who was also in his fifties. Later that same year Smith left American to serve as secretary of commerce in the Johnson Administration, and Spater became chief executive. Although Seawell might have been next in line for the top job, he didn't wait around long enough to find out. But in retrospect it could have been worth his while to wait. Spater was forced to resign in 1973, following the disclosure that his company had illegally contributed to President Nixon's reelection campaign. Old C. R. Smith came back to run things for a few months until a new chief executive could be found. If Seawell had been on the scene he might have gotten the job, but instead it went to Albert Vincent Casey.

In November 1968, Seawell became president of Rolls-Royce Aero Engines, Inc., the U.S. sales subsidiary of Rolls-Royce, Ltd., the British manufacturer of luxury cars and aircraft engines. Rolls-Royce had been awarded a contract to supply its RB-211 engine for the new Lockheed wide-body jets, and it was anxious to establish what Seawell calls "a full presence" in North America. It already had two plants in Canada, and there was talk about building a major plant in the United States. But the company soon got into grave financial difficulties, in large part because of cost overruns on its Lockheed contract. The company declared bankruptcy in 1971 and was placed in receivership. The British government stepped in, splitting off the automotive operations into a separate, publicly held company, while transforming the engine operations into a government-owned company. Seawell took a hand in reorganizing Rolls-Royce, but he was more than ready to leave. The experience convinced him that he would rather be back in the airline business.

He received an offer late in 1971 to serve as president and chief operating officer of Pan American. The offer came from Najeeb E. Halaby, then the chairman and chief executive, who has since gained additional fame as the father-in-law of Jordan's King Hussein. Seawell and Halaby had been both friends and adversaries over the years. They had first met during the fifties, when Halaby was an official in the Defense Department, and they got to know each other better during the sixties, when Halaby was chief administrator of the Federal Aviation Administration, while Seawell represented the domestic airlines as an officer of the Air Transport Association. In those days, as regulator and regulated, they frequently argued opposite sides of the issues at public hearings and in the press.

Pan Am had fallen on hard times. After prospering during the mid-sixties, it had slipped into the red during 1969—Halaby's first year as chief executive—recording a loss of $26 million. The loss grew to $48 million during 1970, and the company was heading for another large loss in 1971—$45 million, as it turned out. Like most airlines, Pan Am had been hurt during part of that period by a recession, which curtailed the travel plans of many potential customers. But it also had some large, persistent problems of its own. For example, it had prematurely committed itself to a large fleet of jumbo jets. It ordered thirty-three of the new Boeing 747s in 1966, when industry prospects seemed bright, but the planes arrived in 1969, when things had turned gloomy. Pan Am had trouble filling even half of the airplane's 350 seats, and this dragged heavily on its earnings. What's more, the 747 wasn't a very reliable performer in its early days. Seawell recalls that the plane weighed more than Boeing had originally planned, forcing the engine manufacturer, Pratt and Whitney, to boost the power "earlier than they would have liked." For a while the 747 was plagued with mechanical problems that caused Pan Am to delay or cancel many flights.

The company was also seriously handicapped by its route structure. Pan Am was exclusively an international airline, with no service at all between cities in the contiguous United States. Juan Terry Trippe, who organized the airline in 1927, had sought to make it "the chosen instrument" of international aviation. Through a tacit understanding with the federal government, Pan Am was able to obtain the best international routes, while yielding any claim to domestic service. This was fine so long as the U.S. thoroughly dominated commercial aviation, but eventually the foreign airlines came into their own, and Pan Am found itself with a lot of competition. Pan Am also lost its political clout over the years, and other U.S. airlines—especially TWA—were given the right to compete along Pan Am's most treasured routes. The other airlines had an advantage, since they could carry international passengers from cities in the U.S. interior, where Pan Am did not operate. Pan Am also began to face formidable competition from chartered airlines with their cut-rate fares. The company was squeezed particularly hard in the Caribbean, where its business had started, and where it was still heavily committed. In the jet age, quick trips to the Caribbean became all the rage, and many other airlines horned in on Pan Am's territory. In just a few decades Pan Am had gone from a virtual monopoly to "the most competed-against airline in the world," as Seawell described it.

The company suffered from a host of internal problems as well. It had never fully made the transition to modern management. Juan Trippe, as is often the case with entrepreneurs, wanted to run the company all by himself. At the start, when Pan Am had only a single plane and a single route—Key West–Havana—he could bring it off. But long after Pan Am had become a multi-million-dollar giant, Trippe was still trying to do it all. He had ordered the fleet of 747s on a hunch, without consulting anyone in the marketing and scheduling departments. Although Pan Am had an organization chart of sorts, it wasn't very meaningful while Trippe was the boss. Trippe finally stepped aside as chief executive in 1968, but he remained on the board of directors, and his presence was strongly felt.

Trippe's successor as chief executive was Harold Edwin Gray. A pilot during Pan Am's early days, Gray had been president of the company under Trippe for the past four years. Soon after getting the top job, he discovered that he was gravely ill, and he stepped down in favor of Halaby. Halaby, recruited into the company a few years earlier by Trippe, had served as president and chief operating officer under Gray, and he retained those titles even after taking over as chairman and chief executive. When Pan Am began losing money, the directors perked up, and some of them suggested that Halaby was trying to do too much by himself—shades of Juan Trippe! Halaby finally responded in June 1971 by appointing four men as group vice presidents, with the understanding that the best performer would eventually become president. But Pan Am's management became more chaotic than ever as these men jockeyed frantically for position. Seawell, who came upon this scene after a few months, recalls that there was "confusion as to who was managing what. There were special segments of the company, and their functions were competitive, not cooperative. They were not acting as a team."

Halaby seemed certain to lose his job if things didn't improve soon, and he was counting on Seawell's talents as an operations expert to save him. However, Seawell was not the first man to be offered the presidency of Pan Am during this period. Halaby had first tried to recruit Samuel Logan Higginbottom, the president of Eastern Air Lines, but Higginbottom didn't think it was worthwhile to make what he considered a lateral move. He would come to Pan Am only if he could be appointed chief executive, and that was a concession Halaby didn't care to make. Meanwhile, Pan Am's board had assigned three of its members to examine the company's management structure, and this special committee, whose members included Donald Kendall of PepsiCo, Frank Stanton of CBS, and Thomas J. Watson, Jr., of IBM, felt that it had authority to seek a new president as well. Unknown to Halaby, it made an offer to "Bud" Wiser, who at this point was serving as president of TWA. Wiser seemed interested, but TWA improved the terms of his contract, and he decided to stay put.

Before Seawell would accept the presidency of Pan Am, he wanted to be assured that he would have all the authority he needed to improve its operations. As he told a friend at the time:

"I'm positive Pan Am can be turned around, but if it has to go down, I want it to go down my way, not Jeeb's." Halaby had promised him a written contract, and Seawell arrived at the negotiating session accompanied by a lawyer—his brother-in-law from Little Rock. Halaby was surprised to find that Seawell wanted the contract to spell out not only the financial terms, but also the assignment of duties. "This irritated me somewhat," Halaby later wrote, "but I assumed it would make Seawell secure and satisfied." Seawell demanded and got authority over flight operations, engineering, marketing and the controller's department. "I wouldn't personally call it hard bargaining," he says, "but Jeeb might have classified it that way. I was gonna have authority to run it." At any rate, Seawell was secure and satisfied enough to hand Rolls-Royce his resignation, and he went to work for Pan Am in December 1971.

Halaby predicted that his new president would be "a healer, a team leader, a bringer-together of people." Although Halaby later revised his opinion of Seawell, Seawell did his best to live up to Halaby's billing. He visited with Pan Am's managers and its rank-and-file workers, delivering pep talks and listening to gripes and suggestions, and he impressed everyone with his cool, methodical approach to even the scariest problems. Seawell made some fundamental changes in management, separating the staff and line functions, which had become confused and entangled, and strengthening the financial controls. "We had a very weak financial department," he says. "We didn't have a good data system, or good controls, so a lot of decisions had to be gut reactions."

Once Seawell arrived, some of Pan Am's directors were ready to dump Halaby. Although most of the airline's problems couldn't really be blamed on Halaby, he had obviously been unable to solve them. But the majority of the board was willing to let Halaby remain—provided he didn't make any mistakes that might hinder Pan Am's recovery. By Halaby's own account, he *did* proceed to make what the board members considered a serious mistake, getting into a dispute with Seawell over the hiring and firing of a couple of vice presidents. This was interpreted as interference with Seawell's operating authority—something Halaby had earnestly promised to avoid. Donald Kendall, one of Halaby's sternest foes on the board, got wind of the dispute in March 1972 and summoned Seawell before the special management committee. Halaby says he later learned that Seawell not only failed to support him, but even threatened to resign—"thereby putting the members under terrible pressure." Seawell has declined to comment on this episode, which is described in Halaby's book *Crosswinds*.

At the initiative of the directors, the monthly board meeting scheduled for early April was moved ahead to March 22. Pan Am had lost more than $23 million during January and February, and a $270 million line of credit with its bankers was up for renewal at the end of March. The board apparently considered it necessary to impress the bankers with some decisive action before the month was out, and Halaby was now deemed expendable. Halaby opened the meeting with a defense of his record as chief executive, coupled with a discussion of his plans for the company's future. He asked the board to give him both a vote of confidence and some time to turn the company around. Halaby, Seawell and two other inside directors were then asked to leave the room while seventeen outside directors deliberated Halaby's fate. After a couple of hours they informed Halaby that they wanted his resignation, and they informed Seawell that he had been promoted to chairman and chief executive officer. "Seawell seemed briefly to choke up with emotion," Halaby later recalled, ". . . and then gained control of himself and the situation."

It would be nice to report that Seawell quickly restored the airline to health and that it lived profitably ever after. But, in fact, it wasn't until 1977—after several harrowing years on the brink of bankruptcy—that Pan Am finally made it into the black. By cutting down on personnel and trimming other costs as well, Seawell seemed on the way to making Pan Am profitable as early as 1974. But sharp increases in fuel prices, triggered by the Arab oil embargo of 1973, not only wiped out the anticipated profit, but left Pan Am with an $82 million loss.

Seawell decided that merging with another airline might be the best way to save Pan Am. One likely prospect was TWA, Pan Am's chief rival. If the two airlines were joined, they could eliminate any conflicting or overlapping routes, which presumably would mean a mutual improvement in financial results. But Seawell found that a merger with TWA would have involved large "start-up" costs and that they couldn't obtain the necessary financing. Instead, with the approval of the federal government, the two airlines agreed to swap some routes to reduce the competition between them. Pan Am held merger talks at various times with three other airlines as well—Eastern, Continental and American. Each of them had an extensive network of domestic flights that would have nicely complemented Pan Am's international business. He couldn't work out a satisfactory agreement with either Eastern or Continental, but he was all in favor of merging with American. The plan fell through, however, when the two airlines couldn't get the necessary approval from the federal regulatory agencies. Seawell did arrange some route swaps with his friend C. R. Smith.

For a while it seemed as though Pan Am might be saved by the Shah of Iran. The company had special ties with Iran, having contributed technical assistance in the development of Iran Air, the state airline. Seawell says that in the fall of 1974 one of Pan Am's New York employees, an Iranian by nationality, came back from a trip to Iran with a "somewhat garbled" message suggesting that the government would like to help out. Seawell got on an airplane and flew straight through to Iran to talk with Lieutenant General Ali Mohammed Khademi, head of Iran Air, "to try to confirm whether the rumor had any validity." Khademi in turn talked to the Shah and relayed word that the government would indeed like to help Pan Am. Under the terms of a tentative deal made public in May 1975, Iran would pump $300 million into Pan Am. Of this sum, $245 million would consist of loans payable after ten years, while the remaining $55 million would go to buy a majority interest in the Intercontinental Hotel chain, which Pan Am owned. Iran would also receive warrants to buy up to 13 percent of Pan Am's common stock. But by July the deal was dead. Seawell visited Iran that month with two investment bankers, Peter Peterson and George Ball of Lehman Brothers, and learned that the Iranian authorities had some serious second thoughts about their rescue mission. Although the deal wasn't formally canceled, the discussions never resumed. It was a great disappointment at the time, but as Seawell now observes: "In retrospect, we can all heave a sigh of relief."

By 1976 there was a boom under way in air travel, and Pan Am nearly managed to break even. The fleet of Boeing 747 jumbo jets, which had seemed such a burden during hard times, suddenly became a great asset when all the seats were filled. The company tailored its schedule to the 747—which is most efficient on long-range flights—by shedding some of its short- and medium-range routes, while adding to its long hops. In 1977, Pan Am reported a profit of $45 million.

Seawell was convinced that the company would also need some domestic business if it hoped to survive in the long run. After the federal government deregulated the nation's airlines in 1978, Pan Am could have unilaterally decided to fly any domestic routes that it considered worthwhile. But Seawell shied away from this solution, estimating that it would cost a billion dollars to become competitive starting from scratch. Instead he resumed his efforts to join forces with an established domestic airline, and he found a willing partner in National Airlines, which is best known for its flights between New York and Miami. Pan Am's bid for National, amounting to somewhat more than $400 million, was contested by two other suitors, Eastern Air Lines and Texas International Airlines, and the dispute went before the Civil Aeronautics Board for adjudication. Pan Am ultimately won, and it completed the acquisition of National in 1980.

It is a tricky matter to judge the "outsiders" as business executives. Because they are usually summoned to rescue companies in distress, they don't always enjoy unqualified success. Con Edison's record has improved under Charles Luce, and so has Pan Am's under William Seawell, but neither company has been exactly scintillating. It may be that these men have performed as well as anyone possibly could, but that would be hard to prove. Certainly they have done better than their predecessors, which should count for something.

The case of Frank Borman presents a somewhat different aspect of the same conundrum. When he took charge of Eastern Air Lines in 1975, it was losing a huge amount of money. The next year it became profitable, and it has remained so ever since. But how much of the credit should go to Borman? The year 1975 was horrendous for practically all the major airlines, but the industry's fortunes abruptly changed for the better starting in 1976.

On the other hand Donald Rumsfeld's experience at Searle leaves no room for doubt or hesitation. His success in turning that company around so completely and so rapidly has been spectacular by any standard.

By and large, it appears that the tycoons who come late to business can hold their own with those who make business a life-long career. The managerial skills necessary to run a large company can be acquired in other disciplines, and the qualities of mind essential to a successful tycoon are not limited to businessmen alone. Ideally, the head man in a company should be totally dedicated to his work. He should be ambitious and aggressive in pursuit of the company's goals. He should be an expert at analyzing problems and organizing their solution. He should be masterful in his personal dealings with subordinates, able to both manipulate and inspire them. He should have enough stomach to be tough and even merciless at times, but also enough humanity to be fair at *all* times. In the real world, alas, some tycoons fall a bit short of that ideal. But the crucial point is that business training and business experience are not enough. It is intelligence and character that make the tycoon.

Chapter Eight

Entrepreneurs

WHY WOULD anyone want to go into business for himself? The question is neither idle nor obvious, for this is the age of professional management, and the professional managers appear to have a lot going for them. Unlike the entrepreneurs, they aren't required to risk their own money to reach the top. By investing only time and toil, a professional can become the master of a vast empire with thousands of employees and shareholders, billions of dollars in assets, and the power to stimulate or undermine the economies of cities, states and entire nations. Almost all our largest companies are headed by professionals. The men who built General Motors, Exxon, Du Pont, U.S. Steel and the rest are long since gone, and it is the professionals who are reaping the fruits of their success.

The entrepreneurs *do* have one large advantage over the professionals. If they succeed, they can make a lot more money than any professional ever dreamed of making. The professionals who head even the largest companies rarely accumulate as much as $10 million in a lifetime of high salaries and generous stock options. But personal fortunes of $50 million and more are fairly common among entrepreneurs whose companies are relatively modest in size. Take for example the case of Henry Ross Perot, who quit his job as an IBM salesman in 1962 to start his own computer-service company on an investment of a few thousand dollars. When the company, Electronic Data Systems, went public in 1968, he kept 81 percent of the stock. And when the stock reached its peak price in 1970, Perot was worth *one and one-half billion dollars,* which probably made him the richest man in America at that point. The stock has gone way down since then, but Perot can still tally his wealth in the hundreds of millions.

While Electronic Data Systems is a thriving enterprise, its revenues amount to just $300 million a year. The mighty Exxon Corporation grosses about three hundred times as much; yet the head of Exxon, Clifton Garvin, is worth a mere million or two. The difference is that Perot got in at the beginning and held onto his stock as the company grew. Garvin came to Exxon seventy-seven years after its founding by John Davison Rockefeller, and he owns less than a hundredth of one percent of the stock. Although Perot doesn't happen to be a big spender, he is certainly in a better position than Garvin to make a splash at Tiffany or Cartier. Garvin, however, runs a company that can shape the destiny of the nation and the world. Which of them is better off? It's a matter of taste.

Of course there is no guarantee that an entrepreneur will succeed—and in fact the odds are heavily against it. For every person who becomes rich by founding his own business, there are thousands upon thousands who go broke or who merely scrape along at the subsistence level. The big winners—men like Perot, or Edwin Land of Polaroid, or Ray Kroc of McDonald's—get all the publicity, obscuring the fact that the chances for a rousing success are very slight indeed. Still, most budding entrepreneurs probably know what they are up against when they risk their capital on a company of their own. And yet they do it all the same.

Many of them have no alternative. They are the ones who lack the academic or social credentials to get ahead as professional managers. If they are to succeed in business at all, it *has* to be in an entrepreneurial role. Some of the more successful entrepreneurs of modern times were high school dropouts—among them Robert Forman Six, the founder of Continental Airlines, Rex David Thomas, founder of the Wendy's International restaurant chain, and Carl Henry Lindner, founder of American Financial, a diversified holding company. For all their natural talent and business savvy, they probably could never have gotten past the personnel offices at most blue-chip companies. Meshulam Riklis, founder of the Rapid-American Corporation, a retailer and manufacturer, and Charles G. Bluhdorn, who founded the Gulf and Western conglomerate, both went to college, but they still would have found it nearly impossible to reach the top in someone else's company. They are both Jewish and immigrants to boot—Riklis having come over from Israel in 1947, and Bluhdorn from Austria by way of England in 1942. Of Bluhdorn, *Fortune* once observed: "His manner changes swiftly from persuasive explanation to table-thumping assertion, all enunciated in mile-a-minute Viennese-American. His single-mindedness about the rightness and logic of his mission in the business world can display itself in rudeness and irascibility as well as in sudden charm." Here is a man who has built a conglomerate that really works, with revenues totaling more than $5 billion, while amassing a personal fortune of some $50 million. Yet it is difficult to imagine him attaining even a vice presidency in the prim, WASPish *milieu* of so many major companies.

There *are* some businessmen whose academic and social backgrounds would qualify them for careers at even the most discriminating of the large, established companies, but who nevertheless choose to become entrepreneurs—with all the risk and uncertainty that this entails. On close inspection, it usually turns out that these are people who are imbued with what is called the "entrepreneurial temperament." To put it in plainer English: they can't get along with bosses. They are just too outspoken or volatile or rough-mannered, or full of bright ideas or simply too full of life to play the slow, civilized games required for advancement in a business bureaucracy. This is not necessarily something that they know instinctively. Many of them try at first to follow careers as hired hands, because that is the way things are done in this day and age. Only after this fails do they go off to make a fortune on their own. When Ross Perot left IBM after five years, it was in frustration over a company policy limiting the commissions that a salesman could earn. In 1962 he had sold his quota of computers by mid-January, whereupon his superiors insisted that he spend the rest of the year in an office job. IBM seems to have a knack for discouraging its brightest people. Gene Myron Amdahl, the man who designed the Series 360 computer, left the company twice. He vowed to create a company of his own that would produce large computers to compete with IBM's, and in

1970 he did. Today the Amdahl Corporation has revenues of
$300 million.

Charles "Tex" Thornton, cofounder of Litton Industries, had
all the talent and training necessary to be a top-flight professional
manager, but temperamentally he was unsuited for the role. He
was so good at professional management that he fooled even
himself for a while. It took seven years as a professional—first at
Ford, then at Hughes Aircraft—before he acknowledged that he
couldn't be happy working for someone else. Once that became
clear, he moved with dispatch to organize Litton. The company,
founded in 1953, was a pioneer conglomerate, and today its revenues of more than $4 billion place it among the one hundred
largest industrial companies in the U.S. Thornton continues to
serve as chairman and chief executive. Whatever his earlier problems with superiors, Thornton gets high marks from most of the
people who have worked *under* him. "Tex is one of the greatest
industrial managers of the postwar era," said a former officer of
Litton. "He is a great motivator."

At Ford, Thornton cherished ambitions that were much too
grand and totally unrealistic. With the other Whiz Kids, he came
breezing into the company in February 1946 and found it a shambles. Thornton evidently saw himself as Ford's messiah who
would take full charge of operations and, with his followers, re-
store the company to a respectable place in the automotive industry. But young Henry Ford II had no intention of putting
Thornton in charge of operations. As Nevins and Hill point out
in their massive history of the company, Henry considered the
Whiz Kids "a useful reservoir of talent," but felt that "however
high the abilities of the newcomers might be, they were mere
infants in the automotive world, and would remain so for some
time to come." Even before the Whiz Kids arrived, Henry had
been casting about for a director of operations who would be put
in over their heads. Someone suggested the name of Ernest Robert Breech, who had been a vice president of General Motors and
was serving as president of Bendix Aviation, which was partly
owned by GM. Breech agreed to join Ford as executive vice president starting in July 1946.

A few weeks before Breech arrived, Thornton was appointed
director of planning, a position that had been created at his own

urging. He had appeared before Ford's Policy Committee to protest that the company needed a central planner to coordinate the activities of the various departments. Under the old setup the departments each did their own planning, and they were often working at cross-purposes. Thornton was assigned to work directly under Henry Ford, but it was expected that he would also discuss his activities with Breech. According to Nevins and Hill, Thornton asked Ford to sign a letter "which gave him very broad authority," but Ford hesitated, suggesting that he first show it to Breech. Breech felt that his own authority would be seriously impaired, and he told Ford: "If you sign this letter, there is no use for me to join the company." Ford didn't sign it, Thornton was made clearly subordinate to Breech, and any messianic impulses were effectively squelched.

It was all downhill from there. Breech brought in a lot of his old colleagues from General Motors, and they quickly upstaged the Whiz Kids. Lewis D. Crusoe, who had been with both GM and Bendix, was given direct authority over Thornton and his group. He admired their intelligence, but regarded them with something less than awe. "They knew nothing about business and the automotive industry," he said. "Their knowledge was from books." He set about giving them a practical education. Thornton, however, couldn't abide Crusoe—"a cost accountant with about as much imagination as this table [rapping on table]. He couldn't take criticism." Not all the Whiz Kids felt that way. "I could not have had better experience than I got under Mr. Crusoe's direction," one of them remarked. One day in the summer of 1948, Thornton went to Crusoe's office and said, "I don't want to work for you anymore."

He joined Hughes Aircraft, in Culver City, California, where he served as assistant general manager under Harold George, a retired Air Force general, and had charge of the day-to-day operations. When Thornton joined the company it was a barely discernible subsidiary of the Hughes Tool Company, the major holding in the Howard Hughes empire. As just one of many airframe manufacturers, Hughes Aircraft had been losing money on revenues of less than $2 million. Thornton, along with others, persuaded Howard Hughes to get Hughes Aircraft out of the airframe business entirely—though Hughes never did agree to change the company's name. Hughes Aircraft began to concentrate on electronics, a field that was only beginning to reveal its fabulous potential.

The company began making electronic devices exclusively for the military. Under two outstanding research scientists, Simon Ramo and Dean Wooldridge, it developed fire-control systems for fighter planes, and air-to-air missile systems for the defense of bombers. Thornton found that it was difficult at first to recruit many scientists for defense work. "The war was over," he recalls, "and everyone was thinking there would be at least thirty years of peace, like between World War I and World War II." But with the outbreak of the Korean War in 1950, the company's business skyrocketed, and it was able to attract what Thornton calls "the cream of the scientists." Hughes Aircraft's revenues soared to around $200 million in 1953, the final year of the war, and its net income reportedly reached $8 million—four times greater than the *revenues* of just five years earlier.

During 1949, Thornton hired a brilliant young man named Roy Lawrence Ash as a financial planner for Hughes Aircraft. "He could multiply in his head as fast as someone else could do on a calculating machine," Thornton recalls. It was the beginning of a business partnership that was to last for the next twenty-four years—through the best of times and the worst of times. Under Thornton, Ash rose to assistant controller and chief financial officer of Hughes. They both left Hughes in 1953, and shortly afterward they founded Litton Industries, with Thornton as the top man and deal-maker, Ash as the second in command, in charge of operations. They remained together until Ash joined the Nixon Administration in 1973 as director of the Office of Management and Budget. Ash did not return to Litton after leaving the government, but instead became chief executive of A-M International, a manufacturer of business machines.

Ash had actually worked under Thornton even before he joined Hughes Aircraft, though they didn't really know each other. He had been one of the 2,800 Army Air Corps officers who belonged to Thornton's Office of Statistical Control during World War II. Before the war Ash had spent six years with the Bank of America, working his way up from messenger boy to operations officer at a branch in Los Angeles. "I had a sense of wanting to get into an environment that had a ladder with lots of rungs," he recalls. "This has its advantages and disadvantages. In a little entrepreneurial business, whether you're a druggist or a dentist, at sixty-five you end up doing what you did all along."

Born in L.A. in 1918, the son of a grain broker, he had gone to work for the bank directly out of high school. Although a top-notch student, he didn't consider it imperative to attend college. "There were not the pressures we have today, especially on the West Coast," he remarks. "It wasn't necessarily considered the thing to do." He did attend night classes in economics and business law sponsored by the American Institute of Banking. After the U.S. entered the war, Ash enlisted in the Army as a private with the Finance Corps and became a staff sergeant within a year. He attended an Air Corps Officer Candidate School in Miami Beach, then was transferred to the Harvard Business School, where Thornton had established a training program for the best financial minds in his outfit. Ash finished first in his class and joined the Fourth Air Force as a statistical-control officer, rising to the rank of captain. In 1945 he returned to Harvard to conduct a strategic-bombing study that was supposed to prove useful in an invasion of Japan. When the atomic bomb abruptly ended the war, Ash sought admission to the business school's regular program, leading to a master's degree in business administration. The school had never admitted a student without a college degree, but the authorities were happy to make an exception in his case. He earned the MBA in 1947 and went back to the Bank of America—which is where Thornton found him two years later. They were brought together by a mutual acquaintance from Harvard.

In recent years the circumstances surrounding the departure of Thornton and Ash from Hughes Aircraft have become clouded by controversy. It is one of those peculiar events that becomes more difficult to fathom as more light is shed upon it. At this stage it seems unlikely that any outsider will ever be able to determine precisely what happened. At the time, however, the reasons for the departure seemed clear and unequivocal. Thornton and Ash were said to have left—in September 1953—as part of a general exodus protesting interference in the Hughes Aircraft operations by Noah Dietrich, the executive vice president of the Hughes Tool Company. Nine executives left Hughes Aircraft, among them General George and the scientists Ramo and Wooldridge.

After a while word began circulating that Thornton and Ash had in fact been forced to resign because of irregularities in the accounting procedures at Hughes Aircraft. That, at least, was the version of events promulgated by Dietrich, who said that it was he who did the forcing. Dietrich's story received little public attention at first, but in 1973 it suddenly became a *cause célèbre*. Ash had been asked to join the Nixon Administration, and his background came under intense scrutiny in the press. Morton Mintz, an investigative reporter with the Washington *Post,* gave new life to the old charges in an article appearing on January 2, 1973. Drawing on records in the Superior Court and the Court of Appeal in Los Angeles, Mintz recounted accusations that the Air Force had unwittingly overpaid Hughes Aircraft millions of dollars for weapons-control systems. Ash was said to have condoned and encouraged recordkeeping practices that led to the overpayments.

The accusations were based largely on testimony by James O. White, who had been chief accountant in the controller's organization of Hughes Aircraft. White said that in 1951, Ash had issued orders to overstate the withdrawals of materials from inventory. The company was working on the basis of cost plus 10 percent, so if material costs were exaggerated, Hughes Aircraft would receive considerably more than its due. White said that Ash also told him to disguise the overcrediting of inventories in the monthly financial reports issued by Hughes Aircraft to Hughes Tool. According to White, Ash made it clear that he himself was carrying out orders from Tex Thornton. White testified that during 1951, Ash had relaxed the physical control of inventories at Hughes Aircraft. Until then, parts had been kept locked up, with employees specially assigned to dispense them in exchange for requisitions. But under the new system the production workers themselves were able to withdraw the parts, and they were expected to simply leave their requisitions on file. White said that before long a lot of parts were unaccountably missing. He said the cost of the missing parts was then charged to the Air Force. According to the testimony, Ash brought in a group of cost accountants to cover up the shortage by determining exactly which parts were missing, then making out thousands of false requisitions. White said the requisitions were stamped with time clocks that had been turned back, and that they were deliberately soiled and wrinkled to make them look authentic. Eventually, he said, he and some of his fellow accountants complained to the people at Hughes Tool about the irregular financial practices. He said they were promised that Thornton and Ash would be fired and that when this didn't happen promptly, the accountants resigned.

These scandalous charges first came to light only because of a lawsuit that had nothing to do with the activities of Hughes Aircraft. In 1959 a man named Emmett T. Steele, who had been associated with both Hughes Aircraft and Litton Industries, sued Litton and its top officers, claiming that he was a cofounder and was entitled to a large block of stock. He said that Thornton had orally promised the stock to him, but had never delivered. A jury awarded Steele $7.6 million in 1965, but the verdict was overturned on appeal and a new trial was ordered. Steele died shortly before the retrial was to begin in 1972, but his family continued to press the claim, and the defendants agreed to pay his widow $2.4 million in an out-of-court settlement.

In preparing for the original trial, Steele's attorney, Harold Rhoden, asked Noah Dietrich to comment on Thornton's character. In a sworn deposition, Dietrich mentioned the revolt of the accountants and made some other hostile comments about Thornton as well. Dietrich explained that he wanted to fire Thornton after the accountants complained, but that he needed authorization from the elusive Howard Hughes and couldn't get it for *two years*. Dietrich's statements prompted Thornton to sue him for slander, but the case was dismissed because a deposition is considered a privileged document. However, Dietrich himself sued Thornton for libel. It seems that Thornton had counterattacked with a press release and with a memorandum sent to Litton's employees in which he questioned Dietrich's veracity. The libel suit went through two trials, and finally resulted in a total settlement of slightly more than $250,000 in Dietrich's favor. It was in the first libel trial that James White, as a witness for Dietrich, put his story on the public record.

In a recent interview Ash had some ready replies to all the accusations. He flatly denied that either he or Thornton had is-sued the orders about costs and inventories attributed to them by James White. He acknowledged that there had been a dispute with the accountants, but described it as a power struggle, not a matter of ethics. "There were political contests as to who would be responsible for the financial administration of Hughes Air-craft," he says. "I won, and there were some losers. Probably to make the losers feel worse about it, I wasn't an accountant—and everybody *knows* one should be a CPA. One can always para-phrase Clemenceau: 'The finance function is too important to be left to the accountants.' But they were still able to throw a lot of red paint." Ash also commented on the Steele case. He pointed out that the jury which awarded money to Steele in the first trial had determined that Steele was *not* a cofounder of Litton. It made the award because it believed that Thornton had given an oral promise to Steele, although Steele could produce no witnesses to any such conversation. Ash says that after Steele died, there was really no choice but to settle out of court, since juries tend to be extremely generous to widows and orphans. "We settled as the better part of valor," he insists.

It is all very complicated—and likely to remain so.

At any rate, Thornton and Ash *did* leave Hughes Aircraft. They wanted to build another company that would sell the products of advanced technology, but they intended to go a step beyond Hughes Aircraft by seeking commercial customers as well as mil-itary. Rather than starting from scratch, they decided to buy an established electronics company and use it as a base for expan-sion. The company that caught their fancy was Litton Industries of California, based in San Carlos, a producer of magnetrons, which had 250 employees and revenues of about $2 million a year. They already knew the company well, since it was a supplier to Hughes Aircraft.

Small as the company was, it seemed too costly for Thornton, Ash and a third partner, Hugh W. Jamieson, who had headed the Hughes Aircraft radar-development group. The owner, Charles V. Litton, wanted more than a million dollars, while the partners had a combined net worth of perhaps $200,000. They went looking for backers, and among the financiers they approached was the legendary Joseph Patrick Kennedy. Finally in November 1953 they worked out a deal with Lehman Brothers, which raised $1.5 million for them by selling stock and bonds in the new venture. Having acquired the company, the partners decided to change its name to the Electro-Dynamics Corporation. But this drew a protest from the giant General Dynamics Corporation, which had an Electro-Dynamics division. So they reverted to the original name, Litton Industries, with the words "of California" deleted. Why not Thornton Industries? " 'Thornton Industries' is not easy to say," says Thornton.

Under the new management Litton Industries began expanding and diversifying at a furious pace. By achieving most of its early growth through acquisitions, it set an example that came to be imitated by many other companies during the fifties and sixties. Litton acquired seventeen companies in its first five years, propelling its total revenues to $82 million for the fiscal year ending July 1958. Approximately half of those revenues came from a single acquisition, the Monroe Calculating Machine Company, a manufacturer of desk calculators and other small office machines. By the end of its first decade Litton Industries had completed forty acquisitions and its total revenues had soared to $553 million. Just five years later the acquisitions totaled about a hundred, while revenues reached $1.8 billion. "We will never reach our destination," Thornton stated at the time. "The opportunities were there," he now recalls. "We wanted to grow fast and take advantage of them. If you grow too slowly and the opportunities are there, someone will see them and take the step. New technological advances were being made every six months or a year. We were back in a time when technology was exploding."

The company's tremendous growth was accompanied by a phenomenal surge in its earnings per share—the ultimate measure of business success. From the end of fiscal 1957 to the end of fiscal 1967, for example, Litton's per-share earnings increased at an average annual rate of more than 33 percent, placing it sixth in that category among the *Fortune* 500 companies. The rise in earnings per share produced, naturally enough, a boom in Litton's stock. Someone who had bought $10,000 worth of Litton in

1954, when it first traded in the open market, could have sold it for over a million dollars at the all-time high in 1967. Thornton and Ash, as cofounders, had been able to buy substantial amounts of stock at just ten cents a share. At the peak price, Thornton's stock was worth more than $100 million, while Ash's was worth more than $30 million. Each of them had invested only a few thousand dollars. Hugh Jamieson also did well in Litton stock, but he felt that he should have been allowed to buy more of the ten-cent shares. He left Litton to start his own electronics company in 1958, and the next year he sued Thornton and Ash, who settled out of court for an amount said to be in the millions. Jamieson's suit was roughly similar to the one filed by Emmett Steele, although Thornton and Ash never denied that Jamieson was a cofounder.

Litton's days of glory came to an abrupt end in 1968. The company reported that its earnings for the January quarter that year had declined by more than 50 percent from the corresponding quarter of 1967. It was the first earnings drop in Litton's fourteen-year history, and it stunned the investment community. Thornton and Ash had been doing so well for so long that their company seemed immune to business cycles, production breakdowns, marketing errors and all the other reversals that beset ordinary enterprises. There had always been the risk that the company, by expanding and diversifying so rapidly, might outgrow the ability of its top officers to keep it under control. But Thornton and Ash had seemingly worked out an effective *modus operandi*. They had delegated a great deal of autonomy to the heads of Litton's diverse operations, but they kept close watch on the monthly financial reports so they could move in at the first signs of trouble. Nevertheless, there had been some serious problems, and for some reason they hadn't been caught in time. The company acknowledged setbacks in its business-equipment and shipbuilding operations and admitted in a letter to its shareholders that there had been "deficiencies of management personnel." Many shareholders responded by unloading their stock, and the price plummeted. Ash recalls watching in fascination and horror as "my net worth went down a million a month, twenty-four months in a row." Litton's problems triggered a reaction against the stocks of other conglomerates as well, and the very word "conglomerate" became an obscenity on Wall Street.

Thornton insisted at first that the earnings decline was only temporary and that the stockholders were overreacting. "To us it's not anything," he declared. "There were fifty-seven quarters when it didn't happen. Two, three or four years from now, that one little dip in there will be practically meaningless." But some of the problems that cropped up at Litton during 1968 turned out to be chronic, and the company's earnings curve went into reverse. In the ten years after fiscal 1967, Litton's earnings per share *declined* at an average annual rate of more than 4 percent, this time placing the company 428th out of 500 on *Fortune*'s list of industrials. Indeed, it seemed for a while that the 1967 per-share earnings might stand forever as the company record. The figure finally was surpassed in 1979, but by that time inflation had whittled away more than half of every dollar.

Roy Ash contends, not without justification, that Litton Industries has made an impressive record on balance. "We didn't do badly," he says, "considering that we went from a standing start. Litton is now a darn good company, and it was when I left." The stock price never again approached the heights achieved in 1967, but Ash says the stock was simply overvalued in those days. "For us and others, expectations ran well ahead of realities. What's really at issue is the earnings multiple. You can't charge that to Litton. The multiple was forty times earnings."

Tex Thornton, who doesn't much enjoy talking about the past, believes that Litton has long since gotten over what he calls its "digestion problem." "Those things that didn't work out—we disposed of those. Now we are in good shape. Even with our size now, we've got this going." Thornton turned sixty-five in 1978, but he hasn't yet announced any plans to retire from Litton Industries. "I will," he says. "I don't know when. Maybe when I feel it will do better if I'm not here. I wanta see it a real blue chip, considered in the same category with the GMs and GEs. I feel it's a blue chip today. But that has to be more broadly accepted. You take the benefits that come from Litton Industries. There's 90,000 people employed, and if you include their dependents and the vendors and service people we deal with, there are upward of a million people whose economic livelihood comes from Litton. I take satisfaction from that. The world is a little bit better because I did it."

In its early days Litton Industries attracted and developed a lot of extraordinary young managers. They were drawn to the company by its dazzling growth and generous stock options, and by management's willingness to delegate a great deal of authority to the operating units. There was, however, a clear limit to the managerial opportunities at Litton. Thornton was only forty when the company was founded, while Ash was thirty-five, and neither of them seemed likely to step down for quite a long time. There were plenty of choice positions at the vice presidential level, but anyone who hoped to become a chairman or a president would have to look elsewhere.

That is just what many of Litton's best people did. About two dozen executives left Litton to become chairmen or presidents of other companies—a record that no other company comes close to matching. The defectors became widely known by the whimsical name "Lidos," which stands for Litton Industries dropouts. (Ash says he prefers to call them "Ligs"—Litton Industries graduates.) Most of the Lidos went to companies that seemed puny or insignificant alongside Litton, and for the most part the companies stayed that way. But a few Lidos, taking their cue from Litton, built their companies into giant conglomerates. Fred R. Sullivan, who had been president of Monroe Calculating Machine when it merged with Litton in 1958, stayed with his new employer until 1964, when he was hired as the chief executive of Walter Kidde and Company, a manufacturer of fire extinguishers and fire-detection equipment. Sullivan went on an acquisition spree that raised Kidde's revenues from less than $50 million to over $2 billion within fifteen years. Another Lido, George Thomas Scharffenberger, who served with Litton from 1959 to 1966, has built City Investing Company from a real-estate operation with revenues of some $8 million into a conglomerate with revenues of $5 *billion*. Harry Gray, who had been a member of Litton's management from 1954 to 1971, joined United Technologies, which was already about Litton's size, as chief executive. United was mainly involved in aircraft production when Gray took over, but he proceeded to acquire Otis Elevator, Essex International (a wire manufacturer) and a few other sizable companies as well, more than quadrupling United's revenues by the end of the decade, which made it more than twice as big as Litton.

Of all the men who have departed Litton for greater glory, none can surpass the achievement of a tall, lanky Texan named Henry Earl Singleton. An engineer by training, Singleton had come to Litton in 1954 and was responsible for one of the company's greatest technological developments—a reliable lightweight inertial-navigation system for use in long-range missiles. When he left in 1960 it was not to join an established company, but rather to start one of his own, called Teledyne. He wanted, he said, to build "a great corporation. GM, AT&T, Du Pont—I want to build a company of that type."

In the Litton style, he built Teledyne into a conglomerate with heavy emphasis on advanced technology. The company, based in Los Angeles, still trails Litton in revenues; in 1979 it grossed $2.7 billion. But in the growth of its earnings per share, and in the buoyancy of its stock, Teledyne has outclassed not only Litton but most other large companies as well. In the ten-year period ending with 1979, Teledyne's per-share earnings grew at an average annual rate of more than 35 percent, good enough for eleventh place in that category on the *Fortune* 500 list. Teledyne's average annual return to investors—a measure that includes stock appreciation plus any dividends—came to nearly 18 percent, placing the company forty-third on the *Fortune* list. Singleton himself has done very nicely as a result of the sprightly stock-market performance. From an original investment of $225,000, his holdings have appreciated in recent years to around $200 million. Singleton lives in appropriate splendor, in a huge mansion of the antebellum style, behind a heavy iron gate in Bel Air.

He values his privacy. He only rarely submits to interviews, and even more rarely to questions from financial analysts. He thus remains, after all these years, something of an enigma. The consensus holds that he is brilliant. One can cite not only his business achievements, but also the fact that he is capable of playing several games of chess simultaneously—*while wearing a blindfold.* He is also frequently described as arrogant. Although his company has been publicly held almost from the start, Singleton is sternly proprietary by nature and not overly responsive to the will of his shareholders. *Forbes,* while not quoting him directly, once summed up his attitude this way: "If you don't like the way I am running the company, get out of the stock." Teledyne ultimately is controlled by a board of directors, of course, but it is a small one—six members including Singleton—and each member has been a close friend of the founder for many years.

Singleton is reputed to be something less than gracious with his subordinates. Once, when it was suggested that he congratulate a division manager for an outstanding financial performance, Singleton replied: "The fact that I didn't comment otherwise should be congratulations enough." A former Teledyne executive suggested that Singleton had a fondness for "managing by shock treatment." "Singleton's technique," he went on, "is to do something big, to do it abruptly, to let everybody know who's boss, instead of trying to negotiate on a low-key basis."

In my own encounter with Singleton, at his office in Century City, I found him to be shy, perhaps a bit nervous, but friendly. Although well past sixty, he remains in excellent shape—thanks, no doubt, to his penchant for jogging and calisthenics. A man of handsome, rugged countenance, he smiled a good deal, though it seemed to require an effort. His voice, of medium depth, just barely betrays his Texas origins. Preoccupied for much of his life with scientific and financial matters, he is not an eloquent speaker.

He was born in 1916 in the little town of Haslet, near Fort Worth, the son of a well-heeled farmer and cattle rancher. "I probably had an orientation toward business all along," he recalls. "My father was an independent businessman who never had a boss from the time he was eighteen years old." As a youth Singleton enjoyed reading about the early titans of American business, the men who built the railroad, steel and oil industries. He was intrigued by the critical works, like Matthew Josephson's *The Robber Barons,* as well as by the more sympathetic biographies. Today he laments the fact that business books aren't used more widely in the public schools. "Those accounts were more interesting to me than some of the political histories that dominate the classrooms," he says.

Despite his interest in business, a military career seemed more appealing when Singleton graduated from high school. He entered the U.S. Naval Academy at Annapolis with the Class of 1939, but he developed an ulcer and received a medical discharge after his junior year. He switched over to the Massachusetts Institute of Technology, where he majored in mathematics, receiving both his bachelor's and master's degrees in 1940. When the U.S. entered the war he signed up with the Navy Department in Washington, working first to develop anti-mine devices, and later participating in a study of anti-submarine tactics. One of his colleagues was Reuben Fine, a grandmaster of chess who ranks among the greatest American players of all time. Singleton got to know Fine, and his interest in chess was stimulated. He joined a club in Washington and played in several dozen tournament games during the war years. He doesn't play much anymore, but a decorative chess set is a conspicuous feature in his office at headquarters.

After the war Singleton found it difficult to settle down. He spent a year and one-half working on patents and inventions for the International Telephone and Telegraph Company, then returned to MIT to earn his doctorate. Today he likes very much to be called *Dr.* Singleton, and you may be sure that his subordinates oblige him. At MIT he served as a research assistant in electronics and as an instructor in electrical engineering. "I thought of pursuing an academic career," he recalls, "but I never could stay with that. I didn't really like it. A big institution—I don't like to be part of a big institution, with all these rules and things you're stuck with. No, it isn't that I don't like that. It's just that something else pulls me away from it—the idea of trying unpredictable things. Some people go out and travel around in the jungle, but business is sufficiently unpredictable for me."

After receiving his doctorate in 1950, Singleton spent seven months as a research scientist with General Electric. Then he joined Hughes Aircraft as a project engineer, working on fire-control systems. He stayed only a year at the company, which he dubbed "Howard Hughes College" because so many talented people went elsewhere to make a name for themselves. Although he worked at Hughes while Thornton and Ash were there, he didn't get to meet them until after he had "graduated." From Hughes, Singleton moved to North American Aviation, the aerospace company, where he was assigned to the electronics division, developing navigation equipment for aircraft.

In 1954 he was offered an opportunity to work on related projects at Litton. The job offer came from Hugh Jamieson, the one Litton founder he *had* met while working at Hughes Aircraft. Because Litton gave its operating people so much autonomy, Singleton saw this as a chance to build, in effect, a business of his own, without risking his own money. It seemed the best of all possible worlds, and he was delighted to accept.

Other scientists and other companies had been working for years to develop inertial-guidance systems for long-range missiles. The systems were supposed to automatically regulate the course and stability of airborne missiles, while resisting any attempts to jam them. Some systems had in fact been devised, but they were ruled out because they were too complicated to be reliable, and because they weighed too much—upward of 500 pounds. Singleton was given a team of six scientists and engineers and was instructed to come up with a practical system. Within three years, a phenomenally short time, they produced a working model that weighed just fifty pounds. Litton went on to become a leading manufacturer of inertial-guidance systems not only for missiles, but also for aircraft, both military and commercial. Singleton was proclaimed a hero, and was given a major promotion to vice president and general manager of the Electronic-Equipment Division. From practically nothing the division's sales surged to $80 million during his time at Litton.

There are conflicting explanations for Singleton's departure from the company in August 1960. Some sources say that he became contemptuous of Litton's top management, considering himself "better qualified" to run the company than Ash and Thornton. Others say that there was a more specific cause—a "personality clash" with Ash. Singleton himself explains that he was simply satisfying his youthful urge to have "a business of my own." "When I went to Litton," as he once remarked, "I needed money and experience. I got both there." He says that he got along "extremely well" with both Ash and Thornton and that he was "treated very well." Ash and Thornton, for their part, have been respectful if not effusive in their public comments about

Singleton. Thornton called him "a very able scientist, a realist, and a straightforward guy."

Singleton was already forty-three by the time he founded Teledyne—rather old for a rookie entrepreneur. "I've always felt I had to be really fairly deliberate about everything," he explains, "and I guess that's part of it. I thought on numerous occasions about starting companies before Teledyne. In the past I couldn't quite see how I was likely to succeed. I think I wanted to have better feelings for how problems would work out." He thought his best course would be to concentrate on electronic components and equipment, his specialty at Litton, and to build a solid base of customers within the federal government—as Litton had. "Eventually I felt I knew enough about how to obtain government contracts, and that I would be given a fair amount of business," he recalls. "I felt very confident that there would be no problem about maintaining at least *some* level of business—that it would be successful in a business way. It wasn't a major thought—could I have a business that would survive. I felt sure *that* would happen. The problems came later, in how do you keep on growing and building up."

He started out with a partner. George Kozmetsky, who had been Singleton's deputy at Litton, matched him dollar for dollar when it came time to make the initial investment. A financial man by training, but well versed in scientific matters as well, Kozmetsky had received his doctorate in commercial science at Harvard, had taught at Harvard and Carnegie-Mellon University, and had also worked for Hughes Aircraft before going to Litton in 1954. Both Singleton and Kozmetsky had become fairly wealthy from their Litton stock options. They each put down $175,000 in cash at the beginning, and they each added $50,000 later on. They used the money to buy three tiny companies in the Los Angeles area—Amelco, Inc., a job shop that would give them "a place to work"; Handley, Inc., which made potentiometers; and the Mercury Transformer Corporation. The total revenues of these companies came to about a million dollars. Singleton and Kozmetsky needed a lot more cash if they were going to make all the acquisitions they wanted. They obtained $1.8 million from a stock placement arranged through Lehman Brothers and also received backing from Arthur Rock, a venture capitalist. There was never any doubt as to who was boss. Singleton started off as chairman, chief executive, president and treasurer, while Kozmetsky settled for executive vice president and secretary. Having become a millionaire many times over, Kozmetsky left his job with Teledyne in 1966 to become dean of the College of Business Administration at the University of Texas. He has continued to serve as a director of the company.

It took Singleton only a few years to build Teledyne into a major company. Like other conglomerates, it was a great favorite of investors during the sixties, and its stock usually sold at more than forty times earnings. It could therefore use relatively small amounts of stock as "currency" to buy up companies selling at much lower price-earnings multiples. Teledyne made 145 acquisitions in all, and its revenues leaped to $32 million in 1963, to $257 million in 1966 and to $1.3 billion in 1969.

When investors turned sour on the conglomerates, Teledyne's stock was driven way down. Singleton then ceased to acquire other companies. Instead he had Teledyne buy huge amounts of its own stock, which he considered grossly undervalued. During the early and middle seventies Teledyne made a series of tender offers for its stock at prices ranging from $14 to $40 a share. The offering price was always above the market price, so the offers evoked a tremendous response. By the time Teledyne had ceased buying, the number of outstanding shares had declined from more than 40 million to around 13 million. This had a dramatic effect on Teledyne's earnings per share. With the number of outstanding shares reduced by two-thirds, the per-share earnings would have risen sharply even if *total* earnings remained flat. But total earnings did not remain flat—they more than sextupled between the end of 1969 and the end of 1979. The combination of a sharp gain in earnings and a massive reduction in shares produced a 1,990 percent rise in earnings per share for the ten-year period, and this in turn was reflected in the stock market. Those investors who considered themselves fortunate to bail out of the stock at $40 watched in chagrin as the price topped $150 by the end of 1979.

With all the acquisitions that Teledyne made, it was perhaps inevitable that some would cause the company trouble. In 1968 it purchased Packard-Bell Electronics, a manufacturer of television and stereo sets and defense products—only to find that it couldn't make a go of the television and stereo operations, which had to be shut down. Teledyne also has had some scary moments with its Argonaut Insurance subsidiary. It bought Argonaut and another insurance company, United Insurance Company of America, in 1969. This seemed a radical departure from the original plan—to acquire high-technology companies—but Singleton explained that he wanted "the stable, growing base it gives us to continue our growth." In fact, insurance dealt the company's earnings growth a temporary setback. In 1972 Argonaut, which had been involved primarily with workmen's compensation and liability insurance, moved in a big way into medical-malpractice insurance, becoming one of the major underwriters in that field. But it was just around this time that juries began awarding huge sums to the victims of medical malpractice, and Argonaut was badly shaken. Argonaut raised its rates sharply, causing some doctors in California and New York to start a job action. Singleton stepped in and fired most of the top executives at Argonaut, and in 1974 he pulled the company completely out of the medical-malpractice business, leaving Argonaut with a $104.5 million write-off for the year. This weighed heavily on Teledyne's overall earnings, which slumped by 52 percent from 1973.

At the peak of the insurance crisis, Singleton liquidated Argonaut's investment portfolio, in case the losses turned out to be even worse than anticipated. After the crisis passed he found himself with about $400 million in cash to reinvest. He shunned the bonds and other fixed-income securities favored by most insurance companies, sinking the money instead into the common stocks of more than a dozen large companies. In several companies he wound up with more than 20 percent of the stock, giving him effective control. This naturally provoked a great many rumors. Was Singleton planning a forcible takeover of any of these companies? Singleton himself denied it, insisting that he simply considered the stocks undervalued and that they were all straightforward investments.

Still, many people found it intriguing that Singleton made by far the largest investment—well over $100 million—in Litton Industries, giving Teledyne more than a quarter of the stock in his erstwhile employer. "Maybe," as A. F. Ehrbar speculated in *Fortune,* "Henry Singleton will decide that he really would like to try his hand at running Litton after all." Whatever Tex Thornton might privately feel about such a prospect, he has kept his cool in public. Thornton, who owns only 3 percent of Litton's stock himself, says he felt "flattered" when he heard that Teledyne had bought so heavily into his company. "Henry having been with Litton a number of years, I didn't think there was anything wrong with it," he remarks. "I see him socially now and then, and we never talk about the company. We say, 'How are you?' 'Fine, how are you?' "

Thornton may actually be fortunate to have so much of his company's stock in Singleton's care. Very few companies are safe nowadays from hostile takeovers, and Litton, with its stock selling below book value, was a likely target. Singleton, on the record at least, is not a predator. He has hardly ever tried to take over another company without the consent of its management. But many other tycoons are considerably less scrupulous, and Thornton might easily have fared worse. For example, his company might have attracted the interest of Thomas Mellon Evans.

Evans, who has been active in business since the early 1930s, used to be described as the last of the corporate raiders—that is, until corporate raids became popular again during the seventies. He still qualifies as perhaps the most feared American businessman of the twentieth century. As the proprietor of not one but two *Fortune* 500 companies, H. K. Porter and the Crane Company, he has presided over more than eighty acquisitions. Some of those acquisitions have been friendly enough, but many others were completed over the terror-stricken protests of the incumbent managements. Evans is anathema to professional managers —or at least to those who don't meet his standards. When Evans moves in on a company, the top executives are usually sent packing. He concentrates on companies that he considers grossly undervalued in the stock market, and in his eyes a low stock value is often a sign of mismanagement. Evans has the entrepreneur's inherent disdain for professionals—and then some. He estimates that among today's major companies, "a good percentage, maybe 20 or 30 percent, are not well run." Evans can also be rough on the professionals that he himself hires, and there is reportedly a heavy turnover in the executive ranks at his companies. "He'll call somebody a dumb bastard or an ignorant son of a bitch," a former Porter executive recalled, "and the guy has no choice but to put up with it—until he can find another job." One of his executives used to keep a sign near the window that read: "Happiness is just three feet away." And there is an old saying that an optimist is an Evans employee who brings his lunch to work. But Evans himself denies that he is unduly harsh with the people who work for him. "All we want is for somebody to do well," he says. "As long as a guy is honest and trying, and gets reasonable results, that's all you can do in a business." When he talks that way, Evans seems a model of sweet reason.

After a company comes under his control, Evans sends in a team of handpicked subordinates to overhaul it. They will spruce up the product line, modernize the financial controls, install new machinery, liquidate the inventory and other surplus assets, and whip the sales staff to new heights of enthusiasm. Above all, they will cut costs. Evans is absolutely ruthless about excess costs— which often means excess *people*. It isn't only the managers who get fired when he takes over; his specter is just as fearsome to the rank and file. The fundamental purpose of an Evans takeover, as one writer so aptly described it, is to "generate cash in every conceivable way to buy outright other companies, which are then amalgamated into the parent to generate cash in every conceivable way to help buy outright more companies . . . etc."

Whatever one may think of his methods, there is no question that Evans has succeeded brilliantly. He is a financial genius with a mind that has been compared favorably to a high-powered computer. His sense of a company's underlying value is practically infallible. He almost never loses money on an investment. Porter's revenues have risen from less than a million to more than a half-billion since Evans took over the company in 1939, while Crane's revenues have soared from around $300 million to well over $1 billion since he became the boss in 1959. Although neither Porter nor Crane is involved in glamorous, high-technology industries, both of them consistently rank among the biggest gainers in per-share earnings, and the growth of their stock has been outstanding.

The greatest single beneficiary of all this success has been Evans himself, who continues to hold a majority of Porter's stock and a substantial minority of Crane's. His personal fortune, which also includes ownership of a horse-breeding farm and majority ownership of a brokerage firm and a television station, has been estimated at more than $100 million. His hobbies, naturally enough, are a rich man's hobbies—not only racehorses, but also art and antiques, hunting and travel. He reads a lot—"novels, best-sellers, not serious reading. I like to read about histories of business. I've read books about Andrew Carnegie that they tried to squelch, how he started the corporation. I haven't seen many business histories lately. Not enough of them are done."

Evans is addicted to the stock market, and he spends a lot of his time at the headquarters of his brokerage firm, Evans and Company, on Park Avenue in Manhattan. No matter what else he is doing, he keeps a steady eye on the stock prices as they slide across two viewing screens, one at each end of his office. Sitting there in his dark blue pinstriped suit, he could pass for a Soviet cartoonist's caricature of an American capitalist. Only the top hat is missing. An interview with Evans can be disconcerting. The interviewer is seated well off to the side, to give Evans a clear view of the screen, and what with the stock symbols and the fact that Evans seems hard of hearing, many questions must be repeated. When the answers finally come, they are usually curt, and delivered in a gravelly voice that is close to a growl.

He was once described as "the corporate embodiment of Jaws, the great white shark" by a New Jersey congressman who resented the closing of some Crane Company plants in that state. The gibe was meant to characterize his business methods, not his appearance, but it seemed gratuitously cruel, since Evans does look something like a shark, with his broad head, wide mouth and relentless eyes. He is of medium height, stocky and practically bald, with a corona of white hair—not handsome, certainly, but formidable.

Evans was born in Pittsburgh in 1910 and was orphaned at the age of eleven. He belonged to the famous Mellon family of Pittsburgh, his paternal grandmother having been a cousin of Andrew Mellon, the longtime secretary of the treasury. But neither Thomas nor his parents shared in the multi-billion-dollar fortune amassed by the principal family members. His father, a banker, left him an inheritance of just $15,000. Thomas and his sister went to live with an aunt, and his inheritance helped put him through school. But he *was* affluent enough to afford the very best, attending the Shady Side Academy, Pittsburgh's most exclusive private school, and earning his bachelor's degree in 1931 at Yale, where he majored in economics. He had a strong interest in sports and played on the football and basketball teams at Shady Side, but he couldn't qualify for any of the teams at Yale, and he even failed in an attempt to become manager of the tennis team.

Above all, Evans loved business. "It just always appealed to me. It was the fun of making money, the challenge—the usual reasons." This attitude was to prove crucial to his success. The most successful businessmen do not merely put business before pleasure. They actually take pleasure—often their only pleasure—from business. The workaday world is their heaven, and the jangle of the cash register is the music of the spheres.

The name Mellon was practically synonymous with Big Business in Pittsburgh, so it is hardly surprising that Evans was pulled in that direction. With a bankroll that was slender by Mellon standards, he had every inducement to prove himself. He denies, however, that he felt any compulsion to compete with the wealthier members of the family.

He started off actually working within the Mellon empire. He had been quite friendly with William Larimer Mellon, Jr., a distant cousin whose father was chairman of the Gulf Oil Corporation. Evans wanted to follow in his own father's footsteps as a banker, and he approached William, Sr., in the fall of 1931, to seek his aid in obtaining a job with the Mellon National Bank. But it wasn't exactly a prosperous time for the banking industry. "He said he couldn't get me a job at the bank, they were laying people off," Evans recalls. Instead he was given a job at $100 a month as a clerk and assistant in William Mellon's own office. He filed papers, made out payrolls and learned at the master's knee, picking up from William "the practical fiscal knowledge that made his economics major at Yale come to life," as one observer wrote. It looked as though he might spend his career at Gulf. "Anybody was lucky to have a job at all in those days," he recalls. "I thought it would be great to have my own business, but I couldn't figure out a way to do it."

He didn't have the capital to go into business for himself, but by chance he discovered a way to get it. While perusing the September 1935 issue of *Fortune,* he came across an article about Floyd Odlum, the bootstrapping entrepreneur who had founded the Atlas Corporation, a holding company. The article mentioned that Odlum had raised capital at a crucial moment by renting collateral from a wealthy friend. William Mellon had always encouraged Evans' own entrepreneurial ambitions, so Evans told him about Odlum's money-raising scheme. Mellon was fascinated, and he agreed to try a similar arrangement with Evans. He let Evans borrow 1,000 shares of his Gulf Oil stock, which at the time had a total market value of more than $50,000. Evans could use the shares as collateral to borrow money from a bank, provided he invested the money in more Gulf stock. In return for the loan, Evans would pay Mellon an annual fee equal to 3 percent of the value of the borrowed shares. It was a reasonable interest rate, but if the deal was to be worthwhile for Evans, the value of Gulf's stock would have to rise. And if the value of the stock dropped sharply, the bank would sell out the borrowed shares to recoup the loan. "That would have been very bad," Evans says, chuckling. "We didn't discuss that. Heh, heh." Evans speculates that Mellon had reason to believe that Gulf's stock would not go down. "He may have known that earnings were going to be better. I don't know what influenced him." In fact, Gulf and a lot of other stocks made nice gains during the general market recovery of 1936 and 1937. Evans wound up with a $40,000 profit.

He soon found a use for the money. An old Pittsburgh company, H. K. Porter, stood on the brink of bankruptcy. Once a leading manufacturer of steam locomotives, it now had only forty employees and was losing money on revenues of just $700,000 a year. Porter had put out a $1 million bond issue in 1926, but it hadn't been able to pay interest on the bonds since 1931. A committee of bondholders was seeking to reorganize the company, and one of the members was a friend of Evans. Porter looked like an interesting gamble, and Evans shelled out $15,000 of his stock-market winnings to buy some bonds, which were selling at 10 to 15 cents per dollar of face value. The creditors finally pushed

Porter into bankruptcy, and in 1939 the courts formally declared that the stockholders had been wiped out, turning the company over to the bondholders. The bondholders received new convertible preferred and common stock in proportion to their holdings. Evans, who had accumulated more bonds than anyone else, emerged as the largest shareholder of Porter, and he was named president of the company.

Evans made a zealous effort to drag Porter into the black. He moved the office workers into the factory and sold the headquarters building and other real estate to generate cash. He expanded the company's product line, on the theory that "you can't live on locomotives, because they never seem to wear out." Using the existing facilities, Porter began making pressure vessels and evaporators for the chemical, food and oil industries. His connection with the Mellons once again stood him in good stead. Charles Veatch, an officer of the Mellon Bank, agreed to lend Porter $25,000 to help finance its comeback.

Veatch also interceded for Evans when some of the Porter directors mounted a challenge to his leadership. Evans was a blunt fellow even then, and the directors, many of them conservative businessmen who had been connected with the company before the bankruptcy, were offended enough to try ousting him from the presidency. Veatch put down the insurrection by declaring that his bank had made its loan because of its faith in the Evans management, and that the loan would be recalled if Evans fell. Evans was chastened by the experience. He converted his preferred stock into common shares and also used much of his spare cash to buy more common stock and gain full control of the company.

Evans realized that no matter how hard he drove his employees, and no matter how sharply he cut back on costs, Porter would never grow very large unless it acquired some other companies. In pursuing acquisitions, he developed a procedure that was to prove repeatedly effective over a period of many years. He concentrated on small, family-owned companies that were faring poorly because of mismanagement. Often he found that the family members were anxious to get their money out and that he could buy these companies for well under their book value. "In the forties and fifties there were many businesses like this that were not well run," he recalls. "Maybe the guy who inherited the job didn't care about it. I generally bought values. I'm not smart enough to know how many times earnings Xerox should be. I check the assets, the fundamental values." He would almost always buy with cash, in part because that was what the families wanted, but also because Evans didn't care to dilute his control of Porter by issuing new stock. He confined himself to industrial companies—"we didn't know merchandising"—and he shied away from those with a particularly long string of deficits, fearing that they might be incurable even under his magic touch.

Porter was still small and a bit shaky when World War II came along. Evans was theoretically draftable, although he was thirty-one years old and a father by Pearl Harbor Day. He says he was "tempted" by the offer of an Army commission, but he felt that he could be more effective on the home front as a defense supplier, and this entitled him to a deferment. Evans took the company into the munitions business by acquiring a plant in Blairsville, Pennsylvania, getting the Navy to equip it, and turning out heavy-caliber shells. Thanks to his knack for cost cutting, his company was able to underbid the competition and get a series of large orders. Porter also bought a pump company in New Jersey which had some contracts from the Navy and the Maritime Commission. Porter's revenues jumped from $2 million in 1941 to $9 million in 1943, largely on the strength of its defense work. During 1944, Evans negotiated a deal to ensure that Porter would remain strong after the war ended. It was his biggest transaction up till then, and one of his shrewdest ever. For $2.7 million he bought an Illinois freight-car company and its subsidiary, a manufacturer of chemical-processing equipment, which between them had net assets of $5.5 million, including a $3.5 million cash horde. While keeping the chemical-processing business (and the cash), he later resold the freight-car facilities alone for $2.5 million.

Occasionally a family would balk at selling its company for less than book value—an essential ingredient of any Evans deal. But with his astounding grasp of finance, Evans usually could devise a deal that satisfied both himself and the sellers. "Negotiating with them, you could get *some* plan that appealed to them," he remarks. During 1954, for example, he wanted to buy the McLain

Fire Brick Company, of Pittsburgh. The company was recommended to him by Charles Veatch, who at that point was a director of both McLain and Porter. The owners of McLain were
asking $4 million, which was a bit more than book value, but
Evans worked out a formula that gave Porter everything it wanted
for just $1,650,000, while netting the family about the same
amount, after taxes, that it would have gotten from a straight $4
million purchase. Evans outlined the deal to Veatch this way:
"Tell 'em we will give them $750,000 for the $2,600,000 in fixed
assets. Then they get back about 80 percent of the difference,
some $1,500,000, as a tax refund. We give them 90 percent for
their $1 million inventory. That's another $80,000 back out of
taxes. So it adds up that they get $1,650,000 in cash from us, plus
about a $1,500,000 tax refund—over $3 million after it's all
worked out. This may be a shade better than if they had got their
$4-million asking price and paid $1 million capital-gains tax.
They keep the corporation intact, make an investment trust out
of it and pass the stock along in their estates. Ask them what more
they want." Veatch, no slouch himself when it came to finance,
had to ask Evans to repeat the offer more slowly so he could write
it down. The McLain family was skeptical at first, but after the
Internal Revenue Service confirmed what Evans had said, the
transaction was completed.

The larger his company grew, the more feared he became.
With his unsentimental, uncompromising views about efficiency,
there was no telling whom or what would be declared expendable
once he took over a company. He began to meet resistance from
management. In 1954 he made an offer for the Laclede-Christy
Company, a publicly held manufacturer of refractories based in
St. Louis. Management campaigned against Evans with newspaper ads and letters to the shareholders, but the rebellion was
easily squelched, since all the executives together controlled only
2 percent of the stock, and Evans had made an attractive offer.
Evans was to face many more battles with many more managements, and he didn't always win.

After operating almost exclusively through H. K. Porter for
two decades, Evans decided to branch out during the late fifties.
A poor cousin of the Mellons could hardly be expected to stop
with just one company. In 1957, using his own money rather than

Porter's, he began buying shares in the Crane Company, a manufacturer of plumbing fixtures and valves based in Chicago. A century-old company with revenues of some $300 million, Crane had been faltering lately, and its stock was selling at less than book value. After spending about $4 million to accumulate 6 percent of the stock, Evans approached a friend on the Crane board, R. Arthur Williams, and asked for an introduction to the top managers. In January 1958 he had lunch with the chairman, Mark Worden Lowell, and the president, Neele Edward Stearns, who served as chief executive. He told them he thought his stockholdings entitled him to a seat on the board, which they did not dispute, but he also suggested that he should be allowed to set policy for the company—which they found troublesome. A few weeks later Evans was told that he could not be a director of Crane, that another investor had come to the rescue of management. The "white knight," as heroes of this type are known, was Gurdon Weller Wattles, a Wall Street operator who controlled several companies. Through one of those companies, Electric Auto-Lite, Wattles intended to buy more than 13 percent of Crane's stock, a move that would make Evans, with his 6 percent, just another shareholder.

Evans was enraged, and he vowed that he would take over Crane in any event. He hired a Washington lawyer named Alfons Landa, the leading expert on proxy fights in those days, and Landa spent the better part of 1958 gathering support for Evans and plotting his campaign. Evans and Landa visited Mrs. Emily Crane Chadbourne, an octogenarian and the only living daughter of the company founder, Richard Teller Crane. She owned about 5 percent of the company's shares, and she agreed to back Evans after Evans agreed to put her grandnephew, Robert Crane, on the board of directors. When Crane's revenues and earnings continued to slide during 1958, even Gurdon Wattles was persuaded to throw in his lot with Evans, and the Crane management capitulated. Chairman Lowell and President Stearns resigned, and Evans became the chairman and chief executive officer at a meeting of the board in April 1959. Three months later, after Crane made a tender offer for a large amount of its own stock, Wattles sold the shares he controlled, and the last potential threat to Evans' supremacy was eliminated.

In his usual swift, decisive manner, Evans set about reforming Crane. By the end of 1959 four of the company's six vice presidents were gone, and so were 2,000 of the 18,000 rank and file. Pickets outside Crane's annual meeting that year carried a sign that read: "Money Mad Evans Has No Heart." Seven of Crane's directors resigned, leaving Evans to deal with a cozy little board of just four members—himself included. One of the directors who left was Alfons Landa, who had been appointed when Evans became chairman. Landa was upset by the adverse publicity the new management was receiving, and he also had gotten into a dispute with Evans about his compensation for the takeover campaign.

Evans used Crane to make most of his mergers and acquisitions after 1959, while Porter, having swallowed more than forty companies, was allowed to relax and digest. In fact, Evans gave up the chairmanship of Porter in 1975, stepping aside in favor of his second son, Edward, who by all accounts is a chip off the old block. Under Edward's leadership Porter sprang into action again, successfully completing a hostile takeover of Missouri Portland Cement and a semihostile takeover of Fansteel, Inc., a metal fabricator, and becoming an unwelcome but dominant shareholder of Macmillan, Inc., the publishing company.

Crane tried to annex some good-sized publicly held companies, but it frequently had to back down in the face of ferocious resistance. In 1967, for example, Crane bought a small block of stock in the Westinghouse Air Brake Company, a diversified manufacturer based in Pittsburgh. Evans approached the chairman of the company, Andrew King McCord, but McCord spurned an offer to merge. Crane extended its holdings to 31 percent of the company's stock, and Evans decided to take his case directly to the other shareholders. But management wouldn't let him have the shareholder list, and he had to sue to get it. Westinghouse Air Brake finally escaped Crane's embrace by finding another merger partner instead, American Standard, Inc.

Though it failed to win the company, Crane didn't lose out entirely. It made a nice $5 million profit when it unloaded the shares it had accumulated in hopes of a merger. In fact, this became the pattern for most of Evans' deals during the sixties and seventies. He would buy a minor but significant amount of stock in a company, announce himself to management and make a tender offer for more shares. Management would panic and seek another suitor, and the other suitor would buy back the shares held by Crane for considerably more than they cost. Evans thus found that his frightening reputation, far from being a handicap, was in fact an asset that could be used to generate quick, easy profits in the stock market. He was rebuffed by the Chemetron Corporation, the Diamond M Company and the Morrison-Knudsen Company, to name just a prominent few; yet he made money every time. He says he has suffered only one loss after buying another company's stock—less than $100,000 in the case of the Zapata Corporation, an offshore-oil driller.

Crane made a huge profit in the stock of Anaconda, the copper producer, without even proposing a merger. In August 1975, Evans approached John Bassett Moore Place, Anaconda's chairman, to inform him that Crane was planning a tender offer for up to 5 million common shares, or 22.6 percent of the total. Evans insisted that it was just "a good investment"—Crane was offering $25 worth of subordinated debentures for shares with a book value of $53 each. But it was well known that he had tried unsuccessfully to take over two other companies in the industry, Inspiration Consolidated Copper and Copper Range—making a total profit of more than $2 million in the process. "I thought it would be good to have something under the ground," Evans says. The Anaconda management, fearing that *it* might end up under the ground, immediately swung to the defensive, suing to block the offer and even persuading a congressional committee to start an investigation. Anaconda hired Joseph Flom, a lawyer specializing in takeover battles. Evans claims that Flom arrived at the Crane Company to take a deposition "with twelve other lawyers." Evans asked, "Who's paying for this?" but the question was ignored. A court ruled in favor of Evans, and he went ahead with his tender offer, managing to buy 4.1 million shares of Anaconda—18.6 percent of the total—while paying 20 percent less per share than he had originally intended. The total cost was $82.4 million.

Anaconda began looking for a merger partner and received an offer from Tenneco, a large company that is heavily involved in natural resources. Tenneco wanted to exchange a new convertible stock for Anaconda's common, but Evans found the proposal objectionable, describing the Tenneco stock as "a big roll of wallpaper." He himself sought out another potential buyer, the Atlantic Richfield Company, which was headed by his fellow entrepreneur and good friend Robert Orville Anderson (no relation to Robert Anderson of Rockwell International). Atlantic Richfield obtained 27 percent of Anaconda's shares through a tender offer, and it completed a merger late in 1976 by paying out $34 worth of cash and securities for each remaining share. That gave the Crane Company a profit of $14 a share—or $57.6 million—on its $82.4 million investment. "It's one of the best investments I've ever made," Evans gloated.

By the late seventies tender offers and corporate raids, once considered highly improper by most businessmen, had become thoroughly commonplace. In a period of strong inflation, it was no longer practical to expand companies internally—whether by building new plants or by entering new markets from scratch. While inflation raged, the stock market remained stagnant, and many sound companies in promising industries began to look like bargains. Pressed to perform in a difficult economy, and with all those bargains available, many tycoons simply could not resist. It amuses Evans to see what he calls the "big, establishment" companies doing the sorts of things for which he was ostracized ten, twenty and thirty years ago. "When we made the tender for Westinghouse Air Brake," he remarks, "no New York bank would act as the clearinghouse. Now the Morgan bank is in there every day." It isn't every outcast who enjoys vindication in his lifetime.

The self-made man is the great hero of American folklore. It is more consistent with all the rhetoric about the free-enterprise system to build a company on one's own than to hop onto someone else's bandwagon. The professional managers, probably feeling just a bit guilty, offer the most generous lip service to the entrepreneurs. They are full of praise for the more daring entrepreneurial exploits—while making no particular effort to emulate them.

Some professionals like to suggest that they are really entrepreneurs at bottom. Walter Wriston, for example, speaks of the hierarchy at Citicorp as though it were just one big entrepreneurial convocation. "Most bureaucracies smother entrepreneurship," he says. "But here, if you have an idea and you're tenacious enough, you can get it accepted. . . . Sure, I could have gone and started a chainsaw factory someplace. But if you're in an organization that will honor entrepreneurship and has the capability to absorb the mistakes we all make, it's fun."

The entrepreneurs—the genuine ones, that is—are not necessarily nature's noblemen. As we have seen, many of them had entrepreneurship thrust upon them. And while some of them courageously risked their own money, others relied instead primarily on silent partners. Entrepreneurs are often negligent about developing and encouraging successors. They identify so strongly with their companies that they simply can't bring themselves to share any significant amount of authority. They want to do it all—long after that has become impossible. Retirement rules usually don't mean very much at companies headed by entrepreneurs. The entrepreneurs tend to remain active in their companies even after their mental powers and physical stamina have waned, and this can be a grave disservice to their fellow stockholders. Sometimes the directors have to step in and pry the company loose from the founder's grasp—which is about as much fun as stealing a cub from a mother lion.

If the entrepreneurs have an edge over the other tycoons it is in the boldness of their imaginations. At the core of almost every entrepreneurial success is some brilliant new insight, some masterstroke of originality, that alters the way in which business is done. It may be a new invention or a new marketing technique or a new financial device. This ability to think new thoughts, and to create something out of nothing, is what people call *genius,* and it really is admirable.

There will always be entrepreneurs. No matter what happens to the economy, no matter how long the odds against success, no matter how boldly the federal government imposes its will upon business, there will always be people with the entrepreneurial compulsion. Entrepreneurship is a state of mind as much as anything. There will always be people who cannot work for others, who are compelled to build their own empires in their own images—and there will always be some who succeed. For that we can be thankful. In their ability to find the right path and to see far along it, and in their willingness to take risks, entrepreneurs are the point men for the American economic system. "If it weren't for these people," as one observer puts it, "we'd still be fighting the Indians with flintlocks."

Chapter Nine

Heirs

YOUNG AMERICANS are constantly being told that this is the land of opportunity, where brains, talent and hard work must inevitably pay off. Many of them take this advice quite seriously and work themselves to a frazzle, only to find their progress foreclosed by a boss who wants to pass the leadership along to a son, son-in-law, nephew—or whatever. Yet it can be argued that nepotism is an inevitable concomitant of free enterprise. If it were outlawed in favor of strict meritocracy, then free enterprise would be less "free." Just as the cost of political liberty is a lunatic fringe, so the cost of free enterprise—*one* of the costs, at any rate—is nepotism.

The chief executives of some of the nation's largest and best-known companies are direct descendants of the founders. Campbell Soup, General Tire and Rubber, Motorola and Reynolds Metals were all founded by the fathers of the present leaders. W. R. Grace and Company is headed by a grandson of the founder, while Anheuser-Busch and Weyerhaeuser are led by great-grandsons. McDonnell-Douglas, the aircraft manufacturer, is currently being run by the founder's nephew, while the chief executive of Deere and Company, a manufacturer of farm machinery, got his job by marrying the daughter of his predecessor, who in turn was the founder's great-grandson.

While there are still plenty of dynasties around, their numbers appear to be dwindling. Many large companies that were dominated for decades and even centuries by their founding families

226

have lately been handing over the chief executive's chores to professional managers. During the sixties and seventies professionals succeeded heirs in the top jobs at Dow Chemical, E. I. du Pont de Nemours, Firestone, H. J. Heinz, International Business Machines, Johnson and Johnson, Monsanto, Rockwell International, the Sun Company and Xerox. These are encouraging developments, and it also is encouraging to find that some entrepreneurs have been turning their companies directly over to the professionals, avoiding even a single generation of nepotism. Nathan Cummings of Consolidated Foods, Norton Simon of Norton Simon, Inc., and the late J. Paul Getty of Getty Oil deserve special credit for suppressing any urge to create dynasties.

Nepotism is unfair to everyone. It is obviously unfair to professional managers, shortening their horizons and squelching their ambitions. It is unfair to a company's shareholders when it denies them the best management available. And it is even unfair to those who seem to be its beneficiaries—the heirs. A man who gets to the top without much effort is bound to be plagued, sooner or later, by self-doubt. Joseph Peter Grace, Jr., who became the head of W. R. Grace and Company in 1945 at the age of thirty-one, has frankly admitted as much. "I never will really know where I could have gotten on my own," he said. "Everyone likes to know what he could do against competition with no unfair advantage." He didn't want to join the company originally. "I didn't want any part of it," he told *Fortune.* As a young man he seemed content to be a stereotype of the idle rich. He even played polo, which is about as stereotyped as you can get. But he finally went to work for W. R. Grace under the compulsion of family duty. And when his father suffered a stroke, Peter was stuck there for good. People who aren't rich like Peter Grace might find it hard to sympathize, but there's a lot to be said for freedom of choice.

Often the beneficiary of nepotism will try to prove himself by putting his own, indelible mark on the company he has inherited. The results of these efforts vary widely from company to company and from heir to heir. Some heirs do very well indeed. It would be hard, for example, to imagine a more colossal success than the one enjoyed by the late Joseph Wilson, grandson of a cofounder of the Haloid Company, who transformed that insignificant manufacturer of photographic supplies into the mighty

Xerox Corporation. Peter Grace is another heir who totally changed his company—although with far less spectacular results. At the time he took charge of W. R. Grace, it ran a shipping business—the Grace Line—was a partner in an airline—Panagra —and was heavily involved in South American trading, merchandising, manufacturing, sugar refining and banking. Through literally hundreds of acquisitions and divestitures, he got the company completely out of its original businesses and into chemicals, natural resources, restaurants, retail stores and other consumer enterprises. Because he bought much more than he sold, the company's revenues increased more than twentyfold—to $5.3 billion in 1979. But Grace's earnings per share have been rather sluggish. During the seventies they rose at an average annual rate of 8 percent—not even a mediocre performance.

Some heirs find that their fears of inadequacy are quite justified. A dramatic case in point is Walton Maxey Jarman, whose father, James Franklin Jarman, founded Genesco, Inc., in 1924. Maxey became chairman of the company—then known as General Shoe—when his father died in 1938. Genesco had revenues of $13 million, which was respectable in those days, but Maxey wanted a much bigger company, and he embarked on an ambitious expansion program, buying out a number of other shoe manufacturers, moving into other types of apparel, and getting into retailing as well. When Maxey retired in 1969 at the age of sixty-five, Genesco was the world's largest apparel company, with revenues exceeding a billion dollars.

But alas, the company he built was highly unstable. Maxey's acquisitions were later described in the bitterest terms by his own son, Franklin Maxey Jarman, who became nominal head of the company after Maxey stepped aside. Frank Jarman accused his father of going on a "binge" and a "billion-dollar ego trip" without due regard for the bottom line. "There was no mention of profit or return on investment," he lamented, "just sales." Frank felt that Genesco had been stuck with "companies that nobody else wanted" or that were "only extensions of personalities" and bound to collapse when their original owners departed. Indeed, Genesco's revenues failed to grow once the acquisitions stopped, even though inflation and a strong apparel market were pushing up the take at competing companies. Meanwhile, the company's earnings declined steadily, until in the fiscal year ending July 1975, Genesco recorded the first deficit in its history.

As Genesco began to falter, Maxey found it impossible to stay genuinely retired. Still a director and chairman of the powerful Finance Committee, he gave orders as though he were the chief executive—and the orders were carried out, for he commanded great loyalty on the board and among the veteran employees. Frank Jarman, president of the company but practically powerless, tried repeatedly to seize control from his father before finally succeeding in 1973. The following year, Maxey left the board, and the company, for good. Frank himself was ousted by the directors in January 1977 after failing to significantly improve the company's financial results. Genesco did show a profit in 1976, but in fiscal 1977 it suffered a horrendous $136 million loss—in part because it had to write off some of the businesses acquired during Maxey's regime.

The problems and controversies raised by nepotism have come to be symbolized in recent years by Henry Ford II, that larger-than-life figure who headed the Ford Motor Company—the creation of his grandfather and namesake—for more than three decades. As chief executive of Ford from 1945 to 1979, one of the longest reigns in the history of American industry, Henry II became the most renowned tycoon of the modern era. His name had been famous even before he was born, of course, but Young Henry came to be a celebrity in his own right as well, a rambunctious social lion friendly with presidents, royalty—the elite of the entire world. One knowing observer suggested that Henry II in his heyday was the "most powerful private citizen in the U.S." He had virtually absolute control over his company, the nation's third largest industrial, and for years he was also the dominant figure in the Ford Foundation, the largest foundation by far. On top of that, he commanded a personal fortune of more than $100 million.

Henry's career deserves the attention of a great tragedian. There was the painful beginning, when he pried control of a dying company away from the senile, tyrannical founder. There were the buoyant early years when the company rebounded from morbidity to prosperity amid the postwar automotive boom. There were the glorious middle years, when Henry fell prey to

hubris and began to take on some of the less desirable characteristics of the man he had displaced. At the end there was a downfall of sorts, though not the cathartic kind favored by the ancient
Greeks. Still, Sophocles might have been interested.

Henry had as much reason as any heir to wonder what he
might have achieved on his own. Before joining Ford he had
spent four years at Yale, but didn't graduate. Henry became a
vice president of Ford at twenty-five and president and chief executive officer at twenty-eight—truly a meteoric rise for a college
dropout. Yet he *was* the right man for the top job at Ford—at
least at the time. Ford Motor was strictly a family company then,
without a single outside shareholder. Henry's father was dead,
and his grandfather, though unfit to govern, was trying nonethe-
less. Nobody but a Ford could have succeeded Henry I under the
circumstances, and Henry II, as the oldest grandchild, was the
logical candidate.

He wanted to reshape the company in the image of General
Motors, the leader of the automotive industry. That meant purg-
ing Ford of its notoriously sloppy managerial practices and instill-
ing in it the modern methods that had been developed with such
extraordinary success at GM. At first Henry had the humility—
and the good sense—to hire outstanding professional managers
and give them the run of the place. He recognized that he didn't
have the know-how to save Ford himself, and he left the brunt of
the task to Ernest Breech, whom he had hired away from the
General Motors organization. Breech and his colleagues, many of
them also lured from GM, resuscitated the company and made it
a force to be reckoned with once again.

That might have been the end of the story—with professionals
running the company forever after, while Henry and his family
stood on the sidelines raking in the dividends. But Henry needed
to be more deeply involved than that. His dynastic impulses kept
conflicting with his desire to build a company in the image of
General Motors. The heir's traditional insecurity showed itself in
his inability to tolerate strong subordinates. He eventually
squeezed Ernie Breech out of the company, and during his thirty-
four years as chief executive seven men all told were to serve as
his second in command, only one of them lasting to retirement
age. The repeated beheadings seemed quaint and even amusing

to the outside world, and for a long time they were quietly tolerated by Henry's fellow directors. Even after the company went
public in 1956, the Ford family retained 40 percent of the voting
power. It was still Henry's company. His name, as he liked to
remind people, was on the building. He could seemingly do whatever he liked.

But finally Henry swung the ax once too often. He disposed of
the popular and talented Lee Iacocca in the summer of 1978. A
brilliant marketer, Iacocca was widely regarded as one of the
greatest figures in automotive history, even while serving as a
perennial subordinate to Henry II. Under normal conditions
Iacocca would have become the chief executive—and he certainly
was better equipped for the job than any member of the Ford
family, including Henry II. Despite Henry's protests to the con-
trary, the dismissal of Iacocca was interpreted as a raw attempt to
perpetuate the Ford dynasty, to clear away an impediment to the
eventual rise of Henry's son, Edsel Bryant Ford II, a young man
still serving as a junior executive. To his shock, Henry found that
the directors of Ford—the outside directors, at least—weren't
about to swallow Iacocca's dismissal without a fight. Fight they
did, though ultimately there wasn't anything they could do. The
Iacocca episode badly tarnished Henry's image, however, and
when he stepped aside as chief executive a year or so later, it
didn't seem a moment too soon.

It is easy to understand why Henry Ford II couldn't be objec-
tive about the Ford Motor Company and his family's role in it.
The company was already a rousing success when he was born in
1917, and from his earliest days he was aware that this made him
special. Both his father, Edsel, and his grandfather were worth
many millions, and Granddad in particular was deathly afraid
that Henry and his siblings—two brothers and a sister—would
fall prey to kidnappers, extortionists or cranks. The Ford security
force established a network of informants throughout the country
to detect possible plots against members of the family, and the
Ford grandchildren were kept under tight security at all times—
"as secluded as in an isolation ward," according to one account.
"At Maine in the summer," Henry once recalled, "I never saw
anybody outside of the family except the men who worked at our
stables."

Young Henry had his first actual encounter with the Ford Motor Company at one of its most glorious moments. Not yet three years old, he participated in the ceremonial lighting of a blast furnace during the inauguration of the vast River Rouge plant. His baptism in fire didn't go according to plan, however. He was supposed to strike the first match, but he couldn't remember how, so his grandfather did the honors instead.

Later on, at an age when most boys are begging their parents for a basketball hoop or a bicycle, Henry had the entire Ford Motor Company as his playground. His doting grandfather would take Henry and his brother Benson, the second of the Ford grandchildren, to visit the plants and laboratories on weekends and would give them the run of the place. An executive recalled that the boys, neither of them old enough to have a license, would hop into a car and drive it helter-skelter through a building, "zig-zagging in and out of the columns, seeing how close they could come without hitting." They also enjoyed scrambling the employee time cards, which were arranged in alphabetical order. On Monday mornings the arriving employees would waste time milling around in front of the rack, trying to find their cards so they could punch in and get to work. On one occasion Henry and Benson took charge of the cash register in the plant cafeteria and gave out more in change than they received in payment. "Let them alone," said their grandfather. "They run wild when they're with me because the rest of the time they're cooped up like caged lions."

Henry was sent to the exclusive Hotchkiss preparatory school in Connecticut, but only after an FBI agent, at the family's request, determined that the place would be safe enough. Never a dedicated scholar, he graduated without distinction. "This boy was not notable for his intellectual brilliance," as the headmaster put it. He was a good-natured fellow, however, and made a fair number of friends. Two of his schoolmates tried to get him to run away to sea—a popular form of youthful rebellion in the 1930s—but he regretfully declined. "I'd like to, but I just can't," he said. "Why, my grandfather would get out the militia."

At Yale, another favorite sanctuary for the sons of the rich, he was a member of the Class of 1940. To graduate he had to write a senior thesis, and he chose as his topic "Folkways and Thomas

Hardy." But he had been too busy with his social life and other extracurricular activities to read much Hardy, so he got someone to help him with the paper. His professor recognized that the work was too good to be Henry's, and Henry confessed. He was offered a chance to redeem himself by writing another paper on another subject, but he decided it wasn't worth the effort. He certainly didn't have to worry about the contents of his job résumé. Many years later, while addressing the Yale Political Union, Henry suddenly ad-libbed: "I didn't write this *speech* either."

Henry was married for the first time in July 1940, and at his father's urging he went to work in the River Rouge plant. But he was soon pronounced draftable by his local board, and he joined the Navy in April 1941, just days after the birth of his first child. He was stationed at the Great Lakes Naval Training School in Chicago, with at least the hope that he might go off to sea after all. Instead he remained at the school for two years, becoming assistant to the training director.

His father, only forty-nine years old, died of multiple illnesses in May 1943. Edsel Ford had been president of the Ford Motor Company, and theoretically its chief executive for twenty-four years, but he continued to languish in the shadow of his own father. Now, with Edsel gone, Henry I, pushing eighty, became president of the company once again. This alarmed the authorities in Washington. Ford Motor was a major defense contractor, producing bombers at its Willow Run plant and tanks at River Rouge. The government had advanced $350 million to Ford to expand and adapt its operations for this vital work, and it was worried about what might happen to the production—and its investment—under the senior Ford. Old Henry was unpredictable in the best of times, and he had lately been debilitated by two strokes. The War Production Board seriously considered either nationalizing the Ford plants or putting them under the direction of the Studebaker Corporation, another defense contractor. But it stopped short of these drastic remedies. Instead, Young Henry was given a premature discharge from the Navy in August 1943. As the oldest of the Ford grandchildren, he was expected to take over the company and keep the production lines humming.

He became a vice president of Ford, and the company did fulfill its obligations to the government, but it wasn't until after the war that he really took charge. His grandmother, Clara, and his mother, Eleanor, both worked on Old Henry, urging him to yield the presidency. Old Henry was reluctant, and according to legend he backed down only after Eleanor Ford threatened to sell the huge block of stock she had inherited from Edsel. The vision of outsiders getting a piece of his precious company was too much for Old Henry, even in his dim state of mind.

Before he could assert himself effectively, Young Henry had to get rid of some strange characters who had been an integral part of Old Henry's regime. The most formidable of the lot was Harry Bennett, who as head of Ford's Service Department was in charge of hiring and firing, the payroll department, transportation and communications. Bennett, a onetime sailor and prizefighter—and a crack shot with a pistol—joined the company in 1916, and over the years he became Old Henry's closest associate and most valued adviser. Not even Edsel Ford enjoyed the kind of trust that Old Henry lavished on Bennett. Under Bennett's leadership, the Service Department became, by one account, "a secret police force of gangsters and shady ex-policemen and football players." Bennett and his men used brutal tactics to suppress opposition within the company and challenges from without. In 1937 they severely beat Walter Reuther and other union organizers in the famous "Battle of the Overpass" at River Rouge. When the Ford grandchildren were young, it was Bennett's men who were assigned to protect them. But as an adult, maneuvering for power in his grandfather's company, Young Henry felt it necessary to carry a gun to the office each day, to guard against his former guardians. Within minutes after the board of directors appointed Young Henry as president, he told Bennett to clear out—and once Bennett fell, so did his appointees, more than a thousand by one estimate.

There was serious doubt that Ford Motor could survive for very long. Once the unchallenged leader of its industry, it had declined to a poor third—behind not only General Motors but Chrysler as well. The company's executive talent was woefully weak, its product development was unimaginative, most of its plants and equipment were obsolete, and its financial controls were nonexistent. Although business had been bolstered tremendously by $3.9 billion worth of wartime contracts, Ford was losing money at a rate of more than $9 million a month when Young Henry became president in September 1945.

Henry took a step in the right direction when he hired Tex Thornton and the Whiz Kids to spruce up the financial department, but bringing in Ernie Breech as executive vice president a short while later was his masterstroke. As a high-ranking executive with two decades of experience in the GM organization, Breech, a dapper little man, was thoroughly imbued with the methods that had turned that company from a loose confederation into a unified force unmatched anywhere in American industry. Under Breech and the other GM transplants, Ford made a miraculous recovery. The company jumped solidly into the black in 1947, clearing $63 million after taxes, and the profit rose to $96 million in 1948, to $177 million in 1949, and to $260 million in 1950. By 1953 the company was once again selling more cars than Chrysler. Ford was helped, of course, by the public's desperate hunger for new cars following the wartime moratorium on production. But as Henry himself was to observe many years later: "The credit for pulling this place together and operating it and making it tick and getting us onto an even keel belongs to Ernie Breech. He really did a superb job here and it pulled us through." Breech was rewarded with the title of chairman and alternate chief executive in 1955.

Before Breech came on the job, Henry had to overcome some serious misgivings about hiring him. There was little doubt that Breech could help the company—but where would that leave Henry? Henry was still in his late twenties, with little practical experience in the automotive business, and the company clearly needed an expert administrator. But with a strong, self-confident man like Breech running things, would there really be a place for Henry in the organization, or would he be a mere figurehead? In a worried conversation with his uncle, Ernest Kanzler, who was helping to draw up Breech's contract, Henry wondered whether he would be "abdicating"—telltale word!—by bringing Breech in. Kanzler reassured him, and everybody signed the contract with a reasonably steady hand.

Although he held the title of president and chief executive officer, Henry seemed content at first to simply play goodwill ambassador. He would travel throughout the Ford empire, joking with the troops and dispensing homilies, and he would deliver jolly, self-deprecating speeches to gatherings of outsiders. But the young man who had been such an indifferent student at Hotchkiss and Yale was in fact studying intently now, absorbing every bit of pertinent information about Ford. By the late fifties he was asserting himself forcefully at board meetings and in conferences with his subordinates. He eventually began to undercut Breech's authority, and Breech recognized that he was helpless to do anything about it. It has been suggested that the final break between Henry and Breech, which occurred in 1960, was precipitated by a dispute over the proposed styling of the company's 1962 models. But there didn't have to be a specific cause for the inevitable. "I've graduated, Ernie," Henry finally told his colleague. Breech himself, resigning in July 1960, sagely observed: "Henry doesn't need me anymore."

With Breech gone, Henry took over the chairmanship, and he held onto the presidency as well for a few months, until he could decide on an appropriate Number Two man. He chose Robert McNamara, one of the Whiz Kids who had joined the company fourteen years earlier and who was serving as a group vice president. But McNamara held the presidency of Ford only a few weeks before he was called away to become secretary of defense in the Kennedy Administration. McNamara, as the world knows by now, is a very strong personality, and there undoubtedly would have been a collision with the boss sooner or later if he had remained at Ford. McNamara's successor as president was John Dykstra, who had been recruited from General Motors after Ernie Breech came to Ford. Dykstra turned sixty-five less than two years after he got the job, and according to one executive he "pitched like hell to have his term extended," but Henry wouldn't change the rules for him. Dykstra was succeeded in 1963 by Arjay Miller, another Whiz Kid and a mild-mannered, scholarly sort, who seemingly posed no threats—real or imagined—to Henry Ford and his ego.

Miller held the presidency for five years, and he might have held it still longer if there hadn't been an upheaval in the executive ranks at General Motors. Ford's gigantic rival had undergone one of its periodic management changeovers, and Edward N. Cole had won out over Semon E. Knudsen for the presidency.

"Bunkie" Knudsen remained an executive vice president, and at age fifty-five he wasn't apt to go any further at GM. Rather than drift along in a subordinate role for ten more years, he talked about quitting, and Henry got wind of this before any action was taken. General Motors was always on Henry's mind, of course, and he jumped at the chance to recruit a top executive away from the competition. Early in 1968 he visited Knudsen's home in Bloomfield Hills, riding alone in a GM car to avoid attracting attention from the neighbors, many of them auto executives themselves. He offered Knudsen the presidency, and Knudsen eagerly accepted, signing a contract the following week. Miller was "promoted" to vice chairman, with responsibility for public information, the financial and legal departments, and corporate development. His authority diluted and his pride hurt, he quit a few months later to become dean of the Graduate School of Business at Stanford University. "I thought I was a better man than Knudsen," he remarked.

Nineteen months after he joined Ford, Bunkie Knudsen was fired. Henry walked into his office and brusquely declared, "You'll be leaving." It wasn't the first time that a member of the Knudsen family had come out second best in an encounter with a man named Henry Ford. Bunkie's father, William S. Knudsen, had been in charge of production at Ford, but he left in 1921 and joined General Motors after Old Henry undermined his authority. "Big Bill" Knudsen became the head of Chevrolet, did an outstanding job of building that division, and later became president of GM. His son followed him into General Motors in 1939 and became boss of the Pontiac division in 1956 and an executive vice president of the company in 1966.

Young Henry gave a cryptic explanation for Bunkie Knudsen's dismissal: "Things just did not work out." Years later he elaborated on this theme, observing that "the people that were here and had been here for a long time just didn't accept Knudsen. . . . It was impeding progress and we just had to do something about it." Knudsen undoubtedly did offend some of the men working under him. There were many complaints about his high-handedness. For example, Eugene Bordinat, Jr., the vice president in charge of design, felt that Knudsen meddled excessively in his department, dictating styling changes that didn't necessarily improve the appearance of Ford's cars. Knudsen also insisted that Bordinat, a late sleeper, should get to the office by 9 A.M. Bordinat offered a stylish *double entendre* in appraising his boss: "Knudsen expresses a great interest in our vineyard, and helps me toil it." Knudsen also alienated Lee Iacocca, who at that time was executive vice president of Ford. Twelve years younger than Knudsen, Iacocca was considered next in line for the presidency. He was a master politician with a huge constituency in the executive ranks. He and his allies reportedly helped to sabotage Knudsen by going around and "undoing" his instructions.

Some observers felt that Henry used discontent within the ranks as an excuse—that he actually fired Knudsen because he perceived him as too strong, too presumptuous in his use of power, and therefore a threat to his own rule. Not a palpable threat, perhaps—for Knudsen could hardly have mustered the support to overthrow Henry—but rather a psychological threat, impinging upon the Chairman's sense of security and well-being. "Bunkie thought he had been given the keys to the kingdom," as one Ford executive put it. "He didn't recognize what we all know —that Henry Ford doesn't give the keys to anybody else." Knudsen himself exclaimed: "I think Henry was afraid of losing his Tinker Toy."

After the Knudsen affair, Henry wasn't in any hurry to appoint a new president. He divided the responsibility for company operations among three men. Iacocca became the head of North American operations, Robert Stevenson took over international automotive operations, and Robert Hampson was put in charge of the tractor operations and the Philco subsidiary. Everyone assumed that Iacocca, with his brains, drive and talent, would eventually emerge as the undisputed Number Two man at Ford. And indeed, after a little more than a year of the troika arrangement, Iacocca was named president of Ford.

Lido Anthony Iacocca had leaped from one great triumph to another on his way to the presidency. Born in 1924 in Allentown, Pennsylvania, the son of Italian immigrants, he graduated in 1945 from Lehigh University—where he favorably impressed a visiting Ford recruiter. He joined an eighteen-month training program at the company headquarters in Dearborn and completed it on schedule even though he took nine months out to earn a master's degree in mechanical engineering at Princeton University. He was assigned as an automatic-transmission engineer at a plant in Edgewater, New Jersey, but found that he preferred sales to engineering. He convinced Charles Beacham, Ford's district manager at Chester, Pennsylvania, to hire him as a salesman, and he later became Beacham's assistant. In 1956 he concocted an advertising campaign that attracted the delighted attention of Robert McNamara, then serving as general manager of the Ford division. Iacocca came up with the slogan "56 for 56"—meaning that buyers could finance a new 1956 car with payments of $56 a month. The slogan helped to boost sales in Iacocca's district, and McNamara adopted it on a national scale. McNamara later claimed, in that precise way he has with figures, that the advertising campaign sold 72,000 extra cars.

Once Iacocca was under McNamara's wing, the promotions came quickly. He was rewarded with the job of sales manager for the District of Columbia, but he held it only a matter of days before he was promoted again. He became manager of truck marketing in the Ford division, based in Dearborn, where he once again worked for Charlie Beacham, who had become head of the division's car and truck sales. Shortly afterward, Iacocca was made manager of car marketing, and in 1960 he was called to the office of Henry Ford himself, who appointed him general manager of the Ford division—and a vice president as well. He was only thirty-six at the time.

Iacocca's greatest contribution to Ford was his exploitation of the growing youth market. As the babies born during the postwar boom approached maturity, they became a powerful buying force, worthy of special attention. Under Iacocca's direction the company made bold overtures to youth in its advertisements and in its product development. Ford put new life into the demure Falcon model, giving it a V-8 engine and bucket seats, and coming out with a convertible version as well. In 1962 the company got heavily involved in racing, on the theory that its exploits at the track would lure young people to the showrooms. The grand climax of Iacocca's youth program was his introduction of the sporty but inexpensive Mustang automobile at the opening of the New York World's Fair in April 1964. It was one of the most sensational launchings in automotive history. The public bought

418,000 units the first year, and the demand rose to more than 600,000 a year in 1966. Ironically, the car almost didn't get off the drawing boards. Iacocca had to push it persistently on a wary Henry Ford, who was still smarting from the dismal failure of the Edsel a few years earlier.

The Mustang's success pretty much ensured that Iacocca would rise one day to the presidency of Ford. It got him an immediate promotion to vice president of the car and truck group, and in that capacity he developed yet another best-selling new car, the Maverick. Iacocca had some influential backers in the Ford family, including Henry's mother and his youngest brother, William Clay Ford, who served as a director and vice president. Having them on his side certainly didn't hurt Iacocca's chances for promotion. It also helped that Iacocca, unlike Knudsen, knew his place, plainly appreciating and accepting the proper role of the Number Two man at Ford. As Iacocca himself put it: "Hell, Mr. Ford is Number One in my mind. Always has and always will be. He hired me, he brought me along, he gave me my opportunities."

In January 1976, Henry Ford II suffered an attack of angina pectoris, and it set him to thinking. "I suddenly discovered that I wasn't going to live forever," he later recalled. "I asked myself, 'Where does the Ford Motor Company end up without me?' I came to the conclusion that Iacocca could not succeed me as chairman. He wasn't the man to run the company—no way. He was not capable of being chief executive of the Ford Motor Company." The conclusion that Iacocca was "not capable" of running the company must have been based on evidence that has never been made available to the rest of the world. At any rate, Henry waited fifteen months before actually taking steps to derail his second in command. In April 1977 he elevated Philip Caldwell, the executive vice president in charge of international automotive operations, to the rank of vice chairman. Usually the vice chairmanship of a company is reserved for highly placed veterans who have outlived their usefulness—witness Ford's own Arjay Miller —but Henry made it clear that this would not be the case with Caldwell. He announced that when he was unavailable to make top-level decisions, Caldwell would have that responsibility. Iacocca, though he retained the presidency, had been demoted to

Number Three in the hierarchy. At that point he wanted to quit, but he held back after a friend told him: "Think of your stock and of your salary."

Henry demoted Iacocca to Number Four on June 8, 1978. He put William Clay Ford, best known as the owner of the Detroit Lions football team, in over Iacocca's head as chairman of the Executive Committee. Henry also solidified Philip Caldwell's position as the second in command by officially designating him "deputy chief executive." Iacocca bluntly told Henry, "I think you're making a mistake," and Henry replied, with equal bluntness, "That's my decision and the board's." In fact, the board was not quite so compliant as Henry suggested. The outside members questioned him closely about his moves and expressed their concern until he gave them an ultimatum: Approve the changes in thirty minutes or he would resign.

Five weeks later, on July 13, Henry fired Iacocca. He explained that Iacocca had done something that he couldn't tolerate, but he refused to go into detail, saying he didn't want to "wash dirty linen in public." Pressed to elaborate, Henry would only add: "If he could have accepted his role and played on the team . . . But he wouldn't do it. He didn't want to play on the team."

The evidence suggests that Henry became incensed at Iacocca for complaining to the company's outside directors. It is unclear whether Iacocca went to the directors or whether they came to him, but at any event he is supposed to have told them that he was angry enough to quit, and they found this alarming. The company faced severe marketing challenges in an energy-conscious era, and it could ill afford to lose one of the great marketing geniuses of all time. Henry accused Iacocca of "conspiring" with the directors and reportedly told the man who had been president of his company for more than seven years: "I just don't like you." Iacocca, however, has said that the sentiment wasn't phrased that concisely. "Ford is the last of the great family dynasties," Iacocca mused in an interview with *New York* magazine, "and if you read history you know that the first thing you do is protect that dynasty. Anything, *anything*—good, bad or indifferent—that might affect that dynasty becomes a problem in the mind of the man who heads it. It's that simple. When I went to Ford thirty-two years ago, I knew it was a family empire. But it just never entered my mind that I could have a problem someday. I thought if I was the best, I'd be all right, dynasty or not."

Iacocca's dismissal had to be cleared with the board, but the outside directors were unanimous in urging that he be allowed to stay. Again Henry issued his ultimatum: "Gentlemen, enough. It's simply him or me." Iacocca was kept on the payroll for three more months, during which he received scores of unsolicited job offers. In November 1978 he became president of the desperately ill Chrysler Corporation, and in September 1979 he moved up to chairman and chief executive—Number One at last.

Henry had fired high-ranking executives before, of course, but this seemed different. Iacocca was special, a towering business figure in his own right, and the firing left a strong feeling of revulsion not only among the directors, but also within the company's executive ranks, where there were many Iacocca partisans. In fact, as Iacocca established himself at Chrysler, he was able to lure several key men away from Ford. Henry's motivations and even his rationality came under question from respected commentators in the press. Walter Guzzardi, Jr., of *Fortune* suggested that the Iacocca incident "made Ford seem more an irascible tyrant than a cool executive weighing the best course of action." "What is most disturbing about the Iacocca firing," Guzzardi went on, "is . . . the revelation of the depth of Henry Ford's commitment to family domination over the company. He has often repeated his conviction that 'the public wants to see somebody called Ford somewhere right near the top of this company.' In fact, no such ground swell of public opinion is discernible, especially since there is no one named Ford around with anything like Henry's abilities. The inescapable conclusion is that the need for 'somebody called Ford right near the top' is not the corporation's need but Henry's, arising from a sense of family loyalty and a desire to perpetuate dynastic power."

At the time of the Iacocca incident, Henry already was embroiled in several other large controversies. The gasoline tanks of Ford's Pinto cars allegedly had an abnormal tendency to explode in rear-end collisions, and the company was being sued for enormous sums by the victims or their survivors. Not only money, but also Ford's reputation for quality engineering, was on the line. Henry himself was the target of two suits, one by his second wife, who wanted a divorce, the other by some stockholders, who accused him of abusing his position as head of the company. The stockholder suit charged that he used Ford's money to pay for his homes, that he authorized a $1 million bribe to an Indonesian general to obtain a contract for the company, and that he *received* a $2 million bribe to do business in the Philippines. The charges seemed incredible to those familiar with Henry's reputation for business integrity—to say nothing of his great personal wealth. But the suit was being hotly pursued by Roy M. Cohn, the flamboyant and highly effective New York lawyer, and the Indonesian matter was being investigated as well by the Department of Justice and the Securities and Exchange Commission. Henry's own nephew, Benson Ford, Jr., soon joined his tormentors. Benson, Sr., who had been a vice president and director of Ford, died of a heart attack in July 1978, and Benson, Jr., who was in his late twenties, demanded a seat on the board. Henry denied the request, and young Benson hired Roy Cohn to press his cause.

Henry had often talked about stepping aside as chief executive before reaching the age of sixty-five, and now he had every possible reason. The job couldn't have been much fun for him anymore, and the death of Benson, Sr., two years his junior, was an ominous reminder of his own angina condition. He relinquished the chief executive's post in October 1979, after passing his sixty-second birthday, but remained as chairman. Philip Caldwell was given the title of president and chief executive officer, but many people doubted that he could function with full freedom while the senior member of the Ford clan remained at his shoulder. In a joint press conference with Henry, Caldwell, according to one account, "was hard pressed . . . to describe how he would overrule Mr. Ford in cases where they differed. After repeated stabs at it, most of which drew laughs from the audience and an observing gaze from Mr. Ford, he gave up." In March 1980, Henry relinquished the chairmanship to Caldwell, but stayed on as a director and head of the Finance Committee. "I shall be looking in," he promised.

Despite Henry's denials, it appears that he deliberately designed the succession at Ford to favor the ambitions of his son Edsel. Lee Iacocca might not have cared to pass the company along to the younger generation of the Ford family, but Caldwell, who reaches the mandatory retirement age in 1985, is likely to give Edsel every consideration, particularly with William and Henry standing by to prompt him. Edsel wants very much to become the head of Ford, but he evidently doesn't expect to be Caldwell's *immediate* successor. Born the day after Christmas in 1948, he has publicly declared that he hopes to become a vice president by age forty and chairman by age fifty. Like his father, Edsel struggled a bit to get through school, but he did earn a degree from Babson College in 1973. He served as a sales trainee with Ford during his college years, and after graduation he became a product analyst, holding marketing positions in Boston and Los Angeles. In 1978 he began what was billed as a three-year stint as assistant managing director of Ford's affiliate in Australia. Henry publicly conceded that he would "like to see" Edsel become chief executive of Ford, but insisted that his son would have to work hard and earn the job. "There are no crown princes in the Ford Motor Company, and there is no privileged route to the top," he declared. Maybe so—but don't count Edsel out just yet.

Chapter Ten

Awash in Washington

WHEN W. MICHAEL BLUMENTHAL was appointed secretary of the treasury at the start of the Carter Administration, a friend of mine asked me how I thought he would fare in the job. Like Blumenthal, my friend had fled Nazi Germany as a child, and he felt a fraternal concern for his countryman, though they had never met. I had written a lengthy magazine article about Blumenthal a few years earlier, shortly after he was named chief executive of the Bendix Corporation, so I could pass as a minor authority on the new cabinet officer. I told my friend that I thought Blumenthal would quickly come to grief. Although he was brilliant and an able administrator, he was much too egocentric to be content as a subordinate—particularly to the likes of Jimmy Carter.

Blumenthal hadn't been in office very long before word began leaking out that he was uncomfortable in his new role. He reportedly differed with the President on economic policy, and he was continually battling with the White House staff for power and recognition. In January 1979, after two years on the job, Blumenthal poured out a long account of his frustrations in an interview with *Fortune*. Although he was reticent about any power struggles within the White House, he still had plenty to lament. He complained about the publicity that surrounds a cabinet officer's activities, about meddling from congressmen and other outsiders, and about his inability to control the Treasury Department bureaucracy. Six months later Blumenthal resigned, though it was a case of jump or be pushed. He was a victim of Carter's effort to purge the Administration of anyone who might not serve as a lockstep loyalist during the 1980 election campaign. After a few months of unemployment Blumenthal returned to the congenial confines of business—as a vice chairman of the Burroughs Corporation, with the promise that he would be promoted to chairman and chief executive at the end of 1980.

It is the rare tycoon who can make the jump from business to government without winding up frustrated and humiliated. No matter how commanding and forceful a tycoon may be in the executive suite, he doesn't stand much chance when he goes up against the political professionals. The contrast between business and government is simply too great, and the talents needed to succeed in each are almost totally different. The tycoon is accustomed to an authoritarian system in which his word is law. In Washington, things just don't work that way. The kind of swift, decisive action favored in business is ruled out by constitutional checks and balances, and by the pushing and tugging of a multitude of special-interest groups. It takes deals and compromises to get things done in politics, and many top businessmen consider that beneath their dignity.

Blumenthal discovered that there was nothing in government to compare with the power wielded by the chief executive of a business enterprise. "In the government," he told *Fortune,* "no one has the power to decide that this is the policy he wants to develop, these are the people who are going to develop it, this is how it's going to be decided, and these are the folks who are going to administer it. No one, not even the President, has that kind of power." He found that he couldn't even make administrative decisions—let alone policy decisions—strictly on their merits. He had to consider whether a decision might lead to conflict with an influential congressman whose help he needed on more important matters. The congressman might get into the act because he had friends in the Treasury Department who opposed the decision, or because the decision would offend the congressman's constituents. As Blumenthal explained: "You may have to maintain government jobs in a particular locale, which may be very inefficient, because a member of Congress from that area wants that bit of extra service and can make life difficult for you on a totally different issue. That kind of interplay, of accepting inefficiency in one area to achieve certain goals in another area, is foreign to a businessman." Blumenthal also complained that he exercised scarcely any authority over the vast majority of his subordinates—the 120,000 men and women who work for the Customs Service, the Internal Revenue Service, the Secret Service and the various other agencies that lie in Treasury's domain. Seniority rules and Civil Service laws make it virtually impossible for the secretary of the treasury—or any other cabinet officer—to determine who will be hired, fired or transferred, except at the top of the hierarchy. Blumenthal said he was able to appoint about twenty-five high-ranking Treasury officers, but the remaining 119,975 employees were "outside my control."

Like most tycoons, Blumenthal had been accustomed to carrying out his duties pretty much in private. A company may be well known—even a household name—but it is rare for the head man to receive much publicity if he doesn't want it. He has public-relations men to shield him from intrusions, and when he doesn't care to talk, the press has no effective recourse. Business is, after all, "the private sector." But when a tycoon moves into government, things change dramatically. He suddenly finds himself in a goldfish bowl, scrutinized by high-toned pundits and bubble-headed gossip columnists alike. Many tycoons find it extremely difficult and unpleasant to cope with this situation. Even Blumenthal, though he was no stranger to government, having spent six years as a minor official in the State Department during the Kennedy and Johnson administrations, professed himself shocked by the contrast. He had received some attention from the press during the mid-sixties as a negotiator in the Kennedy Round of tariff talks. But as a cabinet member his publicity was magnified a hundredfold. "What you say suddenly takes on wide significance that it didn't have before," he observed. "Suddenly, when I say I think interest rates will rise, or I think the stock market will rise or fall, that's in every newspaper. Your words suddenly become important, and nobody is more surprised than you are, because you know you don't know that much more than you did before."

Blumenthal didn't receive particularly harsh treatment from the press while he was in Washington. He seems to have been handled with respect, if not reverence. But he happens to be more sensitive about his public image than most tycoons of my acquaintance. For example, when I wrote about him in 1973, while he was at Bendix, he wanted me to let him review the manuscript so he could censor his own statements before they appeared in print. It was an uncommon request even for a businessman—and it wasn't granted. It is hardly surprising, then, that Blumenthal seemed downright obsessed by the exposure he was getting as secretary of the treasury, and that his comments on the subject carried an almost hysterical ring. "You learn in this job that everything you say is weighed and stored and may be dragged out and used against you," he told *Fortune*. ". . . Not only is what you say used against you—it is also distorted, and you are quoted as saying something you did not say. . . . When you see silly things in the paper about yourself, when you read lies, when you read distortions, accusations, accusing you of stupidity, banality, you say why am I doing this, why?"

Why indeed? Why, in fact, would any tycoon give up his precious power and privacy, not to mention his salary and his stock options, to engage in the rough-and-tumble of politics? Blumenthal himself explained, rather lamely, that he enjoyed "the thrill of serving your country in a really tough job," and he even urged other businessmen to try it. But by his own account his stewardship was more chilling than thrilling, and his ability to *serve* was curtailed beyond the limits of his tolerance.

A tycoon nominated for a position in government can expect trouble even before he assumes office. Appointments at or near the cabinet level require confirmation by the Senate, and this often turns into "an excruciating ordeal of self-exposure and public criticism," as one commentator describes it. More than any other species, the businessman is considered fair game for the politicians, the public-interest advocates and—laying aside the question of accuracy raised by Mike Blumenthal—the press as well. Outsiders often look upon business as grubby and selfish and view its practitioners with suspicion and hostility. It is assumed, at the very least, that a businessman is automatically prone to conflicts of interest, that he will favor business in general—and his own company in particular—while administering the affairs of government.

To prove his good faith, a businessman is expected either to sell his stock or to place it in a blind trust before joining the government. But selling the stock may cause him financial hardship, producing capital gains or losses that spoil his tax planning, and placing the stock in a blind trust leaves the businessman at the mercy of the trustee, whose investment judgment may be faulty, and probably is. If a tycoon happens to be a major shareholder in his company, a forced sale can severely depress the market for that stock. When David Packard, cofounder of the Hewlett-Packard electronics company, became deputy secretary of defense in 1969, he held more than 3,600,000 shares of stock, worth the staggering total of $300 million. The Senate recognized that it would be unfair to other Hewlett-Packard shareholders if this huge block were dumped on the market. On the other hand, Hewlett-Packard was a defense contractor, and Packard, as the Number Two man in the Defense Department, would theoretically be in a position to give the company's fortunes—and his own —a big boost. Packard ultimately agreed that he would donate his dividends to charity while he was in office and that if the stock price rose he would donate the incremental value as well. His three years in office cost him $22 million under this arrangement —surely some sort of record.

As a proprietor, Packard had no trouble getting his job back when he left the government. But a professional manager who serves in government is unlikely to return to the same company. Someone had to replace him when he left, and in fact there might have been a complete reshuffling of the top executives. It wouldn't be either proper or sensible to demote everyone else to make room for the wandering tycoon, and it is unlikely that the board of directors would stand for it. When a professional leaves his company for a fling at government service, he must reconcile himself to the fact that he has written off his past and is beclouding his future. By any reckoning, service in the government is a very real sacrifice for the tycoon.

Few tycoons have been more severely disillusioned by government service than John Connor, who served as secretary of commerce for two years during the Johnson Administration. When he took office in January 1965, Connor was bubbling with enthusiasm and optimism. Even as a college student, he had concluded that Washington offered the kind of power and action that suited him, and before going into business—as an executive with Merck and Company—he had spent several enjoyable years as a government lawyer, working for the Office of Scientific Research and Development during World War II, and as an assistant to James V. Forrestal, the secretary of the Navy, after the war ended. When Lyndon Johnson tapped him to head the Commerce Department, Connor was overjoyed at what he considered this splendid chance to represent business within the Administration and to help shape the nation's economic policy. He left the Administration two years later so thoroughly overcome with revulsion that he resolved never to seek or hold public office again— and he never has.

Connor did not suffer from most of the problems that afflict tycoons when they enter government service. He got along well with the press both before and after he took office, and he breezed through confirmation by the Senate without a harsh word from either side of the witness table. He *did* have at least one dispute with some members of Congress after he took office —over an administrative decision affecting their constituency— but such incidents were notable mainly for their rarity. And his relations with the White House staff and his fellow cabinet officers were courteous and even friendly.

What soured Connor on the job was President Johnson himself. The two men were simply incompatible. Connor had started out believing that Johnson was an admirable man with whom he shared a goodly number of fundamental principles. But before long he realized that they thought differently about many vital issues—and that the President wasn't especially admirable either. Connor was dismayed by the escalation of the Vietnam war and by what he considered Johnson's favoritism toward labor. And he was appalled by Johnson's personal style—particularly his penchant for bullying and haranguing his subordinates. Most significantly, perhaps, they differed on the role of the secretary of commerce. Johnson seemed scarcely interested in Connor's suggestions about the economy, preferring to rely on other advisers within the Administration. And he made scant use of Connor as a liaison with business, choosing instead to deal directly with the business leaders when he had something important to say or ask. It sometimes seemed as though Connor held his office strictly for the sake of form—because it wouldn't do to leave a cabinet position unfilled.

Connor's government service cost him heavily, not only in pride, but also in cash. He took an immediate pay cut from $129,880 a year to $35,000, so he lost nearly $200,000 in salary, before taxes, during the two years he remained on the job. In leaving Merck he surrendered his right to stock options that would have made him richer by $1 million. He put the Merck stock he already owned—31,982 shares, worth about $1.5 million —into a trust administered by the Morgan bank and gave the bank full authority over his investments. He asked the bank to make out his income-tax returns without showing him the details, so he wouldn't be able to deduce the contents of his portfolio. After he left the government, Connor was "absolutely horrified" to discover that the trustee had sold a third of his Merck stock, costing him a small fortune in capital-gains taxes. The sale of Merck shares was all the more "horrifying" because the stock went on to perform exceedingly well in the market during Connor's two years in public office, its value rising by more than 50 percent. As a final blow, Connor took a loss when he sold his house in Washington at the end of his government tour. The transaction made him, as he likes to put it, "the only person in the last decade or so who lost money on Washington real estate." After reciting all his financial hardships in meticulous detail, Connor added, philosophically, "I have never had a desire to be the richest man in the cemetery. To fulfill the responsibility of a comfortable home and educating your children—that's the best you can do."

Connor recalls that his father always warned him not to get

involved in politics. As the head of an oil-distributing firm in Syracuse, the elder Connor had a modest place in that city's establishment and saw at close hand just how dirty politics could be— at least on the municipal level. He was friendly with some of the political figures in Syracuse and served as campaign treasurer when one of them ran for a judgeship. "He was a very upright man, a man of character and integrity, honest and law-abiding," his son relates. "He did not participate in such practices as seeking political favors. But he was discerning. Through his eyes I could see some of the things that went on." Despite his father's advice, Connor concluded that honest, able people had a duty to participate in politics, if only so that public jobs wouldn't all go by default to the crooks and incompetents.

Like his father, he was a Democrat. He would occasionally work for Republican candidates on the state and local level, but he was usually faithful to the Democratic Presidential nominees. He had supported the Kennedy-Johnson ticket in 1960, donating $500 to the campaign, and had taken an active role in 1964 as co-chairman of the National Independent Committee for President Johnson and Senator Humphrey, while raising his donation to $2,000. His efforts during the 1964 campaign angered some doctors who supported Barry Goldwater, and they tried to organize a boycott against Merck's drugs. The boycott never really took hold, but Merck salesmen were occasionally berated as they made their rounds.

Lyndon Johnson had met Connor only a few times before tapping him as secretary of commerce. Connor, as vice chairman of the Business Council, an organization of several dozen chief executives of major companies, would sometimes attend group meetings with the President. But Connor was close to a couple of people who *were* intimates of the President—Sidney Weinberg, the investment banker, and Henry H. Fowler, the Washington lawyer who was later to become secretary of the treasury. Both Weinberg and Fowler touted Connor as a replacement for Luther Hodges, the departing commerce secretary, and that undoubtedly made the difference in getting him the job. LBJ summoned Connor to the White House shortly after the 1964 election, took him for a walk around the grounds, and popped the question. Connor eagerly accepted.

He was sworn into office on January 18, 1965, by Chief Justice Earl Warren, while LBJ beamed his approval. In announcing the appointment, the President had praised Connor in extravagant terms: "He is smart and he is loyal and he is patriotic. He will never discard a principle nor despair of doing what is right and ought to be done." Connor said he was gratified to serve as secretary of commerce in an administration headed by a man who understood businessmen "better than any President since God knows when."

But the honeymoon ended before the couple could even turn back the covers. Given the chance to view Johnson close up and in private, Connor was repelled. "I did not get along with Lyndon Johnson from Day One," he later remarked. At his first cabinet meeting, Connor was shocked to hear the President "talking about our effort in Vietnam as if everyone knew we were deeply involved." The U.S. had not yet openly committed itself to war, and Connor opposed any such move. "The trouble is, I believe what people say," he remarks. "When Johnson said he would not get us into a shooting war in Vietnam, I believed it." Connor turned to another cabinet member, Anthony J. Celebrezze, the secretary of health, education and welfare, and asked what this was all about.

"Don't you know?" Celebrezze replied. "We're at war."

"No," Connor said, "the President said we weren't."

"Well, the election's over," said Celebrezze.

Connor challenged Johnson's Vietnam policy several times— "particularly the use of draftees and inexperienced men as cannon fodder, instead of calling up the Reserves." But his objections had no discernible impact.

As the U.S. became more deeply involved in Vietnam, Connor urged Johnson to propose a tax increase that would meet the rising costs of the war and stave off inflation. Johnson vigorously opposed such a move at first. He was committed to his celebrated "guns-and-butter" policy, not wishing to risk the wrath of the American taxpayer. When Connor advocated a surtax on incomes during a cabinet meeting early in 1966, LBJ replied that he didn't believe a surtax could get through Congress in an election year, but he suggested that Connor and Treasury Secretary Fowler go over to Capitol Hill and talk to Wilbur Mills, head of the House

Ways and Means Committee. They did, and Mills told them that he probably couldn't even get a surtax out of committee. Connor says he later learned that LBJ had telephoned Mills and offered his own opinion before the delegation arrived. Johnson did finally call for a surtax on personal and corporate income in January 1967, in his State of the Union address, and Congress finally approved one in 1968, an election year.

The President and his secretary of commerce found themselves at odds on a broad variety of economic questions. When the aluminum industry raised prices during the fall of 1965, the Administration, despite Connor's objections, took a hard line against the move, threatening to flood the market with aluminum from the federal stockpiles. The industry leaders, after much grumbling, capitulated. Connor also objected when Johnson sought to turn the Administration's voluntary wage-price guidelines into mandatory controls, under the war powers of the President. Connor felt that LBJ was much keener about holding down prices than wages. They also disagreed when Johnson proposed legislation to liberalize the minimum-wage laws. Connor objected to a provision that would have provided double pay for overtime.

While most of their disputes remained private, Connor did take some public positions that LBJ found politically embarrassing. Connor denounced the shipping strike of 1965 as "against the public interest" and contended that some of the union demands were "quite unreasonable." He offended liberals, intellectuals and the academic community all rolled into one with a jocular speech attacking John Kenneth Galbraith, who had disparaged businessmen in some congressional testimony. And he distressed the Democratic delegation from Ohio by rejecting its chosen candidate to head the Commerce Department field office in that state.

Connor had the usual problems of a tycoon adjusting to the role of subordinate. One observer wrote at the time: "A tough-minded forthrightness . . . has survived into his tenure as a public servant, and sometimes that does not make things easier." As Connor himself recalls, "I wasn't the kind to get up every morning, salute, and say 'Yessir.' " He was, in short, a man with a large ego, but he was contending with the Greatest Ego of Them All. Connor says he had been deceived, after the assassination of President Kennedy, by the warm and even humble public image of the new President. "I was very favorably impressed when he said, 'Let's sit down and reason together,' " Connor recalls. "But once elected in his own right, he reverted to type. Once he put his uniform on, he felt you were beholden to him. President Johnson didn't want you to be a yes-man—at least in those situations where he wanted you to say 'no.' "

LBJ antagonized several other cabinet officers as well, Connor says. He figures that the President was no longer on speaking terms with half the people who worked with him by the time the Administration ended. He recalls that Johnson had the "merciless" habit of bawling out staff members "in a very personal way" in front of others. After he calmed down, he might try to make amends. "He would never apologize," Connor says, "but he would recognize if things hadn't gone well, and would do something nice. But there would be a cumulative effect beyond which most of us wouldn't go." Connor expresses his admiration for LBJ's wife, Lady Bird, "a wonderful, wonderful person" who was "able to control the President in a nice sort of way when he got out of bounds talking to people."

Connor did manage to make a few significant contributions to government during his time in office. Along with Labor Secretary Willard Wirtz, he helped avert a nationwide steel strike in 1965, and he also had a hand in settling some wildcat strikes by dock workers that year. His greatest achievement was to establish a program that reduced—if only temporarily—the deficit in America's balance of payments. At the time he became secretary of commerce, the Administration was considering harsh, mandatory measures to cut down the flow of American capital to foreign countries. One of the proposals being discussed was a 15 percent tax on all investments abroad. Connor persuaded LBJ to try a voluntary program instead, with Connor providing close supervision. He concentrated on several hundred of the largest American companies, cajoling them to make improvements, but letting them choose the means—whether by increasing exports, raising capital abroad, repatriating their foreign funds, or simply decreasing foreign investments. The program worked well, perhaps because the businessmen feared that mandatory controls might follow if they failed to cooperate. The U.S. balance-of-payments deficit dropped from $2.8 billion in 1964 to $1.3 billion in 1965, and held at about the same level in 1966. But by 1967 the Vietnam war had stimulated a tremendous new flow of American capital abroad, and Connor's program did not survive his departure from office.

The wonder of it all is that Connor stayed in office as long as he did. Why didn't he quit sooner—or why didn't Johnson ask him to leave? Connor says that he was ready to quit on several occasions. He had vivid memories of his days as an assistant to Secretary Forrestal, back in the forties. Forrestal got into some bitter battles with Congress and with President Truman, who eventually fired him. His physical and mental health deteriorated, and he committed suicide by jumping out a window at the Bethesda Naval Hospital. Connor feared that his own health was in jeopardy. "I was under a lot of strain," he says, "and I was unable to sleep for the first time." It was only at the urging of Secretary Fowler that Connor refrained from walking out on the President during the first year. "I decided to make it a two-year tour of duty—like the military." Connor speculates that LBJ didn't fire him because he didn't want to admit defeat. Connor was Johnson's first cabinet officer—excluding those he had inherited from the Kennedy Administration—and it would have looked bad to drop him so quickly.

But at last Connor broke the stalemate, bluntly telling the President, "I just don't want to work for you anymore," and he left office in January 1967, his "military" tour concluded. Ten years later Connor was able to declare, with a straight face, that he was "a better-rounded, more interesting person as a result of my government experience." And still later he remarked, "I was really glad to serve my country. I feel a great debt to the U.S. for the opportunities I've had." But it seems that his father knew best after all.

As one might expect, Connor couldn't *completely* withdraw from politics. He felt that Hubert Humphrey would have been "the truly great president of our generation" and actively supported him in the 1968 campaign. Since then, however, he has been voting less like a Democrat and more like a businessman. In 1972 he chose Nixon over McGovern. "McGovern, though idealistic, was even dangerous," he says. "Watergate was a terrible thing, and I believe Nixon *should* have been run out of office. But Mc-

Govern might have had an even more harmful effect." In 1976, Connor was ready to deliver speeches on behalf of Carter, but he changed his mind and switched to Ford after studying the Carter program. "He was making commitments which had the effect of extending government controls over just about every form of human existence." Connor says he is still registered Democratic, and that the party, in its civil-rights programs, "reflects my philosophy to some extent." But he has a high contempt for the liberals in the party, such as Ted Kennedy. "When I was younger I used to think of myself as a liberal, till I realized that most of the so-called liberals revel in the name without living up to it. Being liberal now is to be for more government control, particularly over business. Under the true definition of a liberal, the new kind was the kind we had to defend ourselves against in the Magna Carta and other liberalizing documents."

In the weeks and months before he resigned from the cabinet, Connor slipped word of his intentions to some of his more influential friends. Still in his early fifties, he was anxious to find a big, challenging job. He received offers from several institutions, not only businesses but also law firms and universities. The offer that seemed most appealing came from Allied Chemical, once the dominant force in its industry, but by then suffering from inadequate management. Although its revenues had been increasing, its earnings were going nowhere. Connor would start as president and chief operating officer, with the understanding that he would soon move up to chief executive. After two years as a virtual figurehead in the Johnson Administration, Connor relished the opportunity to go where he was clearly needed and wanted—and he felt doubly encouraged when Allied offered him a stock deal that seemed extremely attractive. He joined Allied in February 1967, became chief executive in June 1968, and eventually shook the company out of its slump.

After he had been running Allied for a while, Connor got a call from Lyndon Johnson, who by then was out of office and living on his Texas ranch. Johnson was very friendly and complimentary and mentioned that he used Allied's liquid fertilizer at the ranch. It turned out that he wanted a discount on a large quantity of fertilizer for an agricultural project in Mexico that he was planning with a former Mexican president. The fertilizer deal never went through, however. Connor was willing enough, but there were "too many complications getting it over the border at a cost competitive with Mexican products."

Roy Ash, the head of A-M International, presents a striking contrast to Connor, Blumenthal and just about every other tycoon who ever served in government. He not only came through his government service without regrets, but he loved every minute of it. He spent two years during the Nixon and Ford administrations as director of the Office of Management and Budget, a cabinet-level position. "It was like the Olympic Games," he recalls, "a guy satisfying a one time desire. I look back on it as the time I competed in the Olympics. Guys come back after the Olympic Games and don't ever have to feel despondent. They say it was great while it lasted." As director of OMB, Ash was in effect the general manager of the Executive branch of government, prodding the various departments and agencies to administer their programs effectively and at a reasonable cost. "This is the most exciting job in the whole world and the most interesting one," he said upon stepping down in February 1975. "Anything else is going to be anticlimactic."

To those familiar with the details of his government career, it may seem astounding that Ash could come away in such good spirits. He was embroiled in controversy throughout his term in office and even before—the target of constant attacks not only from Democratic congressmen, which is understandable, but also from Republicans within the Nixon Administration. Ash was a deft infighter during his business career, and that talent served him well in government as he engaged in one power struggle after another within that treacherous maze known as the Nixon White House.

But Ash says he thrives on controversy, and this sets him apart from the vast majority of his fellow tycoons. "I believe that people in business should raise their heads and be counted," he says, "yet so many business people are reluctant to do that. They don't want to take any tomatoes." Ash adores politics, and especially the arguments that politics inevitably engenders. He is a staunch conservative, with many conservative friends. "A conservative," he once said, "is a man whose idealism is tempered with reality. A liberal is one whose idealism is tempered with rhetoric." Yet he enjoys the company of liberals, because he relishes the give-and-take of political debate.

Ash is slow to take offense, reacting to even the harshest taunts with cool reason. "I've got self-confidence," he explains. "A lot of people have self-confidence which isn't justified, but that doesn't matter. The important thing is that they don't look to third parties to give them security. Once you draw security from yourself, you're free of factors that control your life. If you depend on third parties, you have to give up some of your security." Shortly before he took public office, at a time when his appointment was being criticized from almost every direction, and both his ability and integrity were being called into serious question, Ash responded with his customary good humor: "A friend told me to bring some extra pints of blood to Washington because I was going to need them. Guess he was right." And yet I wonder whether Ash is really as cool as he would like to appear. In our conversation he struck me as acutely sensitive to everything that is said about him, even though his response was always good-natured. I quoted numerous articles to him that had been written five, six and seven years earlier, and he clearly remembered every last one of them.

I met him in his handsomely furnished office in Century City. He is balding and six feet tall, with a trim but not athletic physique. Over the years he has had a bad press—to put it mildly—and I was more than a little curious to discover what he was like in person. He is commonly portrayed as a cold-blooded financial man, a computer in human disguise, an emotionless loner who much prefers numbers to people. He is said to be remorseless and relentless in his treatment of subordinates, particularly those who fail to meet their financial goals. In his days at Litton, after the company ran into prolonged financial difficulties, Ash and his staff were dubbed "The Murder Squad" by harassed division managers. It has even been suggested that Ash has the personality of "chilled liver."

None of this came through during the hours I spent with him. He couldn't have been more cordial or accommodating, though he did seem a trifle nervous at first. In breaking the ice, we talked at excessive length about the Los Angeles weather, which had been uncommonly wet that week. But he finally warmed to the main subject—which after all was himself—and he put on a virtuoso performance, smiling profusely, delivering sly quips in his deep, unctuous voice, and tripping lightly from one bit of wisdom to the next. He was extremely bright and articulate, frequently picking up on questions before they had been completed. Our meeting extended far beyond the time originally allotted.

From the start of his government career, Ash had the good sense to realize that he couldn't always have his way, that he wouldn't get anywhere by bossing people around. "You have to use argumentative skills—reason and conviction," he says, "although sometimes reason doesn't get you very far. Some businessmen say, 'The heck with that. I don't wanta convince 'em. I just wanta tell 'em.'" Ash might have been more tractable than other tycoons in part because he had never been the top man in a company before entering government. Although he wielded great power as a cofounder and president of Litton Industries, he had always ranked a notch below Tex Thornton, the chairman and chief executive officer, so his "argumentative skills" were continually being tested. It was only after he left government and went to A-M International that Ash finally became a chief executive himself.

"In government you can't expect to change things substantially," Ash says, "but you can change the course slightly, so things come out different." Given those limitations, he believes that he accomplished quite a bit in public office. Ash is a vocal free-enterpriser, who looks with horror upon most government attempts to regulate business. He claims that he at least made the public more receptive to regulatory reform. "First you take a problem people talk about," he explains, "then you make it an official agenda item—put it on the table. Then the issues crystallize. I can take credit for putting regulatory reform on top of the table." Ash says he made two other major contributions as well. He "articulated the issue" of government transfer payments—i.e., putting tax money directly into the pockets of needy individuals or groups—which he feels have become excessive. And he made a general contribution toward "improving the management of the federal government."

In the course of his government service, Ash learned all the little tricks that politicians use to influence public policy. He didn't find them the least bit abhorrent, and in fact he added a few wrinkles of his own. For example, he found that by drawing on his considerable stamina, and on his ability to outsit most other human beings, he could make a major contribution to Nixon's speeches—literally putting his own words in the President's mouth. "The work of preparing a speech goes on through the night before," he explains. "If it is to be delivered at ten in the morning, they're still working on it at four. The way to have the most effect is to be up at that hour when everyone else has gone to sleep. In that way you have an effect on national policy, since a Presidential speech is a policy speech."

Ash first met Richard Nixon shortly after the Presidential election of 1968. He had been a five-figure contributor to Nixon's campaign, and the two were introduced by Robert H. Finch, Nixon's friend and aide. Ash joined the President-elect and his staff at the Hotel Pierre in New York and helped them prepare to take possession of the White House. Nixon offered to make him, in effect, the manager of the federal bureaucracy, but Ash turned the offer down. "My kids weren't old enough then," he explains.

He did accept a part-time assignment, as chairman of the President's Advisory Council on Executive Organization. The group, which had five other members prominent in business and politics, was instructed to recommend modern organizational and business practices for the federal government, and to sort out the relationships between the federal, state and local governments. The Ash Council, as it came to be known, met three times a month from May 1969 to May 1971, and Ash himself occasionally visited the President to hash out the council's thoughts and recommendations. In its final report the council suggested, among other things, the creation of an Office of Management and Budget, which would supplant the old Bureau of the Budget and take a firmer and more direct hand in administering programs under the jurisdiction of the executive branch. Caspar W. Weinberger, who had been active in California Republican politics, preceded Ash as director of the OMB, but the job opened up after the 1972 election, when Nixon appointed Weinberger secretary of health, education and welfare. Ash, who had once again contributed heavily to Nixon's campaign, was asked to succeed Weinberger, and this time he was ready. He took a pay cut from $195,000 to $42,500, but it made little difference in his case, for he had become quite wealthy as a charter shareholder of Litton. Although the company's stock had plunged to a fraction of its all-time high, Ash was still reported to be worth close to $9 million at the time he entered public office.

Rarely has a Presidential appointment caused such an outcry. Between the announcement of his appointment in November 1972 and the swearing-in ceremony in February 1973, Ash was attacked heatedly and repeatedly from every quarter. One of the earliest and most persistent attackers was Senator William Proxmire, chairman of the Congressional Joint Economic Subcommittee. Proxmire suggested that the shaky financial record of Litton Industries cast doubt on Ash's "competence as an industrial manager." He also charged that Ash's appointment would produce some serious conflicts of interest. The head of OMB had a certain amount of jurisdiction over defense expenditures, and Ash, as president of Litton, had been at "the heart of the defense contracting industry." Proxmire mentioned that Litton was involved in disputes with the Navy over huge cost overruns on some shipbuilding contracts. Ash, as director of OMB, might be in a position to influence the Navy's response in this matter. In fact, some Navy sources had provided Proxmire with the minutes of a meeting held in June 1972 between representatives of the Navy and Litton, in which Ash allegedly threatened to appeal directly to the White House if the contract dispute wasn't resolved to Litton's satisfaction. But Ash brushed aside any suggestions about a conflict of interest, observing that he would be selling his 255,000 shares of Litton stock and placing the proceeds in a blind trust. "When the Washington Redskins trade a football player," he said, "I doubt if in the next match he favors the team he just left."

Proxmire's subcommittee heard testimony from a Navy procurement official, Gordon W. Rule, who also assailed the choice of Ash as director of the OMB. Rule, a civilian who served as director of procurement control and clearance with the Naval Materiel Command, recalled President Eisenhower's warning, in his farewell address, against "the acquisition of unwarranted influence . . . by the military-industrial complex." Rule felt that the appointment of Ash was just the sort of thing the late President had in mind. "Old General Eisenhower must be twitching in his grave," he remarked at one point. His caustic comments didn't budge Ash or Nixon, but they did get Rule himself into trouble. Admiral Isaac C. Kidd, Jr., Rule's boss as chief of the Naval Material Command, tried to force him to resign. When Rule refused, he was transferred to a lower-ranking job, but he did finally get his old job back after three months of purgatory.

Other politicians followed Proxmire's lead. Representative Les Aspin, a Wisconsin Democrat who served on the House Armed Services Committee, deplored Litton's record as a defense contractor and wrote two articles attacking Ash and the company for *The Nation*. When Ash, two months after taking office, reported that he was unable to sell some 12,000 of his Litton shares because they were held as collateral for a loan made to another party, Aspin scolded him, in an open letter, for not telling Congress about this sooner. Even William B. Saxbe, a Republican senator from Ohio whom Nixon later named attorney general, expressed doubt about the appointment, particularly in view of the Navy's contract dispute with Litton. "I don't think it's good to have a president of Litton in the catbird seat," Saxbe said. Ash expected opposition from the Democrats, and he didn't take it to heart. But the criticism from someone like Saxbe seemed an unkind cut. "I sat practically next to him at the cabinet table," he says. "That's the life in Washington."

The movement to keep Ash out of office gathered steam in Congress, and it almost succeeded in the spring of 1973. By then Ash was already on the job, but Congress passed a bill that would have revoked his appointment, subject to review and confirmation by the Senate. In those days the director of the OMB did not need Senate approval, and it is unlikely that Ash could have obtained it. But Nixon vetoed the bill. The Senate overrode the veto, but the House's attempt to override fell short of the required two-thirds majority. Congress then passed another bill making the OMB director subject to confirmation by the Senate, but exempting Ash. Nixon let that one go by.

The political attacks against Ash put the press on his scent as well. Embarrassing accounts of his business dealings began to crop up, most notably in the Washington *Post*, the New York

Times, The New Republic, and *The Nation,* and in the syndicated columns written by Jack Anderson and jointly by Rowland Evans and Robert Novak. Sometimes the critics seemed to be straining mightily to make a very small point, as when the Associated Press reported that Ash and Tex Thornton had been involved in a "controversial" land deal with the Interior Department. It seems that they had bought twenty-two acres of oceanfront land near San Francisco, which the Interior Department needed for the Point Reyes National Seashore. In 1969, Interior traded 14,145 acres of federally owned range land near Elko, Nevada, for the California land held by Ash and Thornton, explaining that it was an even swap in terms of value. The AP report seemed to suggest that Ash and Thornton got slightly the better of the deal, but it didn't point to any conclusive evidence. Some press reports did considerably more damage, however—especially the article by Morton Mintz in the January 2, 1973, issue of the Washington *Post,* which recounted the charges that Ash and Thornton indulged in financial skulduggery during their time together as executives of Hughes Aircraft.

It seems likely that any other businessman in Ash's position would have stepped aside rather than endure the kind of exposure that followed his nomination to public office. If nothing else, the attacks proved that Ash had a hide worthy of a rhinoceros— or even a professional politician. "Before I came to Washington," he wrote gamely in a letter to the *Post,* "I was told it would be normal to be the subject of running press criticism. I was ready; in fact I offered a built-in advantage to the press. My name is hard to misspell and it can be fitted into headlines with considerable space left over for pejorative castigation." But despite his public insouciance, Ash admits that he was privately concerned about how his children—three boys and two girls—would react to the attacks upon him. "You're gonna read some of the most terrible stuff about me you've ever heard," he told them. "I only ask you not to believe it till you come to me and discuss it." He says most of his children "took it okay," but his older daughter was "more sensitive than some of the others."

Within days after assuming office, Ash found himself in the midst of one of the Nixon Administration's epic confrontations with Congress. Vowing to keep federal spending at a minimum, Nixon and his men had devised a theory that the Executive branch was not required to spend all the money that Congress appropriated for public programs—that it had the right to "impound" a substantial portion of these funds. Congress took a different position, of course, and Ash was hailed before a committee headed by Senator Sam Ervin to explain the Administration's case. "I volunteered to defend impoundment," Ash says, "kind of like the volunteer who throws himself over barbed wire so the rest of the troops can cross." It was quite a debut for a public servant—squaring off against Ervin, a leading authority on constitutional law, over a constitutional issue. "Not only tomatoes but hard bullets were coming at me," as Ash describes it.

Ash had been with the Administration for less than three months when H. R. Haldeman, John D. Ehrlichman and a number of lesser Presidential staff members departed. He says that when he took the job at OMB he assumed that the Watergate affair had simmered down, though in fact it had only begun to boil over. "I feel terribly relieved that I wasn't there when it happened," he remarks. "I never really did learn what went on, save only the principals. Why was it done in the first place?" Ash lived in the Watergate apartment complex during his stay in Washington, but in his droll way he insisted on referring to it by its street address—700 New Hampshire Avenue.

The upheaval in the Administration presented an extraordinary opportunity for those who hadn't been tainted by Watergate. Ash, who makes no secret about his craving for power, was able to expand the range of his activities and his influence with the President. By the middle of 1973 he was being described, in a House committee report, as "the most powerful person in the Executive branch." He could never have enjoyed that distinction during the heyday of Haldeman and Ehrlichman—the Scylla and Charybdis of the Nixon White House. But the men who replaced them were considerably less fierce, and they had more to worry about than intramural politics. General Alexander Haig, who succeeded Haldeman as the White House chief of staff, had to devote most of his time to Watergate, and to the controversy surrounding Vice President Agnew, while Melvin R. Laird, who replaced Ehrlichman as the President's chief domestic adviser, vowed that he would only play a stopgap role. In fact, he stepped down toward the end of 1973.

Certainly the potential for great power was inherent in Ash's job. Although the OMB had only 660 employees—small as government agencies go—those employees were intimately involved in some of the most vital activities of the Administration. John Herbers, of the New York *Times,* in an article about the OMB and the men who ran it, offered this impressive summary of the agency's functions:

> It decides to a large extent how much money will be spent for each program. It then oversees how each program is carried out. It reviews all legislation the departments and agencies submit to Congress, with authority to change it. O.M.B. analyzes every bill that is passed and recommends that the President either sign or veto it. Virtually every questionnaire sent to business or other private groups must be cleared by O.M.B. It establishes the broad array of committees that advise the Government on policy . . . and it has access to every study and piece of information gathered by the departments and agencies.

As Nixon became increasingly occupied with Watergate, Ash's agency made the subtle but crucial shift from being an adviser on policy to an initiator of policy. Ash tightened his grip on the agency itself by recruiting management experts from outside the government to supplement the work of the civil servants left over from the old Bureau of the Budget—"a policy takeover," in the jaundiced view of Evans and Novak, that would have been "mercilessly crushed" if Ehrlichman had still been in power.

Although it is widely supposed that Nixon became so obsessed with Watergate during his final months that he could scarcely function as President, Ash insists that this wasn't so—at least where *he* was concerned. He would meet with Nixon as often as three times a day. "One of the things that impressed me with him," Ash says, "is how he was able in his own mind to separate what must have been the tremendous burden of having Watergate issues unfolding, and deal with the substantive issues of government. All my meetings with him at the end dealt with substantive issues, and he gave them intense involvement. Looking back, you say, 'How could he?' " At one point in 1974, Ash received a letter from a close friend, saying "surely you deplore all this," and urging him to quit. But Ash replied that it would have been irresponsible to leave while the Administration was sinking. "I thought I was doing my job pretty well," he says. "At that point, how could Nixon get anyone else in to do it as well?" Ash stuck by Nixon personally as well as professionally. Just days before the President's resignation, Ash threw a party at his mansion in Bel Air for Nixon and 150 friends and supporters. During the festivities Nixon's daughter Tricia earnestly proclaimed: "Innocence is innocence—and my father is innocent. If the committee votes to impeach, it will just be a political move by people who want to get Richard Nixon out of office. But they won't get away with it. This is a country of justice."

Ash ultimately met his nemesis in William E. Simon, a former partner in the Wall Street firm of Salomon Brothers, who had joined the Administration around the same time he did. Simon started out as deputy secretary of the treasury and kept that job while also becoming head of the Federal Energy Office. The energy "czar," as he was popularly known, was a self-confident, tough man who cherished his prerogatives. He had the enthusiastic backing of Treasury Secretary George Shultz, one of Nixon's most trusted and valued advisers. Ash evidently had little trouble dominating the two previous energy czars—James Akins and John Love—and he promptly tested Simon's mettle. According to Evans and Novak, Ash asserted his own agency's right to "run" the energy program, while insisting that Simon would be limited to matters of "policy." "Bullshit!" Simon reportedly replied—and the battle was joined.

The battle became the talk of Washington, and it even flared up on national television. On February 12, 1974, Ash discussed the nation's energy problems in the wake of the Arab oil boycott at a breakfast meeting with some reporters. In remarks that proved to be something less than farsighted, Ash called the energy crisis "manageable" and "short-term" and predicted that the price of crude oil would drop from $10 or $11 a barrel to $7 or $8. He did modify his remarks at another news conference later that day, acknowledging that there would be long-term repercussions affecting the production, distribution and consumption of energy, and he even sketched out a plan for dealing with the problem. Simon himself had been emphasizing the long-term nature of the energy problem, and he was irked—to put it mildly —that Ash had made public statements deviating from this line. Appearing the next morning on NBC's "Today" show, Simon declared: "Perhaps I should call a press briefing on the budget. Maybe I should ask Mr. Ash to keep his cotton-pickin' hands off energy policy." The phrase "cotton-pickin' hands" was an in joke. It had been used a few months earlier by Secretary Shultz to chastise Mel Laird for a public statement he had made about taxes. Ash had been tipped off that the phrase would be repeated by Simon, so when the reporters came running he was ready with his own witty retort: "We don't pick cotton at OMB. We run the plantation."

When Shultz left the Administration a couple of months later, Simon was named secretary of the treasury. It was a bitter blow for Ash, who was said to have wanted the job himself. The two antagonists continued to slug it out, occasionally in public, as when Simon called for cuts in the fiscal 1975 budget and Ash disdainfully replied that it couldn't be done. The bickering became so intense that President Nixon, in the midst of his Watergate agony, sometimes had to step in personally to make peace.

After Nixon's resignation Simon emerged clearly triumphant over Ash. He was appointed chairman of the new Economic Policy Board created by President Ford, with authority to serve as the Administration's spokesman on all matters relating to the economy. Unlike Nixon, Ford chose to meet personally with the members of the cabinet and the heads of the agencies in discussing their policies and budgets, and this further diluted the power of Ash and the OMB. Ash stayed with the new Administration for only six months before going into temporary retirement. "I got one of my best compliments ever from the press," he says. "Eileen Shanahan, of the New York *Times,* said on my last day, 'You're the only person in political life I know who got a better press coming out than going in.' "

Simon, who left office in 1977 along with President Ford, went on to write a best-selling book about his experiences, entitled *A Time for Truth.* Ash obtained a copy of the book, but read only the part about himself—a passing reference to their dispute—

after checking the index. "He was wrong about that," Ash says, "so I figured he was wrong about anything else." Oddly enough, Ash and Simon are now back together again, preparing for the Olympic Games of 1984, which will be held in Los Angeles. Ash is on a local board, while Simon is treasurer of the U.S. Olympic Committee. "We still take our potshots," Ash says. Perhaps the Olympic Committee can arrange a special sporting event—a joust, say—in which these perennial combatants can have it out once and for all.

Ash remained fairly active in politics after leaving office. President Ford appointed him to the Republican National Committee's Advisory Council, Jimmy Carter appointed him to the President's Advisory Committee on Federal Pay, and Governor Edmund G. Brown, Jr., of California, occasionally drew on his services as well. Ash still gives political speeches, and one of his favorite topics of late is the proposed constitutional amendment that would make it mandatory to balance the federal budget. The amendment is favored by many of his fellow conservatives, but Ash opposes it. "It would have bad side effects and it wouldn't work—otherwise it's a great idea," he jokes. "You can't pass a law to tell politicians to stop being politicians. You have to make it politically popular to be against spending. You may be able to slay a five-ton elephant with a single well-placed bullet, but you can't slay five tons of ants that way—and government spending is like five tons of ants."

For a while Ash withdrew with his wife to their ranch in Ventura, California. "I totally decompressed," he recalls. "I did ranch work—fixing fences. I decided I had done my life's work, that I had achieved enough net worth. Why do people like to get back to the land in their old age? Perhaps it gives them a sense of immortality." But a man with his drive couldn't remain totally idle. He started writing a book about how Presidents handle the Executive branch of government. "It would have six readers," he estimates. He didn't get very far, however. "Writing is hard work! You can't just write. It forces you to think, perhaps more deeply than you ever have before." He served as a director of several companies, and he rented an office in Century City, where he received visits from his old friends and associates and managed his stock portfolio. He spent his time "trying to beat the Dow Jones Average by a couple of points and blithely doing so," but he came to the conclusion that "being a passive investor is not so much fun."

During the summer of 1976 he was approached—"out of the blue," he says—by an investment banker named John Birkelund. Birkelund had close ties to a director of Addressograph-Multigraph, a manufacturer of business machines, but he was acting on his own when he asked if Ash would be interested in becoming chief executive of the company. Addressograph-Multigraph, based in Cleveland, was plagued with an outmoded product line, its earnings had been dragging for years, and it obviously needed a change at the top. Securities analysts referred to it, with no great affection, as "Addressogrief-Multigrief." Birkelund figured he could sell Ash to the directors if Ash wanted the job.

Ash inspected the financial statements and determined that the company might at least make a promising investment. The stock was selling for around $9 a share, but Ash figured that the liquidating value was twice that much. "I kind of backed into it," he says, "in the sense of saying I don't know what the upside is, but the downside is 100 percent *profit*. I said if I'm there running it, the worst I can do is liquidate it for $18 a share." It was agreed that Ash would become chairman and chief executive at a salary of $225,000 a year and would buy 300,000 newly issued shares of the company at $9 apiece, making him the largest individual stockholder. One of his first moves was to hire James R. Mellor as president and chief operating officer of the company, pirating him away from Litton Industries. Tex Thornton considered it a hostile act to take Mellor without even asking permission, and he blessed Ash out on the telephone. The two old partners aren't on very good terms these days.

The new management turned Addressograph-Multigraph around with astonishing speed, and the stock price doubled and even tripled without resort to liquidation. Ash changed the name of the company to A-M International—which should lay to rest the unflattering nickname—and he soon moved the headquarters from Cleveland to Century City. A prominent feature of his office there is the leather-upholstered chair he used at cabinet meetings —quite literally the seat of power. Cabinet-level officers are routinely offered the chance to buy their chairs when they leave, and

Ash was happy to shell out the $400. He displays the chair as proudly as any Olympic champion displays his medals.

It certainly is no secret that the political life can be extremely rough—and yet a lot of tycoons are drawn to it anyway, like moths to the flame. Many of them believe that government is at the root of all the problems that afflict business, and they suppose that by joining the government they can change things. Some of them undoubtedly are attracted as well by the glory of performing in a larger arena. And some are looking for immortality—a place in the history books that is denied to the run-of-the-mill tycoon.

The tycoons feel most comfortable with—and within—a Republican administration. In any given Presidential election some 80 or 90 percent of them will support the Republican candidate. It isn't because they think profits will be higher under the Republicans—usually, in fact, it's the other way around—but rather because Republican Presidents tend to keep their hands off business. The tycoons value their power and their prerogatives above all else, and they want as much room as possible in which to expend their creative energies. Though you won't catch any of them saying so, their personal freedom undoubtedly means a lot more to the tycoons than the welfare of their shareholders.

Regardless of who occupies the White House, there will always be a place for tycoons in the federal government. The Treasury Department, the Commerce Department, the Defense Department, the Office of Management and Budget, the Federal Reserve Board—all are customarily headed by skilled, experienced businessmen. When Mike Blumenthal left the Treasury, for example, he was succeeded by G. William Miller, the former chairman of Textron, Inc., a conglomerate. Miller, who had already been serving as chairman of the Federal Reserve, obviously wasn't deterred by Blumenthal's loud complaints about the pain and futility of the office. He might have had second thoughts, however. The ubiquitous Senator Proxmire has publicly questioned his integrity on more than one occasion, and that can hardly have been a pleasant experience.

It is becoming increasingly common for businessmen to reject offers to serve in the government. Robert Thomas Campion, chairman and chief executive of Lear Siegler, a manufacturer of vehicle components, expressed what may now be the prevailing sentiment among tycoons: "The seasoned executive has to be a nut—or very patriotic—to go to Washington." Walter Wriston of Citicorp says he was offered the chance to become secretary of the treasury in two Republican administrations, but he managed to wriggle out. He says he has no great hankering for "the beating that you take in public." He adds: "I think there was a time when the best and brightest, to coin a phrase, wanted to go down and save the world. And I think it's a great shame that they don't anymore. Long-term that's the biggest problem this country's got. . . . I think the attack on American political leadership at all levels has gotten so bad that a lot of people just say, 'Who needs it?' "

Chapter Eleven

Journey's End

In 1960, while serving as a junior executive with General Motors, John DeLorean traveled to Palm Springs to attend a conference of Pontiac dealers. Palm Springs is a welcome change of scene for anyone from the Detroit area, but for DeLorean the trip provided a special and unexpected treat. It happened that Harlow Herbert Curtice, recently retired as chief executive of GM, was also visiting nearby, and DeLorean had the chance to meet him at the El Dorado Country Club, where the conference was being held. Curtice had been the head of GM from 1953 to 1958. The five years of his leadership were among the most bounteous in the company's history, and he had earned widespread admiration and acclaim. "I looked at this guy almost as a god," DeLorean recalled.

If not a god, Curtice was at least a king of kings—complete with the most attentive and obsequious courtiers. The monarchs of old might have envied his many comforts and conveniences, as described in this vivid contemporary account:

> Platoons of subordinates jump when he twitches. Garages filled with gleaming limousines and beaming chauffeurs stand ready to transport him wherever he desires. A private 18-plane air force of multi-engined, red-white-and-blue airplanes is at his disposal. Private secretaries and public-relations men take care of bothersome detail, see to it that Cadillacs, hotel suites, restaurant tables and theater seats are there when and where he wants them. High-salaried assistants smooth his path, greet him wherever he arrives, order his drinks, fetch his newspapers.

In short, he had all the perquisites of a Big Business tycoon—only more so, because *he* was the boss of GM.

As the head of the nation's largest industrial concern, Curtice wielded power and influence well beyond the confines of his own domain. His words carried tremendous weight, and in fact he is credited with literally talking the U.S. out of an economic slump during 1954. The slump had been widely predicted by the economists, and the telltale signs had already begun to appear by January. Business was slowing down, unemployment was rising, and everyone was retrenching. Well, nearly everyone. In a speech before 500 of the nation's leading businessmen, Curtice declared, in solemn tones: "No depression is in my vision." What's more, he put his company's money where his mouth was, announcing that GM would spend a billion dollars on expansion over the next two years in anticipation of a great boom in auto sales. The headline writers dubbed him "Bet-a-Billion" Curtice, and his optimism became contagious as Americans suddenly went on a buying spree. By the middle of the year, GM's dealers were screaming for more cars to meet the public demand, and Curtice announced that he would have to spend *two* billion on expansion. The demand carried over to the other major auto makers, Ford and Chrysler, and they too launched massive expansion programs. The demand for cars breathed new life into the auto industry's many thousands of suppliers, who in turn stepped up their purchases from the suppliers of raw materials, such as steel, copper and aluminum. A genuine economic boom developed, and it carried through all of 1955. "People had money and credit," Curtice later explained. "I think I pushed them off the fence to the right side."

Curtice was cultivated by the powerful and those who aspired to power both at home and abroad. He golfed with Eisenhower and received decorations from the governments of France and Belgium. A building was named for him on the University of Michigan campus. He was selected as *Time*'s "Man of the Year" for 1955, and an idealized rendering of his patrician countenance, with prominent beak and thin, gray mustache, adorned the magazine's cover. His presence was constantly demanded at receptions, banquets, parties and press conferences.

Fortune recounted the details of a single week Curtice spent in New York, immersed in a welter of business and social activities.

The occasion for his visit was the opening of the GM Motorama, the annual display of the company's new models. On Monday he gave a speech at the Waldorf-Astoria on the state of the economy. After the speech he attended a party given by an advertising agency at the Pierre, and that evening he went to another party thrown by another agency at the Savoy-Plaza. On Tuesday he had breakfast with the executives of a steel company, followed by a rehearsal for a television appearance. At lunchtime he held a press conference on the Starlight Roof, and in the afternoon he attended a cocktail party at the University Club. He was the guest of honor that evening at a dinner given by a publisher at Leone's restaurant. On Wednesday morning he attended a special meeting of GM's Financial Policy Committee at the company's New York offices, then the monthly meeting of the board of directors. In the afternoon he appeared at a preview of the Motorama attended by 5,500 selected guests, followed by two cocktail-buffet parties. That evening he kept his date with the television people, appearing on an hour-long special hosted by Bob Hope. On Thursday he posed for photographs, then attended another Motorama preview, two business meetings, a luncheon, and parties at the 21 Club and the Stork Club. On Friday he formally opened the Motorama. Harlow Curtice, the tycoon's tycoon, rarely lacked for companionship.

He actually lived at GM's headquarters most of the time. His legal residence—and his family—were in the city of Flint, just fifty miles northwest of Detroit. But on week nights Curtice didn't bother to go home. After working a ten-hour day, he would dine at the Detroit Club, then return to headquarters and retire to a bedroom just down the hall from his office. He would awaken at seven-thirty in the morning, and appear at his desk by eight, raring to start yet another ten-hour day.

By the time John DeLorean met him, Curtice was a changed man. Just two years earlier Curtice had been a world figure, but now he seemed like a supporting actor in a vampire movie. The leadership of General Motors had been his identity, his purpose in life, and when he was forced to surrender it at age sixty-five, under the company's retirement rules, nothing else remained. His life had been blighted as well by a horrible accident, which occurred about a year after he left office. He and a retired GM vice president, Harry W. Anderson, were hunting ducks on Sainte Anne's Island in Ontario. Curtice spotted a low-flying flock of mallards, and he squeezed the trigger of his 12-gauge shotgun just as Anderson, stumbling on uneven ground, lurched in front of him. Anderson died within minutes of a wound in the back of his head.

DeLorean mentioned Curtice to the El Dorado golf pro, who offered a depressing appraisal of the great man. "That's the loneliest human being who ever lived," the pro said. "He comes into my golf shop for a couple of hours every day and talks to me and my assistant about the automobile business. We don't know anything about the automobile business, but we listen to him. He just seems to want to talk so badly." DeLorean was appalled. Suddenly he had a terrifying glimpse of his own future—like Scrooge confronting Christmas Yet to Come. "You realized he never had been regarded as a human being," DeLorean commented, "but only for his job." DeLorean was moved to ask himself: "What is life all about? You work forty years, and what have you got?" The specter of Harlow Curtice—who was to die of a heart attack a couple of years later—haunted DeLorean throughout his career at General Motors. It was still very much on his mind in 1973 when, not yet fifty years old, he abandoned a $550,000-a-year job in GM's senior management—and with it a chance to become president. Today he is his own boss, the founder and chairman of the DeLorean Motor Company, which manufactures sport cars at a plant in Northern Ireland. One nice thing about being your own boss is that you don't have to retire.

Like DeLorean, Peter McColough of Xerox had a frightening look at the future early in life. His father was on social terms with a lot of prominent Canadian businessmen, and Peter could see at close hand the damage caused by an overzealous dedication to business. "I saw people involved in divorces, estrangement from their children—they had no vacations, no hobbies. I really felt that was failure, not success." Later on, his father moved to Fort Lauderdale, which has a sizable community of retired Canadians, and Peter got to see how things looked at the end of the line as well. "There were men who didn't want to pay for a good meal, who didn't have anybody to leave their money to, who couldn't enjoy their leisure. As my father said, 'Peter, the virtues of your younger life are the vices of later life. Don't think you can abruptly change.' " McColough wasn't deterred from pursuing a business career—and an immensely successful one at that—but he did promise himself that he wouldn't do it "at any price." "I didn't want to end up at age sixty-five with $100 million and that's all I'd done in life," he says. "I didn't have the fear I couldn't succeed. I had a fear whether I could do it without the danger of really concentrating on only one thing, so that I would feel an abject failure at sixty-five."

It is debatable whether McColough really kept his promise to himself. He does demonstrate a certain detachment from the job nowadays by taking long vacations. But he confesses that he was forty years old before he ever took his full vacation allotment. And his schedule when he isn't on vacation sounds pretty demanding. He spends most of his working days on the road, visiting the far-flung Xerox operations or meeting with clients and suppliers. At the office he puts in a nine-hour day, and he usually either takes work home or attends a business dinner. He also works at home every weekend. It remains to be seen whether he will suffer withdrawal symptoms when he reaches retirement age —which comes earlier at Xerox than at most other companies. A top Xerox manager is expected to step aside when he reaches his sixtieth birthday—in McColough's case, during 1982. Although he will surrender the chief executive's job, he will be permitted to remain in an advisory role until age sixty-five, and he has been giving the matter some serious thought. "I could be chairman of the Executive Committee," he muses. "The Executive Committee doesn't play any great role. It meets to do perfunctory things." Of course that could change with McColough running it.

Most tycoons cannot contemplate retirement without a certain amount of anxiety. "People who are at all observant," says Charles Brown of AT&T, "see how quickly the prestige mantle falls away when you retire. The prestige of the job is not something one wants to bank one's feelings on very much." Irving Shapiro of E. I. du Pont, discussing his easy access to the President of the United States, remarks ominously: "The day I step out of this job, it will be a different situation."

A decade ago, when David Mahoney became chief executive of

Norton Simon, Inc., he said he intended to leave before reaching his sixty-fifth birthday in 1988. But today, with the mandatory retirement date no longer so remote, Mahoney takes a different tack: "At times I've thought and thought, and said I could cash in and do what I see fit," he remarks. "I could never figure what the 'see fit' was. I enjoy what I'm doing." He says he might leave Norton Simon if some splendid opportunity presented itself elsewhere. "If you told me you could find a cancer cure, I might drop what I'm doing and pitch in. I don't ever see myself retiring. The word 'retire' means quit, give it up. I'm just going to take other directions, keep right on going until it's all over. They say retirement kills you, but I think there are enough things out there to intrigue me that are exciting." He just hasn't found them yet.

Probably most chief executives would prefer to continue working rather than heading to pasture. The sixty-five-year age barrier is, after all, somewhat arbitrary. There are tycoons who should retire *before* they reach sixty-five, but there are others who remain highly effective into their seventies and even their eighties. A compelling example is Armand Hammer of Occidental Petroleum, who was born in 1898 and still keeps a steady grip on his company's affairs. But only the entrepreneurs—like Hammer—and the heirs—like Peter Grace, who was born in 1913 and still runs W. R. Grace and Company—ordinarily have enough influence to stay at the top indefinitely. The professionals, still burning with energy, still compulsively dedicated to their work, still brimming with plans, are forced to go cold turkey. Some, like Harlow Curtice, take it badly, floundering about in a dream state, unable to cope with leisure. Others make the only sensible choice: they go out and look for another job.

Once past the age of sixty-five, however, it is hard for a professional manager to find a good, challenging job as a hired hand. The better-heeled professionals have gotten around that problem by becoming entrepreneurs. In the final stage of life, desperate for something to do, they are actually willing to risk their own money, and they are shelling out the hundreds of thousands—or even millions—accumulated from years of high pay and generous stock options. John Kenneth Jamieson, for example, who retired in 1975 as chairman of the Exxon Corporation, joined with other investors to form a venture-capital firm that took over the

Crutcher Resources Corporation, a manufacturer of pipeline equipment. He serves as chairman of the firm and has hired a young professional as chief executive. One of Jamieson's fellow investors is John Dickson Harper, who retired in 1975 as head of the Aluminum Company of America.

The most prominent refugee from the ranks of the professionals is Harold Sydney Geneen, the former head of International Telephone and Telegraph. Geneen is widely regarded as the greatest professional manager of all time because of his stunning success in building ITT during nineteen years as the chief executive. He too has formed a venture-capital operation, its investments including a substantial holding in the Pneumo Corporation, which is involved in aerospace and supermarkets.

Because he was so special, Geneen was permitted to remain as chief executive of ITT until he reached the age of sixty-eight in January 1978. He didn't want to step aside even then, but there was concern at the time that he might be indicted for perjury in the wake of his testimony before a Senate committee investigating ITT's role with the Central Intelligence Agency in Chile. Geneen remained as chairman of the board with a contract extending through December 1980, while Lyman Critchfield Hamilton, Jr., the president, became chief executive. Just two months after this transition, the Justice Department decided not to prosecute Geneen. In July 1979, Geneen led a move to oust Hamilton and replace him as chief executive with Rand V. Araskog. In the meantime, Geneen had launched his career as a venture capitalist, and some members of the board suggested that this might pose a potential conflict of interest. Geneen responded by giving up the chairmanship at the end of 1979—a year ahead of schedule. It seemed an ignominious end to a glorious association, but at least Geneen won't be pestering any golf pros in his waning years.

Only in harness can a tycoon be truly happy.

Chapter Twelve

Standard Equipment

WHAT IS special about the tycoons? What distinguishes the men who run the major companies from those who never reach the top? The tycoons differ from one another in so many ways that it is no easy matter to sort out the traits they share. Tycoons occupy the entire spectrum from extroverts to recluses, from free-spenders to tightwads, from libertines to puritans, from charmers to bores. Many of them resist the notion that they might be homogeneous in some way. "No," says Thomas Murphy of General Motors, "I don't think you'll find that common denominator. I guess the thing that always astounds me, when I look at people —even your own kids—they're different. I'd say everyone is an individual, thank God, and so you have to look at it in that light." Murphy can be excused for fancying himself unique, but the tycoons do have many things in common. Indeed, there are certain qualities that appear to be practically essential to anyone who aspires to the top in business. As a gesture to Tom Murphy and his company, we can describe these qualities as the tycoon's *standard equipment*.

It is a well-known fact, if not an outright platitude, that long hours of hard work are required to reach the top in business. The twelve-hour stints at the office, the working lunches and dinners, the homework at night and on weekends, the trips that last days and weeks at a time—all are familiar parts of the ambitious businessman's routine. Probably most people assume that businessmen work hard because they want to succeed—that hard work is the means to an end. But things aren't quite that straightforward, for work can be an end in itself. The tycoons, by and large, are driven by a passion for work that is quite as powerful and compelling as any other human drive. Their work takes precedence over wife, children, pets, vacations and hobbies. That may seem perverse to ordinary mortals, who savor their moments of leisure and the company of their loved ones. But perversion or not, it is a mark of the tycoon. Businessmen who lack an overpowering commitment to their work, who are only going through the motions, will almost certainly be eclipsed by those who *do* have the commitment.

The tycoons will cheerfully admit that they are workaholics. Robert Edward (Ted) Turner III, the flamboyant young Atlanta entrepreneur and sailing champion, is as outspoken on the subject as anyone. Born in 1939, he became a multimillionaire while still in his thirties, and he currently owns a television station, an outdoor-advertising business and two sport franchises—the Atlanta Braves in baseball and the Atlanta Hawks in basketball. "Sometimes I think I oughta pull back and take it a little easier," he declared in an interview with *Playboy.* "I mean, I've provided for my family, I've done what society says you're supposed to do. I don't know what I'm working for now, but I'm still running around like a peg-legged man in an ass-kicking contest. But, God, it's fun. Naw, I couldn't quit. That's why I always win in the end. I could no more give this up than an alcoholic could give up his whiskey."

Sometimes the work ethic can be carried to grotesque extremes. Take the case of Harry Gray, chairman and chief executive of United Technologies. In 1963, while a vice president of Litton Industries, Gray was severely injured in a motorcycle accident. He had been riding with a friend, the actor Keenan Wynn, when his cycle skidded on ice and hurled him against a guardrail, breaking his leg in seventeen places and shattering his hip. Gray was hospitalized and placed in traction, and for six weeks the doctors weren't sure that the leg could be saved. Yet Gray missed only two days of work. He had his office files and a secretary moved into his hospital room, and continued to manage Litton's Electronics-Components Division while flat on his back. After four months in the hospital he was sent home, and, still bedridden, he had his living room converted into an office. He spent four more months working at home, while the doctors periodically predicted that he might be crippled for life. But Gray shrugged them off, and today he brags, "I play tennis, I play golf, I dance and I walk."

Tycoons are often so intent on their work that they look upon vacations as almost a nuisance. This phenomenon was examined in *Fortune* a few years ago by Herbert E. Meyer. One of the people Meyer interviewed was William A. Marquard, chairman of American Standard, Inc. Marquard said he used up most of his vacation time by taking long weekends. "A four-day weekend is great," he observed, "and if I can do that three times each summer it's enough. After the fourth day I start to get itchy." Marquard mentioned that he traveled so much on business that he rarely felt the urge to go away on vacation. As a concession to his wife, however, he frequently took her along on business trips, and on each trip he tried to set aside one free day. Another chief executive, George Scharffenberger of the City Investing conglomerate, told Meyer about the time he let his wife talk him into a seventeen-day tour of Greece. Scharffenberger couldn't bear to stay out of touch with his company, but for the first eleven days the primitive Greek telephone system prevented him from completing a call to the headquarters in New York. When at last the call went through, he was amazed to find that "the company was intact and nobody missed me."

It appears that quite a few tycoons go on vacations merely to placate their families—although some of them can't manage even that. John Brooks Fuqua, founder of the Fuqua Industries conglomerate in Atlanta, once scheduled a two-week vacation in Switzerland as a sop to his wife. But he was back in the office in three days, explaining, "When you've seen one castle, you've seen them all." On another occasion Fuqua, his wife and some friends visited Miami to watch the University of Georgia compete in the Orange Bowl—but Fuqua remained in his motel room reading business publications while the rest of the group went to the game. Fuqua has been described as a man with a "singleminded absorption with business," although he sometimes does try to interest himself in the recreations favored by his friends. He played golf, but gave it up after shooting 167 in his first round, and he retired from skiing after exactly one hour of instruction.

The tycoon needs an extraordinary amount of energy to satisfy his passion for work. Many a talented and eager young businessman has failed to get ahead simply because he wasn't built to take the grind. "It becomes clear pretty soon if you can't do the job, or if you can't do it for very long," remarks Peter McColough of Xerox. "You're born with it," he adds matter-of-factly. Tex Thornton of Litton Industries made the same point, though somewhat more colorfully. "Look at those Thoroughbreds out there," he once told a visitor to his California horse ranch. "Those animals don't make good riding horses, and they don't make good dray horses or cow ponies. They're bred to race. It's the same with people. It's something that's born into you."

One tycoon who demurs on that point is Roy Ash, Thornton's former associate, now the head of A-M International. "Some have the kind of stamina to work extra and stay up all night if necessary, and some don't," Ash concedes. "But one can program himself—it's a form of mind over matter. Don't you think the marathon runner mentally conditions himself to go beyond the normal physical tolerance? He doesn't turn himself off when the signs of fatigue appear." Ash headed a commission to reorganize the Executive branch of government during the first years of the Nixon Administration, and the working sessions sometimes lasted seventeen hours. His colleagues reported that Ash always managed to get through without wilting, and that they couldn't honestly recall that he stopped for a bathroom break. It would be hard to imagine a more impressive triumph of mind over matter.

The tycoons sometimes become so absorbed in a task that they fail to consider the limitations of the people who work with them. "It can be a problem," one of them admits. "You think everyone's on the same wavelength you are, and you find you're wearing out your staff. I notice this particularly on business trips. All of a sudden the staff's falling apart." He can at least be sympathetic in retrospect. But Herbert Meyer, in his article about vacations, points out that most chief executives are contemptuous of subordinates who can't keep pace. To confess physical or mental fatigue—by taking vacations, for example—is often regarded as "an admission of weakness or even a lack of dedication." Meyer concluded that this attitude can have a destructive effect on both the subordinates and the company, and he came out strongly in favor of ample vacations: "Nothing so enhances a man's ability to think productively as a period of relaxation or a simple, but extended, change of pace. So vacations are not a luxury but rather a necessity for any businessman who wants to remain truly effective over a period of years and decades."

Occasionally the tycoons will get so carried away with their work that they will exceed their own capabilities and imperil their health. Malcolm Meyer, the chairman of the Certain-teed Corporation, a manufacturer of building materials, wound up in the hospital some years ago suffering from exhaustion and was forced to take a two-month medical leave. Charles Tandy, the founder of the Tandy Corporation, which operates the Radio Shack retail chain, was stricken with a heart attack in 1968 and underwent a gall-bladder operation in 1972, but his family, friends and associates couldn't get him to slow down. He died in 1978 at the age of sixty.

Charles Jule Pilliod, Jr., chairman of Goodyear Tire and Rubber, is as strong a man physically as you'll find in any executive suite, but as a salesman in South America during the fifties he very nearly worked himself to death. While on a trip to Bolivia he spent a full day touring the dank, chilly copper mines near Quechisla and Oruro, peddling such Goodyear products as conveyor belts and rubber hose. He already was suffering from a bad cold, and by the next morning his voice was gone. But he insisted on visiting still more mines at Oruro, and by the end of the day he was coughing blood. That seemed to be a symptom worth taking seriously, and since there weren't any hospitals in the area, he sought help at the local office of W. R. Grace and Company. The office manager put him in a bedroom on the second floor and called in a physician, who found that Pilliod had a severe case of pneumonia. It was two days before penicillin could be brought in, but after just two more days Pilliod insisted on resuming his sales trip. He traveled to Potosi, suffered a relapse, and spent a day in bed at his hotel. Even then he wouldn't give up. He moved on to Cochabamba, where he visited some more mines before finally returning to his home base in Lima, Peru. "I got some pretty good sales along the way," he remarked, by way of justifying this exercise in self-destruction. I once mentioned to Pilliod that I planned a visit to Brazil and that I had noticed warnings in all the guidebooks against drinking the tap water. "I always did it," he replied. "It didn't bother *me*."

There seems to be a lot of confusion about what motivates the successful businessman. Most people evidently assume that the chief motivation is money, since money is what business is about and since business offers munificent salaries and stock-ownership deals to those who reach the top. But money, like so many other desirable commodities, is most appealing to those who lack it. Money is usually what draws people to business in the first place, but it is not what motivates them to reach the very top in their companies. A businessman can stop short of the chief executive's office and still receive an income that will more than satisfy his worldly needs. The Number Two and Number Three men in some of the nation's largest companies are paid well over a half-million dollars a year, while $100,000 salaries—lofty even in these inflationary times—are commonly offered to the more obscure vice presidents.*

The impulse that drives the businessman to run that extra mile, to make it all the way to the top, is power. A consuming need for power is part of the tycoon's standard equipment.

Some top-ranking businessmen are quite frank about their addiction to power. That in itself is remarkable, because "power" is such a raw word, and the image it conjures up—one man asserting his will over multitudes—does not sit very well with the inhabitants of a democracy. John Weller Hanley, chief executive of the Monsanto Company, a giant producer of chemicals, recalled that

---

* I don't propose to judge whether businessmen actually *earn* their huge salaries, which in some cases now exceed a million dollars a year. Probably some of them do, depending on how effective they are at enriching their shareholders. The question really seems irrelevant, just as it is irrelevant to ask whether Pete Rose earns his $800,000 a year on the baseball diamond. It is a matter of supply and demand. Businessmen, sports stars—and everybody else—will take whatever they can get for whatever they have to offer. Like it or not, that's how a free market operates.

even as a teenager he felt the urge "just to see if you could persuade people to do what you wanted them to do." Working part-
time at a soda fountain, he would use high-pressure tactics to
make his customers take an egg in their malted milk shakes. Donald Nelson Frey worked his way up from laboratory researcher to
group vice president of the Ford Motor Company by the age of
forty-four—but that wasn't enough. "I just have to run a *whole*
business," he explained. "I'm not happy unless I'm dealing with
all the pieces." Because of the special circumstances prevailing at
Ford, he knew that he would never be the top man there. He
went on to become chief executive of Bell and Howell, a manufacturer of movie cameras and other products. It is a mere fraction of Ford's size, but Frey is perfectly happy, because the
fraction is all his.

Power means different things to different tycoons. Most of
them seem content with running their businesses and are not
overly concerned about exerting their influence beyond their own
domains. Donald Frey and Jack Hanley, for example, appear to
fit that description. But there are also some tycoons who derive a
great deal of satisfaction from making an impact, through their
companies, on the world outside. "That's true motivation," says
Robert Beck of Prudential Insurance, "the chance of being able
to work with an organization that can influence things. When this
kind of company decides on a course of action, it can be a force
for good. I like being part of it. That turns me on." David Mahoney of Norton Simon says he is no longer very excited about
wielding power over his subordinates, but he does get a thrill
when he introduces new products that change the buying habits
of consumers, or when he makes a move that might affect "the
real-estate market in Baton Rouge." These imperialistic tenden-
cies would undoubtedly please Winston Churchill, whose photo-
graph Mahoney keeps close by him at company headquarters.

While many tycoons define power in positive terms, as the ability to control others, Roy Ash lays heavy stress on power in the
negative sense, as "freedom from control by others." That may be
too much for a businessman to hope for in this day and age. The
chief executive of a large company must frequently submit to the
will of the government regulatory agencies, which have become
increasingly assertive over the past two decades. Ash has cam-

paigned vigorously against regulation that he considers excessive, even—and especially—while serving in the government itself. Indeed, it is the rare tycoon who isn't aggravated to some degree by government regulation. Henry Singleton of Teledyne, normally a mild-mannered man, spouts pure vitriol when he contemplates "these bureaucrats and clerks who can kick us around." Charlie Bluhdorn of Gulf and Western, who is *not* a mild-mannered man, and who has had his share of run-ins with the government, especially with the Securities and Exchange Commission, is capable of great rages when the question of regulation is raised. Even his more statesmanlike utterances on the subject betray a certain frenzy, as when he told *Nation's Business:* "I am frightened by the unbelievable, bureaucratic, very dangerous government regulations that have engulfed our country. This is the essence of everything that has caused and is causing the change in attitude by American business, in terms of ambition, desire, excitement—all the things that made us a great country. This is a threat to our system." Although Bluhdorn may depict regulation as a national crisis, one of his subordinates suggests that his concerns are in fact somewhat narrower. "A lot of Charlie's fury is that here is some guy from the SEC making $40,000 who is able to make trouble for Charlie Bluhdorn. If that's the case, the world must be upside down!"

It has been suggested that a hunger for power not only drives most tycoons to the top, but makes them better managers as well. This provocative theory was advanced a few years ago in the *Harvard Business Review,* in an article entitled "Power Is the Great Motivator." The authors, David C. McClelland, a Harvard psychology professor, and David H. Burnham, the head of a consulting firm specializing in behavioral science, concluded that "the top manager of a company must possess a high need for power, that is, a concern for influencing people." They came to their conclusion by studying 500 executives from twenty-five different companies who were participating in management workshops aimed at improving their effectiveness as managers.

Through a series of tests, questionnaires and interviews, McClelland and Burnham compared executives with an urge to be strong and influential against those who tried to be friendly with their subordinates. They found that the latter group, which they dubbed "affiliative" managers, were in fact the ones who had the worst morale problems. "The manager with a high need for being liked . . . is the one most likely to make exceptions in terms of particular needs," the authors explained. "If a male employee asks for time off to stay home with his sick wife to help look after her and the kids, the affiliative manager agrees almost without thinking, because he feels sorry for the man and agrees that his family needs him." While this might make one man happy, it builds resentment in the rest of the work force. "This kind of person creates poor morale because he or she does not understand that other people in the office will tend to regard exceptions to the rules as unfair to themselves. . . ." By contrast, the executives who were strongly motivated by power tended to be less sensitive to individual needs and more concerned about the needs of the company. They held their subordinates to a uniform set of rules, and that in turn produced better results from their subordinates. Of course managers who obtain good results from their subordinates are usually the ones who get promoted. The urge for power not only sustains them through the ordeal of climbing to the top, but actually enhances their performance, giving them an extra boost.

McClelland and Burnham emphasized that they were not trying to equate good management with extreme, tyrannical behavior, or with "personal aggrandizement." The best executives, they said, were the ones who harnessed the urge for power, directing it primarily into activities that helped their companies.

The whole system of executive perquisites is tailored to the tycoon's need for power. Perquisites are the tangible evidence that the tycoon has arrived, that he is someone special, that he has been elevated above the crowd and liberated from the petty concerns that afflict the masses.

The array of perquisites available to the tycoons is as boundless as the imagination of man. There are chauffeured limousines to carry the tycoon to and from home, company-owned cars for his personal use, company jets to take him to the far corners of his empire, company helicopters to fetch him from his summer home, even company yachts and houseboats to lull customers— or anyone else—into a compliant mood. The tycoon will receive free memberships in dining and country clubs, free tickets to sporting events, free medical examinations, free legal advice, free financial counseling and free telephone service. His company will insure his life at no cost to himself and will lend him large sums of money at little or no interest. He will have access to private parking, private apartments and hotel suites, private dining rooms, private hunting lodges and private fishing camps. A whole battalion of subordinates will look after his fundamental needs, attending to all the nasty little quartermaster chores that ordinary men must perform for themselves. There is someone to do his Christmas shopping, to take his car to the mechanic, to prepare his tax returns. He need never step among the common people. If he needs a new suit, the tailor will come to *him*. If he needs a haircut, the barber will appear in the executive suite, dragging a caseful of equipment.

Executive perquisites have lately come under special scrutiny from the SEC. On orders from that agency, publicly held companies must now enumerate, in their proxy statements, the perquisites extended to top members of management. The SEC took a particularly hard look at the perquisites enjoyed by Hugh Marston Hefner, that dedicated *bon vivant* who founded and runs Playboy Enterprises. In fact, it launched an investigation of the company and its proprietor early in 1978. One bone of contention was the twenty-nine-room Playboy mansion near Los Angeles, Hefner's principal residence, which was equipped with a swimming pool, a greenhouse, a tennis court and outdoor Jacuzzi baths. Although it cost more than $2 million to operate, depreciation included, Hefner was paying rent of only $36,000 a year. Playboy's own Audit Committee investigated too, and in 1980 announced that it had slapped Hefner with a $796,413 assessment for improperly documented or unapproved expenses. At the same time, four other Playboy officers were assessed a total of $122,000 for similar oversights. At last report, the Internal Revenue Service was wheeling overhead, hungry for a share of the spoils.

At General Motors, where the top man has all the perquisites of a king, there are plenty of managers on lower rungs whose treatment is at least princely. A middle manager at GM, so the reasoning goes, is every bit as worthy as a chief executive somewhere else. The outside world's insight into class and caste at

General Motors has been gleaned largely from the reminiscences of John DeLorean, the company's most celebrated dropout. DeLorean cooperated with the author—up to a point—in the recent best-seller *On a Clear Day You Can See General Motors,* which was written and published by J. Patrick Wright, a onetime Detroit bureau chief for *Business Week.* One of DeLorean's favorite stories, related in that book, concerns a Chevrolet sales official who loved to have a refrigerator full of beer, sandwiches and fruit in his hotel room on business trips. Although he ranked "rather low" in the hierarchy, there still were any number of subordinates willing to go to great lengths to satisfy his whims. In one city the local sales people brought a well-stocked refrigerator up to his suite before he arrived, only to find that it wouldn't fit through the door. After the initial panic subsided they hired a crane operator to lower the refrigerator in through the window.

DeLorean discovered firsthand that subordinates who ignored such details did so at their own risk. In the same book he recalls visiting San Francisco on business while serving as assistant chief engineer of the Pontiac division, arriving ahead of his boss, the chief engineer. He was taking a shower at his motel when the boss burst into the bathroom—without knocking—and bawled him out for not sending anyone to meet him at the airport. "Goddamnit," he declared while DeLorean stood there dripping, "I served my time picking up my bosses at the airport. Now you guys are going to do this for me." The boss, Elliott M. Estes, eventually became president of the company.

Some tycoons insist that perquisites are necessary for the proper conduct of business. Their time is valuable, they point out, and certain perquisites help them devote their fullest attention to the company's affairs. The chauffeured limousine, for example, leaves them free to read reports and documents. Never does one hear of a businessman even glancing at the scenery on the way to and from the office. But as Michael Korda points out in his book *Success!,* the perquisites cited most often as time-savers very often are in fact time-wasters. "In most cases," he writes, "a corporate jet is no more efficient than a commercial airplane—in fact, they are usually slower and more cramped. . . . In New York City, corporate executives use their limousines to make a trip of ten blocks. They could walk the distance in ten minutes, or make

it on the subway in five, whereas the limo may take half an hour."
Korda concludes that the tycoons value their perquisites primarily
because they provide privacy—that "the true test of success is the
degree to which one can isolate oneself from others."

That theory receives a certain amount of support from the
tycoons themselves. David Mahoney, in a characteristically
straightforward interview, told *Money* magazine: "I don't ride the
subway. I grew up on the subway. I know what it's like. I'm not
going to wear sackcloth and ashes about it. Most of us who spent
time standing around on Army chow lines vowed that we weren't
going to do it in the future, and I haven't." Mahoney also acknowledged that he "wouldn't go shopping in the city" and that
he doesn't even go to a theater when he wants to see a movie. He
has "friends in the film business" who provide him with first-run
movies, which he shows on a projector at home. Mahoney has
been known to take the corporate jet on a trip from New York all
the way to Paris. To avoid standing on line at the airport he is
willing to put up with two refueling stops—in Newfoundland and
Ireland.

Joseph Pulitzer, the late press lord, carried executive isolation
to an absurd extreme—though he was outdone many years later
by Howard Hughes. In 1907, Pulitzer bought a 269-foot yacht for
$1.5 million—Ragtime Era dollars, please note—so he wouldn't
have to depend on the White Star Line when crossing the ocean.
"In this luxurious craft," wrote W. A. Swanberg, "he was uncon-
taminated by influences, regulations or persons beyond his jurisdiction and command, out of reach of church bells, trolleys and
drill sergeants, surrounded only by things he desired and by some
75 employees, every one of them trained to cater to his whims.
. . . It gave him *complete control.* It was an absolute monarchy, he
was king, and the 75 employees were his subjects." The yacht's
name, appropriately enough, was *Liberty.*

There is always the danger that isolation will hurt the tycoon's
performance as a businessman by putting him out of touch with
the people his company is meant to serve. Can the chairmen of
Exxon, Mobil, Texaco and the other large oil companies, set apart
as they are by wealth and privilege, really appreciate the problems
of ordinary consumers faced with the mounting costs of heating
oil and gasoline? Can David Rockefeller, who roams the world

with all the panoply of a chief of state, understand the hopes and aspirations of small businessmen or young couples seeking loans from the Chase Manhattan Bank, which he lately served as chairman? Born to great wealth, and catered to from his childhood, Rockefeller simply does not function on the same plane as the common man. Some years ago a feature writer with the New York *Post* spent a day with Rockefeller, recording his comings and goings. At one point Rockefeller actually forsook his limousine to walk the few blocks from Chase headquarters to a meeting with John B. Connally, then the secretary of the treasury. But he became "momentarily lost" while looking for Wall Street, where the meeting was to be held. Imagine how he would have fared in the New York City subway system!

In recent years the tycoons have become seriously concerned about kidnappers and terrorists, and they can argue that their isolation helps to ensure their safety. The argument seems justified, even though businessmen in the U.S. appear to be safer than most. While Europeans and South Americans are being seized, injured and even killed with monotonous regularity, no chief executive of a large American company has fallen into the hands of the malefactors at this writing. The matter of safety is important, of course, but as an explanation for perquisites it is somewhat belated. The perquisites that insulate the tycoon from the rest of mankind pre-date by many decades the current reign of terror.

The tycoons are extremely competitive. They lust for competitive situations and take the most intense pleasure in winning. It is easy enough to appreciate why a powerful competitive urge is essential to success in business. People who disdain or fear competition never get very far, because business really boils down to an endless series of hardfought contests—against one's colleagues for the next promotion and against other companies for the next customer.

Even the American Telephone and Telegraph Company, its name practically synonymous with monopoly, is a highly competitive place. Charles Brown, the chief executive, says the company actively encourages internal competition, viewing it as a way to sustain the quality of telephone service in the absence of external pressures. "Those who have an antipathy or theological contempt for monopolies doubt that," Brown says, "but I don't know how else they think we have the system in as good shape as we do." Brown says he himself greatly enjoyed competing against his peers at AT&T. "There would be similar units all over the company. A person had plenty to compare his unit to. That adds spice to the jobs." Nowadays, of course, AT&T itself is competing to a degree with other manufacturers of telephone equipment, thanks to a landmark decision by the Federal Communications Commission. And in an era of historically high interest rates, AT&T also is meeting stiff competition from other companies and the U.S. Treasury in its efforts to raise capital. "If you're in the right frame of mind, you can find much to compete against as a Bell employee," Brown says.

Roy Ash, who loves to theorize about managers and management, regards the competitive urge as an extension of the urge for power. "Power is no more than winning," he remarks. "Everybody likes to win. Who likes to waste time in a chess game, or a card game, and not win? What's the matter with winning? There's nothing the matter with winning, even though people would say it's *how* you play." Why does Ash feel so strongly about winning? "I think my parents wanted me to win, and perhaps wanted to win through me. My wins seemed to be reinforced. That's true of most of it. I got off to a start in school where I seemed to win all the time, starting even in first grade. I tended to get the lump of sugar when I won. I also had some losing periods—fortunately not too many."

It is surely no coincidence that a disproportionately large number of tycoons competed in scholastic sports—and that they did rather well. Pilliod of Goodyear never completed college, but he was a star wrestler and football player in high school. John Connor, late of Merck and Allied Chemical, was captain of his college golf team. McColough of Xerox, a Canadian by birth, played hockey and rugby at college, while Charles Brown played baseball. Donald Kendall of PepsiCo and Robert Anderson of Rockwell International both attended college on football scholarships, and Mahoney of Norton Simon won a basketball scholarship. Mahoney recalls that "the unnamed coaches I've had in my career" were among the most important people in his life. "What I absorbed from these people," he says, "was probably more meaningful than a lot of stuff I absorbed in the classroom. I mean, their whole idea of trying to help you, and root for you—the idea that you can win, you also can develop, and you have to reach out, the idea that you can, you should, put out your best—and if you put out your best you should win." Mahoney, like Ash, adopts a slightly defensive tone when he discusses his need to win. "I had troops out in the Pacific," he recalls. "I never told them it was fun just to be there. The whole idea was you're supposed to win. You might get your ass shot off!" Mahoney says he hates bitterly to lose. "If you show me a good loser, I'll show you a loser," is his favorite apothegm. He says he can only accept defeat if his opponent is clearly better. "I have more trouble accepting defeat when I screwed it up." Naturally that doesn't happen very often.

Persistence is more important than intelligence for the man who hopes to reach the top in business. "Men of very high intellectual caliber are often strikingly ineffectual," writes Peter F. Drucker, the renowned management consultant. "They often fail to realize that a single insight is not in itself achievement and performance. They may never have learned that insights become effective only through hard, systematic work."

The sentiment is echoed by Henry Singleton, of all people, who happens to be one of the most brilliant men in business today. The founder of Teledyne is becomingly modest about his intellectual capabilities, claims that he has never measured his IQ, and attributes his success largely to a tolerance for drudgery. It took three years of trial and error, for example, before he and his colleagues developed the inertial-navigation system for guided missiles—his big breakthrough as a young executive at Litton Industries. Not everyone has the mental discipline to work at a project for three years, or even for one year, without reaching a successful conclusion. "There are so many people who have done extraordinary things who don't have so much intelligence," Singleton says. "They just keep plugging away. I have a great deal of patience to continue to work on projects for a long time. To stay with it is what is helpful." Singleton says the deliberate, persistent approach served him well when he was figuring out the best way to go into business for himself, and it has served him well in his role as chief executive. Some of his moves have been exceptionally bold and daring—as when Teledyne bought two-thirds of its own shares at more than the market price, or when the company invested $400 million in the stocks of a dozen companies that had fallen out of favor with other investors. But while Singleton may be bold, he is certainly not impulsive. "I have always tried to analyze as carefully as possible what the various outcomes of my activities would be. I figure on numerous outcomes, rather than just choosing the one I want and saying that's the way it's gonna be."

It would be wrong, however, to suppose that success in business has no correlation at all with intelligence. Practically everyone who makes it to the top possesses intelligence well beyond the ordinary. The honor roll of tycoons who finished in the very highest reaches of their college or graduate-school classes is a long one. William Agee of Bendix, Charles Luce of Consolidated Edison, Richard Rosenthal of Citizens Utilities, Irving Shapiro of E. I. du Pont, Anderson of Rockwell International and Beck of Prudential are just a few that spring to mind. Plenty of other tycoons finished well up in their classes, if not at the very top, among them Hanley of Monsanto, Mahoney of Norton Simon, and Murphy of General Motors. When a tycoon doesn't do particularly well at school—as in the case of Kendall of PepsiCo or McColough of Xerox—it is usually for lack of enthusiasm, not lack of brains. It is difficult to think of any successful businessmen who are just plain stupid. And it is impossible to think of any who lack persistence—part of a tycoon's standard equipment.

The successful businessman has the ability to bounce back from his failures, to learn from them where that is possible, and to move on to the next problem with a clear mind. Resilience is essential to anyone who expects to reach the top. "You really have to not be second-guessing yourself," says Peter McColough. "A lot of the business leaders I've observed really have the attitude that all you can do is the best in the time available, and with the brains God gave you."

Brooding over the past is not only pointless, but self-destructive as well. Practically any tycoon can recall some early trauma that had a potentially lethal effect on his career. What distinguishes the tycoon is his ability to rise above the trauma, rather than succumbing to it. Donald Frey, for example, while still a junior executive at Ford, was in charge of engineering for the 1961 Thunderbird model. The car turned out to be, in Frey's own words, "noisy," "shaky" and "a dog." "My pride was wounded," he said, "and there were a lot of meetings where I had to stand up and take the responsibility." Many other businessmen in Frey's place would have skulked off to look for a job somewhere else. But Frey had the resilience—and, one might add, the self-confidence—to drag himself out of the hole. As he put it: "The important thing in a situation like that is: don't lose heart. It's easy enough to come unglued and throw up your hands. Bullshit! Instead, you should sit down and see what you can do to fix it up." Frey applied himself to the problem and managed to partially salvage the sixty-one Thunderbird: "We finally cleaned it up about two-thirds of the way through production." He went on to produce a 1962 Thunderbird that he called "a good automobile."

For some tycoons, recovery from failure takes the form of an almost mystical experience—as when Charles Luce, on the brink of losing his job as law clerk to Supreme Court Justice Hugo Black, regained his confidence by taking long walks and communing with nature during a week-long vacation. Bob Beck, caught in a terrible slump while serving as a sales agent for Prudential Insurance, snapped out of it by climbing to the top of a hill, where he spent three hours daydreaming and debating with himself.

Beck's metamorphosis occurred in 1952, when he was still in his mid-twenties and had been working for Prudential a little more than a year. Luckily he was based in Syracuse, which has lots of hills, none of them very hard to climb. He chose one overlooking Le Moyne College, on the outskirts of town, where he could easily have been mistaken for a graduate student boning for the midterm exams.

He had done well at his job in the beginning, but every salesman has fallow periods, and for six weeks he had been unable to sell a single insurance policy. With each rejection he grew more timid. "It had got so that when I went out on an appointment, if the light was on in a left-hand window when I arrived, I'd turn around and go home, because I regarded it as a bad omen. You get so discouraged, you're rejected so often, and you don't want to take any more risks of people saying 'no'. I really thought I was on my way out of the business." As he later learned, timidity is the customary defense mechanism of slumping salesmen. Instead of battling his way out of a slump by redoubling his efforts, the ordinary salesman will actually reduce the number of calls—to reduce the number of rejections. For many, that is the beginning of the end. Beck was still a tyro at that point, and nobody had bothered to advise him in the subtleties of his craft. And so he sat on the hill puzzling things out for himself.

He reviewed the events of the previous six weeks and recognized the folly of cutting down on his sales calls. "I was letting my mental attitude affect my performance," he concluded. "There's an expression of Charlie Brown's: 'I have found the enemy, and he is me.' " He returned to town—and sold seventeen policies in his next twenty calls. "Nobody could say 'no.' The prospects were the same, and I didn't know any more—it was just my attitude. When I went up the hill, I was in the insurance business, but when I came down from the hill, the business was in me."

The tycoons are compulsively curious. Never satisfied with their knowledge of the business, they are always on the prowl for some new insight or understanding. This is a trait that manifests itself quite early in the tycoon's career—usually to the annoyance of his more hidebound colleagues. The budding tycoon is easy to recognize. He refuses to stay put in his office for very long, and can often be found wandering into other offices and other departments, asking questions, offering suggestions, and generally making a nuisance of himself. There is no detail too obscure to spark his interest, for he is driven by a need to understand his company in the large, to fully appreciate what makes it tick.

Donald Frey was like that at Ford. "All through the years," he said, "regardless of what function I was performing, I had a desire to find out the broader aspects of what I was doing—to see what the next guy was going to do." Frey would visit the marketing and financial managers, the test drivers, the stylists, the production workers—and anyone else who would remain still long enough to have his brain picked. He was trying to satisfy what he describes as an inner drive, but his peregrinations had a practical effect, expanding his range of talents and making him eminently promotable. Curiosity had a lot to do with Frey's rapid rise up the ladder at Ford.

Even after he has moved well up in the hierarchy, the tycoon is likely to remain obsessed with details. John deButts, who preceded Charles Brown as chief executive of AT&T, never hesitated to dirty his hands if it would give him a firmer grasp of the business. While serving as general manager of New York Telephone's Westchester area office, he occasionally tagged along with the service and maintenance men, and he would help them install telephones or repair cables. Later, as the president of Illinois Bell Telephone, he still made it a point to know everything that was going on under his roof. *Fortune,* in a profile of deButts, recounted this telling incident:

> His extraordinary grasp of details sometimes proved embarrassing to subordinates. Donald H. Sharp, who served as a vice president under deButts at Illinois Bell, recalls accompanying the boss down a corridor of the thirty-story headquarters building in Chicago. They passed a room in which seventy or eighty people were working at desks, and Sharp remarked, "John, I wonder what all those people are doing." DeButts, with a slight edge to his voice, replied, "Donald, I *know* what they're doing."

DeButts' need to know happened to mesh perfectly with the Bell System's notions about what a chief executive should be. Only the most versatile managers, thoroughly familiar with the complexities of the vast system, are considered qualified for the top job.

Curiosity continues to be an asset once the tycoon reaches the top. In fact, it becomes an absolute necessity if he is to properly direct and supervise the vast range of activities that fall within his authority. "You have to ask for and listen to the opinions of other people," observes John Connor. "You can't possibly be knowledgeable about everything that goes into making a decision. You have to get recommendations from the people responsible for carrying out the decisions. They have opinions that will prove useful in the final decision. A willingness to listen, to pay attention, and to often accept recommendations that don't jibe with your experience is very important."

The tycoon's standard equipment includes a passion for hard work and the energy to satisfy it, a need for power and the self-control to apply it judiciously, a strong competitive urge, persistence bolstered to at least some degree by intelligence, a resilience that turns failures into mere setbacks, and a compulsive curiosity that doesn't flag even after the tycoon is safely ensconced at the top. Scanning the list, one is struck by the fact that these are traits that are normally present from a person's earliest years. They either spring from the genes or are pounded into the prospective tycoon while he is still highly malleable. This must come as a blow to young businessmen who suppose that tycoonery is a learnable skill and that they can succeed largely by emulating those who are already successful. The evidence suggests that by the time one is old enough to worry about his future in business, that future will have been largely predetermined.

The tycoons possess certain other traits that make them different from you and me. They are masterful opportunists, keenly alert to any chance for personal advancement and quick to capitalize on it. They are tougher and more aggressive than other people, less burdened with scruples, more inclined to let the ends justify the means. They also know how to get along—how to ingratiate themselves with their superiors on the way up, how to parry abuse from the outside world once they have reached the top.

Above all they are True Believers. They believe in their jobs; there is no other job they would rather have. They believe in their products; airplanes may crash, automobile tires may fall apart, cigarette smokers may die lingering deaths, but it is never the product's fault. They believe in their companies; in their loyalty to the organization they would put any patriot to shame. And they believe in the free-enterprise system. And why shouldn't they? It has worked for *them*. These are positive people, optimistic people, people not easily prey to doubts or fears. They cannot be shaken. There is a heavy dose of fanaticism in the tycoon's character.

Sources and Acknowledgments

The bulk of the material in this book was drawn from interviews with the tycoons themselves. My thanks to the following for giving me generous amounts of time, attention and information: Robert Anderson, Roy L. Ash, John D. Backe, Robert A. Beck, Charles L. Brown, Jr., John T. Connor, Thomas M. Evans, Donald M. Kendall, Charles F. Luce, C. Peter McColough, David J. Mahoney, Jr., Thomas A. Murphy, William T. Seawell, Irving S. Shapiro, Henry E. Singleton, Charles B. Thornton and Walter B. Wriston.

I also borrowed heavily from secondary sources—books, magazines, newspapers, public documents and corporate literature. Among the books that proved especially helpful were:

Brough, James, *The Ford Dynasty: An American Story,* Garden City, N.Y., Doubleday, 1977.

Carr, William H.A., *From Three Cents a Week . . . ,* Englewood Cliffs, N.J., Prentice-Hall, 1975.

Elliott, Osborn, *Men at the Top,* New York, Harper & Brothers, 1959.

Freud, Sigmund, *The Interpretation of Dreams,* New York, Modern Library, 1950.

Halaby, Najeeb E., *Crosswinds,* Garden City, N.Y., Doubleday, 1978.

Korda, Michael, *Success!,* New York, Ballantine, 1978.

Nevins, Allan, and Hill, Frank Ernest, *Ford: Decline and Rebirth, 1933–1962,* New York, Charles Scribner's Sons, 1963.

Rischin, Moses (ed.), *The American Gospel of Success,* Chicago, Quadrangle, 1965.

Swanberg, W.A., *Pulitzer,* New York, Charles Scribner's Sons, 1967.

Wright, J. Patrick, *On a Clear Day You Can See General Motors,* Grosse Point, Mich., Wright Enterprises, 1979.

I have quoted more than one hundred articles from twenty magazines, including *Business Week, Cross & Crescent, Dun's Review, Esquire, Forbes, Fortune, Harvard Business Review, Money, Motor Trend, Nation's Business, New York, New York Times Magazine, Newsweek, Playboy, Prudential Magazine, Ramparts, Signature, Sky, Time,* and *U.S. News & World Report.* Also quoted are more than forty articles from six newspapers: New York *Post,* New York *Times,* New York *World-Telegram, Wall Street Journal,* Washington *Post,* and *Women's Wear Daily.* While these sources were extremely valuable—and often crucial—it would have proved awkward to credit them all in the text, and it would be unduly burdensome to list them all here. However, certain articles deserve special mention, in particular the interview with Donald Kendall in *U.S. News* (March 30, 1970); the profiles of Henry Ford II and Lee A. Iacocca appearing in the *New York Times Magazine* on Oct. 19, 1969, July 18, 1971, and Mar. 5, 1978; profiles of C. Peter McColough and Walter Wriston in *Nation's Business* (Sept. 1972 and Apr. 1975, respectively); of Wriston in the Washington *Post* (July 28, 1974); of Irving Shapiro in *Harvard Business Review* (Mar./Apr. 1978); of Tex Thornton in *Time* (Oct. 4, 1963) and *Ramparts* (Nov. 30, 1968); of David Mahoney in the *Wall Street Journal* (July 20, 1977) and *New York* (July 25, 1977); of Robert Anderson in *Signature* (Feb. 1973), the *Journal* (Mar. 29, 1979) and *Fortune* (Sept. 1973). Also from *Fortune:* profiles of Tom Evans (Sept. 1955), John Connor (Feb. 1966), Leon Hess (Jan. 1970), J.B. Fuqua (Feb. 1972), John DeLorean (Sept. 1973), the Jarman family (July 1975), Roy Ash (Feb. 27, 1978) and Donald Rumsfeld (Sept. 10, 1979), as well as the "How They Got to the Top" series, which appeared during 1976 and 1977, and articles entitled "A Group Profile of the Fortune 500 Chief Executive" (May 1976) and "The Too-High Price of Public Service" (Dec. 1977).

I am deeply indebted to Michael Korda of Simon and Schuster, who was not merely the editor of this book, but its guiding spirit as well. His blend of discernment, judgment and tact cannot be matched. My eternal gratitude to Meredith Bernstein, my agent, for making the connection, and for her encouragement at trying moments. And special thanks to Frances Louis and Richard Louis, who read the work in progress and offered many useful suggestions.

A.M.L.
New York, 1980

Index